pilgrimage and storytelling
in the canterbury tales

the dialectic of "ernest" and "game"

pilgrimage and storytelling

in the canterbury tales

the dialectic of "ernest" and "game"

by charles a. owen, jr.

university of oklahoma press: norman

Owen, Charles Abraham, 1914–
  Pilgrimage and storytelling in the Canterbury tales.

  Bibliography: p. 241.
  Includes index.
    1. Chaucer, Geoffrey, d. 1400.   Canterbury tales.
  I. Title.
  PR1874.O93   821'.1   76-53814

To my wife, Mab

foreword and acknowledgments

THE words "ernest" and "game," which recur at intervals in the *Canterbury Tales*, had a special meaning, I think, for Chaucer as he experienced the way his collection of stories developed in its own right. They reflected the shift in the locus of value from the overt morality which the stories frequently laid claim to, and from the conventional meaning associated with pilgrimage, to the experienced value and the implicit meaning we get through watching the pilgrims tell stories.

In this book I attempt to explore the way Chaucer's conception of the *Canterbury Tales* developed over the fourteen years of his work on it, in the belief that such an exploration will help to set forth its special qualities, the form that was emerging, and the artistic effects that gave it substance. I take issue with the direction of much recent criticism, which not only has turned away from the problems of development as insoluble but has tended to emphasize the more conventional, more typically medieval aspects of Chaucer's poetry—in short, to enhance the "ernest" at the expense of the "game."

In keeping with Chaucer's own spirit of "game," I have attempted in the second chapter a less systematic approach to the question of development than the one I took in my previous articles. Those who follow such issues closely will note some important new evidence for the theories advanced. The more casual reader will find the chapter not discordant, I hope, with the rest of the book.

My indebtedness to previous critics and scholars is everywhere apparent. I have acknowledged what I know to be borrowed, yet have inevitably failed to do justice, not only to published sources but also to the students and colleagues who have stimulated my thinking with their questions and comments. I would like to pay special tribute to those generations of scholars who in the fifty years to 1925 made Chaucer so much more available to us all—to Furnivall, Skeat, Kittredge, Tatlock, Root, Lowes, and their many confreres—and to Robinson, whose edition makes possible the assimilation of their work.

For the typing of earlier versions of the book I am indebted to my daughter Lucy and to the Research Foundation of the University of Connecticut. The foundation has also made a grant to aid in publication of the book. To my wife especially, to the other members of my family, and to friends, I owe an inordinate debt for their patience in listening, and for their help in revising what I have written. I am indebted to Vernon Losee for his work on the index.

I would also like to pay tribute to the department head who first gave me the chance to teach a Chaucer course. Leonard Dean encouraged me to add my voice to that parliament of "foules" known as Chaucerians. The name suggests the greatest debt of all—to the poet, who has made scholarship, and art, and life a more meaningful and exciting adventure for so many in the six centuries since he lived and wrote.

CHARLES A. OWEN, JR.

Freedom, N.H.

contents

Pilgrimage and Storytelling in the Canterbury Tales

The Dialectic of "Ernest" and "Game"

I

the impoRtance of the liteRal

"Everich a word"

THE *Canterbury Tales* is a collection of stories. It is also a narrative of some thirty people journeying from Southwark to Canterbury and back. As the first, it reflects a medieval literary convention. As the second, it absorbs the first, suggesting in its imperfections, its contradictions and inconsistencies, the experimental nature of Chaucer's art. As Chaucer worked on the fiction of the pilgrimage, the received meanings of such a fiction gave place to the developing significance of the interacting elements. The stories tended to become expressive of character. Often overtly didactic, they tested themselves against each other and against the increasingly stated and hence objectified purposes of the narrators. From the conflicts and contrasts and consonances, and from the complex relationships thus set up, emerged a series of patterns, which the reader both enjoys and perceives as significant. Though these patterns are only implicitly meaningful, they often contrast with the overt didacticism of the narrators; they come to serve as the standard against which the visions of all the narrators are measured; they constitute a level of value independent of any one story or any narrator; they give the reader a purely aesthetic enjoyment—the kind a creator might have who watches the independent actions of his own creatures. The "game" of the storytelling replaces the "ernest" of overt morality as the source of value. The "game" of holiday travel yields richer meaning than the "ernest" of pilgrimage. Hence the paradox of a "game" more "ernest" than "ernest," of value enjoyed as pattern.

Two things especially contribute to the dynamics of emergent

3

pattern in the *Canterbury Tales*. They appear as two sides of the same coin in the passage where Chaucer first apologizes for some of the words he will have to report:

> Whoso shal telle a tale after a man,
> He moot reherce as ny as evere he kan
> Everich a word. . . .[1]   (A 733)

Here, in disclaiming his own responsibility for what the pilgrims say, he is giving them an autonomy, a freedom from authorial control; he is pointing to their characters as the source of initiative; he is providing the base for the major interactions in the narrative of journey, the relationship of character to tale and the relationship of characters and of tales with each other. He is also proclaiming the most drastic slice-of-life naturalism in the annals of literature. "Everich a word" does not even permit a slicing of reality. The whole pilgrimage will be there—no untruth, no feigning things, no paraphrase. The autonomy of all agents and the literal accuracy of the report—these two ingredients condition what happens in the *Canterbury Tales*. The fiction is that there is no fiction.[2] The result, as in Dante, is a polysemous narrative and an affirmation of beneficent rule by the "sighte above," but in naturalistic rather than supernatural terms. Chaucer fixes his attention on the Canterbury Way, on the words and actions and visions of his pilgrims.

One set of references is especially impressive, not only as showing his intimate knowledge of the whole Canterbury road and his intention to use the road as an element in a meaningful pattern, but also as implying the structural import of the stages of the journey. In the G fragment, as the pilgrims near Canterbury, they are overtaken by a canon and his yeoman at a small village called Boughton, in the Blee Forest. Chaucer not only knows the name of this hamlet but also knows its exact position—the halfway point of the short journey from Ospring to Canterbury—and this detail makes it clear that the day's journey began at Ospring, though he does not mention that town by name:

> Sires, now in the morwe-tyde
> Out of youre hostelrie I saugh yow ryde.   (G 589)

Chaucer makes of Boughton a significant turning point. The pilgrims have been listening to the Second Nun's rendering of the life of

4

St. Cecilia, but they are distracted from the religious commitment appropriate to the day they reach their pilgrimage's goal—distracted by the drama of the Yeoman's conversion and the Canon's flight, and by the Yeoman's account of alchemy as honest but futile experiment on the one hand, and as villainous but effective skullduggery on the other. The base metals are not transformed into gold by the efforts of either of the two canons, nor by proximity to the great martyr's shrine. The Yeoman boasts, before his conversion, of his master's skill:

> That al this ground on which we been ridyng,
> Til that we come to Caunterbury toun,
> He koude al clene turne it up-so-doun,
> And pave it al of silver and of gold.   (G 626)

The boast is vain; the road remains a road. But the events add level on level of meaning to the literal—the Canon's flight from exposure to the community of pilgrims; the Yeoman's pride in what blowing an alchemist's fire for seven years has taught him; his foolish moral fervor against the tricky Canon's con game; the cost in quality of life of the effort to extract wealth from matter; and the contrasting stories on what was probably the middle day of a five-day pilgrimage, a day that began at an inn in Ospring and ended, no doubt, at another inn in Canterbury, a day that included the visit to the shrine of St. Thomas. Far from superseding the literal, the values depend on "everich a word." Chaucer sought increasingly through his art the effect of real pilgrims on a real road, their overnight stops the inevitable punctuation of their storytelling activity.

Through their efforts to create, through their quarrels and discussions and confessions, we see not only their intentions, their conscious image of themselves, but also on occasion the inadvertent self-revelation that gives depth to the character. These occasions constitute the great moments of the pilgrimage. The Prioress, the Nun's Priest, the Wife of Bath, the Pardoner, and the Merchant stamp themselves vividly on our consciousness. That others make a less telling impact does not disturb the potential. At any moment the quarrel may flare up that exposes a Reeve, a Friar, or a Summoner. The Franklin is moved by more generous sentiments to involve himself in the "game," while Chaucer and the Clerk wait patiently to be noticed and pilgrims like the Monk, the Physician, the Second Nun, and the Man of Law seek an anonymity in the stereotypes of genre. The range of vividness from Wife of Bath to Second Nun suggests a planned maximum, but the steps in between are plausibly haphazard. The relationships thus set up between the meaning of the tale, the purpose of the narrator, and his inadvertent self-revelation, compounded as the tales proceed by every conceivable type of cross-reference, create the sense of meaningful pattern that constitutes the equivalent of the anagoge in medieval allegory. The reading of meanings on this level, dependent still on accurate attention to "everich a word," is primarily an aesthetic experience. The naive expression of a mimetic aim by the narrator reflects Chaucer's confidence, to be sensed everywhere in the *Canterbury Tales*, that faithful imitation yields the truest values.

Chaucer's escape from the shackles of medieval didacticism is, as one would expect, not absolute. At some point after he started the *Canterbury Tales*, he was moved to retract his greatest work as a poet. Whether he recovered from this excessive religiosity or ended in it will never be certainly known. What has given his work its humane appeal over the ages is its singular freedom from the excesses associated with *Zeitgeist*. Once its terms are understood and its language mastered, Chaucer's work speaks to us in a timeless idiom with an artistry we need no key to unlock. It can perhaps be seen as an expression of our own *Zeitgeist* that, having contributed so much to the dissemination of Chaucer's poetry, we have tended of late to emphasize its narrowly medieval elements, to derive from it a series of specialized and esoteric meanings, to force it to conform to a thesis-ridden vision.[3] To the extent that we have done so, we have broken with the classical line of critics extending from Dryden through Blake and Coleridge to Kittredge and Lowes and Muscatine. Their emphasis on his richly peopled world and on the skill of the art that projects it, on what Dryden called "God's plenty," reaches back to what one of the first men to read the *Canterbury Tales* saw in it. When ordering illuminations for the several tales, the Ellesmere editor had the artists illustrate each tale, not with a scene from the story itself, but with the portrait of the pilgrim telling it.

The problem that the Ellesmere editor and the men responsible for the other early manuscript arrangements tried to conceal makes the

Canterbury Tales unique among the great literary works of our civilization. Its incompleteness, especially its fragmentary incompleteness, presents a challenge few recent editors have chosen to face. What we have represents at least three different plans for the whole work—an early beginning for the storytelling marked, among other things, by the Wife of Bath telling the *Shipman's Tale*, a later arrangement with the Wife detached from the opening sequence and telling her own tale, and another arrangement in which the number of tales each pilgrim is to tell has been changed from one to four or from four to one. The plausible expedient is to accept one of the early arrangements, ignoring as insoluble the related problems of the proper tale order, the days of the journey, and the development of Chaucer's conception of his work.

Support for this expedient is derived from the extreme unlikelihood that thirty people on horseback could hear one another telling stories on a narrow medieval road.[4] The basic fiction being so totally unrealistic, no notice need be taken of the place names scattered here and there to give an aura of authenticity. Chaucer apparently took some cognizance of this objection himself. A number of times he has the Host call people to him when he chooses them for the next tale. Thus the Host says to Chaucer:

> Approche neer, and looke up murily.
> Now war yow, sires, and lat this man have place! (B 1889)

Similarly, in turning from the Monk to the Nun's Priest, he says, "Com neer, thou preest, com hyder, thou sir John!" (B 4000). And in the Manciple's Prologue, when he spots the Cook riding behind in a drunken stupor, he not only tries to have him wakened but summons him:

> Do hym come forth, he knoweth his penaunce;
> For he shall telle a tale, by my fey.   (H 13)

In the Canon's Yeoman's Prologue the Canon draws near the group at the center to overhear what his Yeoman is telling the Host (G 684 ff.). Had he been aware of the line the Host's questioning was taking, he would surely have intervened sooner and perhaps avoided the necessity for flight. The impression Chaucer gives is of the Host riding in the midst of the group, the current storyteller near him, and some pilgrims

—like the Cook when he is sleeping off a night's debauch—not listening.

In any event, the citing of one improbability does not really justify ignoring the evidence provided by the realistic references to places on the road and to the time of day, especially when, combined with a recognition of development, they provide some explanation for the fragments in which Chaucer left his work. Turning our backs on these interrelated problems ends any effort to understand how the *Canterbury Tales* came to be what it is. The experience of a work in progress, its form emerging from the interaction of the parts in the imagination of the author, underlies and rewards an accurate reading of a work less than a quarter finished.

Strangely enough, the strongest element in the interacting parts that absorbed the creative energies of Chaucer's last years is not the powerful medieval motif of pilgrimage. Once the Host has made a community of the group at his inn, the pilgrims become storytellers. The climax of their activities becomes in the final plan the prize-awarding supper at the Tabard. In a sense, the storytelling contest supplants the pilgrimage. Of course nothing prevents those so inclined from directing their storytelling to the same end as the pilgrimage. Few of the pilgrims in fact choose this option. The Pardoner even mocks it with his cynical performance. Recognition of this opposition between art and religion perhaps motivates in part the Parson's outburst against the Host's swearing. The successful diversion of most of his fellows from the religious concern motivating their decision to go on pilgrimage and their immersion in the "game" proposed by the Host must have irked the Parson beyond silent endurance. That the Host easily turns aside the attack and is not again challenged until, at the end, he must call on the Parson for a tale, speaks more for the enthusiasm the idea of storytelling has aroused in the pilgrims than for any special capacities Harrie Baillie has for his self-imposed duties. In any other context the Host would be no match for the Parson. The same is true of all the associated oppositions created in the work: Canterbury versus Southwark, the Cathedral versus the Tabard, the consecrated wafer and wine paid for in the crucifixion versus the "soper at oure aller cost." The disparities are ludicrous. Yet the "game" dominates.[5] It creates the meanings and values that absorb our attention and compel our imagination. The literal reality of a road, of men and women, of the storytelling and the comment it occasions, of, finally, an organized game, a contest, imitates successfully the complex interrelationships of a society; it generates experienced values that transcend the society and even rational definition. The Host can smugly tell the victims of his crude banter not to be "wroth": "A man may seye ful sooth in game and pley" (A 4355). Or again: "Ful ofte in game a sooth I have herd seye!" (B 3154). One of his victims replies, "But 'sooth pley, quaad pley,' as the Flemyng seith" (A 4357). And Chaucer himself says, "And eek man shal nat maken earnest of game"(A 3186).

the development of the canterbury tales

"Yif me a plante of thilke blissed tree"

1. Direction of Change—"His owene knyf"

THE direction in which Chaucer's imagination moved as he worked on the fiction of his pilgrimage can be experienced in a number of ways.[1] The solemn admonitions of the treatise on penitence known as the *Parson's Tale* turn up in several of the pilgrims' stories, transmuted from didacticism to trenchant comedy. The sober antifeminist literature of the Christian tradition helped to create the indomitable Wife of Bath. Refracted through her nature, this antifeminism acquires a variegated and unwonted spectrum of colors; it is now assented to in order to justify the indulgence of a wife's whims; it is now turned into an accusation of aggression against her feeble old husbands; it is now heard out during long evenings with her fifth hubsand and impatiently absorbed despite the scornful fury of her thwarted libido. Even Petrarch's allegorical interpretation of Griselda's relationship with Walter, which while admitting how insupportable such conduct would be in literal marriage, sees in it a model for man's relationship with God—even this interpretation, which justifies the analogy with Job and touches one of the deepest dilemmas of the human condition—is absorbed into the "game" of the Clerk's song. The patient Griselda becomes a subtly comic thesis for her antithesis the Wife of Bath, and we are prepared for the moment when the Wife will step into the fiction of her fellow pilgrim the Merchant, as well as for the moment when she will step out of fiction altogether into the poet's relationship with Bukton.[2] The placing of overt morality within fiction, and even within the fiction of a fiction, tests it and refines it, and permits it a free play in contexts where its admonitions, missing their targets in varying degrees, alert our perceptions to the comedy of claims and appearances and enliven our appreciation of experienced value.

When the Wife of Bath repeats the antifeminist stories that her fifth husband read to her before their climactic quarrel, she chooses, or rather Chaucer has her choose, the ones that most outraged her. The psychology of his fictional creature reinforces his own artistic motives, and we are regaled with a distillation, the result, first, of the labors of a fictional compiler, then of Jankin's sadistic culling, and finally of Alice's impassioned and ambivalent memory—a distillation of the propaganda against women accumulated through the ages. Small wonder that with such a series of distorting mirrors, Samson, Socrates, Clytemnestra, Livia, and Lucilia lose the dignity of history and legend to become comic figures. The Wife's presence as the last of the reflecting surfaces is everywhere in evidence—in her responding to Pasiphaë's unnatural lust, for instance, before she can even tell the story:

> Of Phasipha, that was the queene of Crete,
> For shrewednesse, hym thoughte the tale swete;
> Fy! spek namoore—it is a grisly thyng—
> Of hire horrible lust and hir likyng.   (D 736)

How far Chaucer's sense of this material was from a typical medieval interpretation of it, is revealed in the treatment by the *Gesta Romanorum* of what is perhaps the most ridiculous of all the stories in Jankyn's collection:

> My beloved, the tree is the cross of Christ. The man's three wives are pride, lusts of the heart, and lusts of the eyes, which ought to be thus suspended and destroyed. He who solicited a part of the tree is any good Christian.[3]

Here is how the Wife remembers the story:

> Thanne tolde he me how oon Latumyus
> Compleyned unto his felawe Arrius
> That in his gardyn growed swich a tree
> On which he seyde how that his wyves thre
> Hanged hemself for herte despitus.

11

"O leeve brother," quod this Arrius,
"Yif me a plante of thilke blissed tree,
And in my gardyn planted shal it bee."   (D 764)

Not by accident is the Wife of Bath involved to such an extent in this transmutation of overt morality. Her influence is almost omnipresent in the period of Chaucer's greatest imaginative commitment to the fiction of his pilgrimage. The Clerk's song swings the patient Griselda into her ambiance. The Friar, the Summoner, the Merchant, and even the Host reflect her influence in different ways. The Pardoner, by his interruption of her confession, puts himself within her orbit. The Nun's Priest and the churls who follow the Knight have a more tenuous relationship with her. The Nun's Priest escapes from a direct expression of antifeminism only when he attributes it to his feathered hero: "Thise been the cokkes wordes, and nat myne" (B 4455). And, as we shall see later, the churls—the Miller, the Reeve, and the Cook—replace the Wife as contrast to an idealistic first storyteller and permit Chaucer to save her impact for a later and climactic moment in the journey.

The "game" of the stories some of the pilgrims tell absorbs material from the treatise on penitence and the seven deadly sins that is known as the *Parson's Tale*. Here we see Chaucer working not only with overtly moral utterances, but with material that he himself had written under a different inspiration. Whether his conception of a marriage group came from the extended passage on the significant placement of Adam's rib, as Sister Mariella has suggested, can never be established. Similarly, we shall never know whether the Parson's dicussion of sex in marriage played any part in the rules that Nicholas devised as God's commandment for John and Alisoun in the predicted second flood.[4] But there can be no question of the influence on the *Merchant's Tale* of the following passage, describing the fourth finger of the devil's hand that grips man "by the reynes" in the sin of lechery:

> . . . and namely thise olde dotardes holours, yet wol they kisse, though they may nat do, and smatre hem. . . . And for that many man weneth that he may nat synne, for no likerousnesse that he dooth with his wyf, certes, that opinion is fals. God woot, a man may sleen hymself with his owene knyf, and make hymselve

dronken of his owene tonne. Certes, be it wyf, be it child, or any worldly thyng that he loveth biforn God, it is his mawmet, and he is an ydolastre. (I 860)

The detail of the knife is certainly from this passage; its transformation into literal harmlessness—

> A man may do no synne with his wyf,
> Ne hurte hymselven with his owene knyf (E 1840)

—one of the many ways the narrator lacerates an old man's folly in marrying a young wife. The details of January's folly go beyond ordinary experience and suggest that Chaucer had in mind as he wrote a narrator with special reason to rue a marriage of old and young.

Chaucer's Pardoner makes use of more material from the treatise than any of the other pilgrims. Since he is preaching a sermon, he takes over the morality directly, but more than our knowledge of his evil purpose colors the performance. Frequently, his condemnations serve as excuse for a vivid reliving of the sinful experience itself. An extravagant rhetoric marks passage after passage as self-indulgent in another way. Thus the treatise's simple statement about gluttony—"This synne corrumped al this world, as is wel shewed in the synne of Adam and of Eve" (I 819)—becomes in the Pardoner's frenetic style:

> O glotonye, ful of cursednesse!
> O cause first of oure confusioun!
> O original of oure dampnacioun,
> Til Crist hadde boght us with his blood agayn!
> Lo, how deere, shortly for to sayn,
> Aboght was thilke cursed vileynye!
> Corrupt was all this world for glotonye.   (C 504)

The treatise goes on to quote Scripture:

> Looke eek what seith Seint Paul of Glotonye: "Manye," seith Saint Paul, "goon, of whiche I have ofte seyd to yow, and now I seye it wepynge, that been the enemys of the croys of Crist; of whiche the ende is deeth, and of which hire wombe is hire god, and hire glorie in confusioun of hem that so savouren erthely thynges." (I 820)

A later passage in the Pardoner's sermon picks up the quotation from St. Paul and again, though more subtly this time, the rhetoric transforms it:

> The apostel wepyng seith ful pitously,
> "Ther walken manye of which yow toold have I—
> I seye it now wepyng, with pitous voys—
> That they been enemys of Cristes croys,
> Of whiche the ende is deeth, wombe is hir god!"
> O wombe! O bely! O stynkyng cod,
> Fulfilled of dong and of corrupcioun!   (C 535)

What these passages show in general terms reveals itself impressively in the more detailed study of the development. The "game" of the storytelling became for Chaucer more important than the "ernest" of pilgrimage; it yielded a more vivid experience of value; in the interaction of its elements it had an almost autonomous growth. Had Chaucer lived to finish the poem, he would have eliminated the evidence that testifies to his changes of plan. The game of the storytelling would have been complete, but Chaucer's game with its elements would have left little or no trace. As it is, we have contradictory evidence on the number of pilgrims, on the number of tales each pilgrim is to tell, and on the ending the *Canterbury Tales* was intended to have. There are other discrepancies as well: the prose tale the Man of Law says he will tell, the famous son-of-Eve reference to herself by the Second Nun, and the triad of priests accompanying the Prioress that becomes a single priest when he is called on for a story by the Host. But the evidence for Chaucer's change in plan that promises the greatest resonance is the sexual ambivalence of the *Shipman's Tale*.

2. The Wife of Bath and the Road—"My joly body"

The *Shipman's Tale*, in outlining the plight of a husband with an extravagant wife, reveals an unexpected sexual affiliation for its narrator:

> The sely housbonde, algate he moot paye,
> He moot us clothe, and he moot us arraye,
> Al for his owene worshipe richely,
> In which array we daunce jolily.

14

> And if that he noght may, par aventure,
> Or ellis list no swich dispence endure,
> But thynketh it is wasted and ylost,
> Thanne moot another payen for oure cost,
> Or lene us gold, and that is perilous.   (B 1209)

Few people question that here we have the Wife of Bath speaking, the only woman on the pilgrimage to whom such language and such sentiments could conceivably be attributed.[5] The tale itself, while not on the theme of female sovereignty, has a resourceful heroine who prevails against her lover's perfidy and her husband's stinginess and gives voice at the end to her sense that sex and money are convertible:

> I am youre wyf; score it upon my taille,   (B 1606)
> .   .   .   .
> Ye shal my joly body have to wedde;
> By God, I wol nat paye yow but abedde!   (B 1614)

That the two women, the Wife of St. Denis and the Wife of Bath, express one another's sentiments and even use each other's language finds confirmation in the references both make to "cosynage" (B 1226, 1599); in the use of the pun on "taille" for the final lines of the story—

> Thus endeth now my tale, and God us sende
> Taillynge ynough unto our lyves ende   (B 1624)

—and in what were originally intended to be the introductory lines for the Wife of Bath's performance,[6] where a phrase her heroine is to use becomes a striking synecdoche for Alice herself:

> My joly body schal a tale telle,
> And I schal clynken you so mery a belle,
> That I schal waken al this compaignie.   (B 1187)

The sense of her body as "joly," as an instrument for pleasure, also informs the Wife of Bath's discussion of marriage in the early part of her prologue:

> And yet with barly-breed, Mark telle kan,
> Oure Lord Jhesu refresshed many a man.   (D 146)

15

. . . .

> In wyfhod I wol use myn instrument
> As frely as my Makere hath it sent.   (D 150)

Two other qualities tie together the Wife of Bath as narrator, her surrogate the Wife of St. Denis, the interrupter in the Man of Law's Epilogue, and the⌐Wife of Bath herself in her theoretical justification of sex in marriage that takes up the first part of her prologue.⌐One is a respect for the forms of religion, which involves, for the interrupter in the epilogue, denouncing Lollardry and springing "cokkel in our clene corn" (B 1183); for the Wife of St. Denis, honoring the "Lord that for us bledde" with expensive raiment at Sunday services (B 1368 ff.), even if it has to be paid for by adultery; for the narrator in the *Shipman's Tale*, seeing that offices are read (B 1281), that mass is said (B 1441), and that respectable surfaces throughout remain intact, whatever betrayals go on beneath; and, for the⌐Wife of Bath, in the first 162 lines of her prologue, finding in Scripture the permission for the pleasure in sex that the Wife has practiced all her life⌐ Accompanying the concern for religious forms, is the no-nonsense downrightness of a person who sweeps away, by the sheer force of her personality, the objections that logic might raise. The surrogate Wife of St. Denis in her final speech has little trouble handling her husband's objections to her extravagance, despite the shock of having just discovered her lover's perfidy. The same confident, logic-flouting tone is to be heard in the already quoted passage that makes the perfect transition between the Wife's anti-Lollardry and her concern about the number of marriages the orthodox Christian might justifiably contract:

> My joly body schal a tale telle,
> And I schal clynken you so mery a belle,
> That I schal waken al this compaignie.
> But it schal not ben of philosophie,
> Ne phislyas, ne termes queinte of lawe.
> Ther is but litel Latyn in my mawe!   (B 1190)
> Experience, though noon auctoritee   (D 1)
> Were in this world, is right ynogh for me
> To speke of wo that is in mariage;
>   For, lordynges, sith I twelve yeer was of age,

16

Thonked be God that is eterne on lyve,
Housbondes at chirche dore I have had fyve,—
If I so ofte myghte have ywedded bee.[7]   (D 7)

Before following the evidence for change further, we should pause to spell out the implications of what we have already seen. The *Shipman's Tale* was originally assigned to the Wife of Bath, and when Chaucer assigned it instead to his piratical sea captain, he did not change the telltale reference at the beginning to "us women." His apparent need to reassign the tale has important implications. Why not leave the tale with the Wife of Bath and obviate the need for change? Perhaps because in writing her another story he was using up her one opportunity to tell stories. This answer, plausible at least, receives support from what happens later. In the tales presently connected to the *Shipman's Tale*, Chaucer and the Monk suffer interruption. The Host and the Knight reach the end of their patience at what they consider less than inspired performances by the two narrators. In both instances the Host gives the offenders another chance at storytelling— offers that make no sense if each pilgrim will have by right three more turns in the competition. A single story for each pilgrim is most likely the pattern, then, when the six stories that form the longest of the fragments (B²) were being linked together, and when the Wife of Bath was being separated from her moorings in the Man of Law's Epilogue and from her original tale.

It is important to remember, as we watch her development as a character and her acquisition of a new story, that the Wife of Bath remains detached from the other fragments, presumably because Chaucer wanted to keep her that way. The best evidence indicates that the stories attached to her own (in the D fragment) and those influenced in part at least by her performance (in C and E-F) were being linked together, and for the most part written, at the same time as B² was taking shape.[8] We even have evidence for dating these developments as occurring about the year 1396, during a period extending a year or two in either direction. These two large groups of tales taking shape at the same time—the one group linked together and the other constituting a group because of connections of various kinds with the Wife of Bath, both groups starting with no introduction or placement of speaker, the one with a tale originally composed for the Wife of Bath, the other with the Wife herself in mid-confession—these two groups of tales contain the heart of the mystery. Why were they kept separate from one another and from the framework of the *Man of Law's Tale*? Which of the other fragments of the *Canterbury Tales* preceded and which ones followed these two groups, both in terms of fictional time, the days of the journey to Canterbury, and in actual time, the years of Chaucer's work on the Canterbury pilgrimage? Evidence exists which will help to answer these questions, but first let us look at the two groups, keeping in mind some places, times, and distances.

The longest fragment of the *Canterbury Tales*, B^2, starts with an unintroduced *Shipman's Tale* and ends with the Host's comments on the *Nun's Priest's Tale*. In between are the *Prioress's Tale*, Chaucer's two tales (*Sir Thopas* and the *Melibeus*), the Monk's tragedies, and the Nun's Priest's mock-heroic fable. When Chaucer's *Thopas* is interrupted by the Host, he is given another opportunity and tells the *Melibeus*, stimulating the Host to an extended account of his shrewish wife, Goodelief. The Monk, also interrupted and offered a second chance, refuses to accede to the Host's suggestion that he tell about hunting. In calling upon the Monk the first time, the Host points to Rochester, thirty miles from London and twenty-six from Canterbury, as "heer faste by"; and when he supports the Knight's interruption, some seventeen tragedies later, he refers to the mud of the road, presumably now beyond Rochester. At the end of his comments on the *Nun's Priest's Tale*, the Host turns to an unnamed pilgrim, and the fragment ends.

The series of tales influenced by the Wife of Bath occur in three disconnected fragments: in D, which includes her own prologue and tale, the *Friar's Tale*, and the *Summoner's Tale*; in C, containing the Physician's unintroduced tale and the Pardoner's Prologue and *Tale*; and in E-F, consisting of the four stories by the Clerk, the Merchant, the Squire, and the Franklin. The Wife's performance stimulates first a response from the Pardoner, in which he says that he is thinking of marrying; then from the Friar, who is immediately jumped on for his interruption, by the Summoner; and finally from the Clerk, the Merchant, and the Franklin, who take up the subject of marriage. The quarrel of the Friar and the Summoner leads the latter to threaten two or three tales about Friars before they reach Sittingbourne, a village forty miles from London and sixteen from Canterbury. The last line of his tale (and of the D fragment) implies that he has carried out his threat: "My tale is doon; we been almoost at towne." Thus the D fragment completes only the most superficial of the Wife's influences on her fellow pilgrims, the quarrel of the Friar and the Summoner.

The *Physician's Tale* and the Pardoner's Prologue and *Tale*, which make up the C fragment, contain no explicit references to time and place. However, since it is unlikely that the Pardoner would interrupt the Wife of Bath with the word that he is considering marriage after his anger at the Host's slurs on his manhood, a position for the C fragment after the Wife of Bath's Prologue is indicated. Several recent critics have found in the Pardoner's confession an effort to emulate the Wife of Bath.

Three of the four tales in the fragment labeled E-F either mention the Wife of Bath explicitly (the Clerk's and the Merchant's) or comment on the theory of marriage she has propounded (the Franklin's). The *Squire's Tale*, which stands third in the fragment, refers to the hour as prime, that is, nine o'clock in the morning. This tale, the only one not connected to the Wife's thematically, breaks off incomplete. It inspires comment from the Franklin on his son's libertinism, a contrast to the Squire's gentilesse. At the end of the *Clerk's Tale*, in a stanza Chaucer may have canceled, the Host wishes his wife could have heard the story of Griselda, but in contrast to his similar wish at the end of the *Melibeus*, he does not explain why. At the end of the *Merchant's Tale* the Host again refers to his wife. Unlike May, she is "trewe as any steel," but a "labbynge shrewe" with a "heep" of other vices. The Host cuts short his comment out of fear that "it sholde reported be," for "wommen konnen outen swich chaffare."

So far, we have been concerned mainly with actual time—with the years of Chaucer's work on the *Canterbury Tales*—and with the way the pilgrims and their tales developed in his imagination. The references to the time of day and to places on the road in the above summary suggest that fictional time and distance were a part of the reality he was creating. Was there a plan for the days of the pilgrimage? Or were these references merely atmospheric? The accuracy of the reference (discussed in the first chapter) that names the small village in the Blee Forest, halfway between Ospring and Canterbury, gives warrant for a closer attention to these details. The accompanying diagram shows the names of the more important towns and villages on the road from London to Canterbury and their distance from the inn in Southwark. Names of towns not mentioned in the *Canterbury Tales* are shown in parentheses.

We have already seen the importance of the reference to Boughton under Blee in the Canon's Yeoman's Prologue. This reference, which gives place, time and direction of travel, as well as indicating an overnight stop at Ospring and an early arrival in Canterbury, accords with the implications of the B² fragment, but not with the group of tales connected with the Wife of Bath. If the pilgrims reach Sittingbourne, sixteen miles from Canterbury, at the end of the *Summoner's Tale*, the mention of its being "prime," or nine o'clock, in the *Squire's Tale*, presumably the next day, at any rate on some later day (see the references to the Wife of Bath at the end of the *Clerk's Tale* and in the

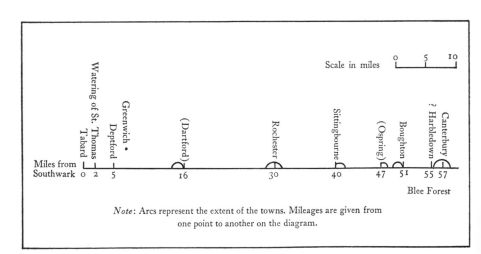

Note: Arcs represent the extent of the towns. Mileages are given from one point to another on the diagram.

Merchant's Tale), conflicts with the other indications. That the Canon and his Yeoman overtake the pilgrims early in the morning, halfway between Ospring and Canterbury (nine miles apart), leaves no room for another morning of storytelling in the sixteen miles between Sittingbourne and Canterbury. On the other hand, the pilgrims' passing Rochester in the Monk's Prologue works in well with all the implications of the Canon's Yeoman's Prologue. It allows for an overnight stop at Dartford, fifteen miles from Southwark, another at Ospring, thirty-one miles farther along.[9] It also suggests a motive for Chaucer's keeping of the two big groups of tales separate from each other. They were intended to provide the nucleus, the one for the outward, the other for the homeward journey. The latter journey, as suggested by the reference to prime, would take two days, with the overnight stop this time in Rochester. The pilgrimage as a whole would last five days, and the sixth night would mark the return to the Tabard, the only repetition of an inn on the journey.

A number of advantages accrue from regarding the pilgrimage as a five-day return journey. As we shall see later, it accommodates every reference to time and place in the links and the tales. It makes sense of the Host's voluble description of his marital difficulties in the Monk's Prologue and his contrasting caution in the Merchant's Epilogue. Not only has he heard Alice of Bath and recognized an ally for his shrew of a wife, but he is also aware of the diminishing time and space between himself and the spouse he dreads. The sudden access of caution on the part of the Host succeeds his initial instinctive response to the Merchant's account of May's cynical perfidy:

> "Ey! Goddes mercy!" seyde oure Hooste tho,
> "Now swich a wyf I pray God kepe me fro!
> Lo, whiche sleightes and subtilitees
> In wommen been! for ay as bisy as bees
> Been they, us sely men for to deceyve,
> And from the soothe evere wol they weyve;
> By this Marchauntes tale it preveth weel.
> But doutelees, as trewe as any steel
> I have a wyf, though that she povre be,
> But of hir tonge, a labbyng shrewe is she,

21

And yet she hath an heep of vices mo;
Therof no fors! lat alle swiche thynges go.
But wyte ye what? In conseil be it seyd,
Me reweth soore I am unto hire teyd.
For, and I sholde rekenen every vice
Which that she hath, ywis I were to nyce;
And cause why, it sholde reported be
And toold to hire of somme of this meynee,
Of whom, it nedeth nat for to declare,
Syn wommen konnen outen swich chaffare;
And eek my wit suffiseth nat therto,
To tellen al, wherfore my tale is do." (E 2440)

Another instance of a relationship that points to the homeward journey for this series of tales occurs when the Pardoner makes his outrageous suggestion that the pilgrims partake of the benefits available to them in his pardons and in his relics:

Paraventure ther may fallen oon or two
Doun of his hors, and breke his nekke atwo.
Looke which a seuretee is it to yow alle
That I am in youre felaweshipe yfalle,
That may assoille yow, bothe moore and lasse,
Whan that the soule shal fro the body passe. (C 940)

The Pardoner is the more likely to make this suggestion if the Cook has already fallen from his horse, an event that happens when he tries to answer the Manciple's comments on his drunken stupor. The little town of Bobbe-up-and-doun, where this episode occurs, has never been certainly identified, but its position "under the Blee" places it close to Canterbury. The separation of the *Manciple's Tale* from the *Canon's Yeoman's Tale*, the Host's attributing the Cook's sleepiness to one of three alternatives, all of which could only have occurred during the night at an inn, and the lack of any mention in the *Manciple's Tale* of the pilgrims' approach to their destination weigh slightly in favor of seeing it as the first tale on the homeward journey rather than the final tale on the way out.[10] Whichever position it was planned for, it would precede the *Pardoner's Tale*, clearly intended to follow the Pardoner's interruption of the Wife of Bath's Prologue.

The Development of the Canterbury Tales

The diagram of the road to Canterbury can now indicate the days of the pilgrimage and the position in the two-way journey of a number of the groups of tales.

This diagram represents the period when the two big groups of tales were taking shape. It concentrates attention on them and on the fragments most closely associated with them, and makes clear the final advantage in regarding the group of tales connected with the Wife of Bath as belonging to the homeward journey.

If Chaucer was to avoid anticlimax after the visit to the shrine in Canterbury, he needed vivid copy for the return to Southwark. The growth of the Wife of Bath in Chaucer's imagination, as reflected in the detailed account of her five husbands and her response to the antifeminism endemic in the Middle Ages, paralleled his recognition of this aesthetic problem. We cannot be sure which came first, the Wife of Bath's development or the awareness of the challenge in the built-in anticlimax of the frame story. The likelihood is that the possibilities in using her to exploit the rich vein of antifeminism took precedence. From

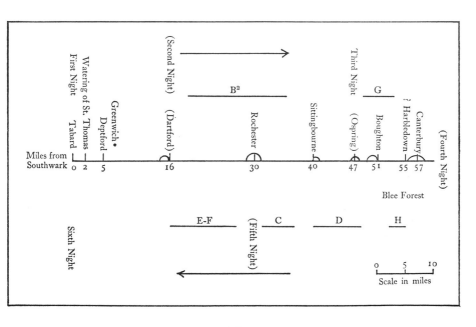

the moment Chaucer decided to cut the Wife of Bath loose from the Man of Law's Epilogue, the interaction between development and problem set in, and the remarkable series of tales connected to the Wife of Bath began to take shape. Just as the position on the road gave special meaning to the sequence Second Nun and Canon's Yeoman, so the details of conduct that Chaucer imagined for a character such as the Host began to relate to the psychology of distance and direction. How else to explain the contrast already discussed between the Host's account of his wife's aggressive conduct in the Monk's Prologue and the one in the Merchant's Epilogue—accounts which show every sign of being written in conjunction with each other? The growth in the Wife of Bath's character, which turned her from a single-faceted, fiercely partisan type to the richly realized woman still on the surface a zealot but with a capacity for experience, change, and even love, contributed to Chaucer's developing sense of the ways in which his fiction could have meaning.

With the dynamics of the relationship between portrait and tale developing, the stories became polysemous. The narrator's conscious purpose, his unconscious self-revelation, and the emergent patterns that only an uninvolved observer could fully appreciate add to the literal story strata of meaning—a match for the complexities attributed by the allegorists to Biblical narrative. Quarrels, discussions, interruptions, autobiographical revelations all contributed. In Chaucer's fiction as it developed, however, nothing compelled the pilgrim to self-revelation. *Sir Thopas*, for instance, focuses attention on questions of taste, genre, and literary technique. The tale becomes a test rather than a revelation of character; the Host's response exposes his limtis as a critic. The meagre commitment of the Monk to the "game" of storytelling reflects itself in the tragedies he threatens to keep on telling. Everything confirms the freedom of both narrators and auditors in the fiction. Our sense of the pilgrims as present, capable of interrupting, capable of replying, capable even of not listening, suggested perhaps to Chaucer the part that the road might play in giving verisimilitude to the pilgrimage. The pilgrims on the road at a specific time and place would add another physical dimension to the frame story; a succession of place names would suggest their movement along the road, give thematic significance to time as they neared the martyr's shrine, create a special problem in the anticlimax of a return journey, and epitomize the inherent conflict between the "ernest" of the pilgrimage and the "game" of the storytelling.

3. The Man of Law and the Parson—"Jerusalem celestial"

Before the *Shipman's Tale* led off the longest fragment of the *Canterbury Tales*, it belonged to the Wife of Bath; it was introduced by the Epilogue to the *Man of Law's Tale* and by a part of the Wife of Bath's Prologue. The miracle that the evidence for this earlier sequence remains, results apparently from Chaucer's habits of composition. When a new and better inspiration took possession of his imagination, he did not pause to tidy up but went forging ahead, leaving for later the busy work of introduction, connection, and consistency of detail.

The framework of the *Man of Law's Tale* has a number of suggestive elements. The Host starts off by observing the length of shadows as equal to the height of the trees causing them and knows that for the latitude he is in on April 18 it is ten o'clock. He seems upset at the waste of a quarter of the day and calls on the Man of Law to keep his promise by telling a tale. The Man of Law delays his performance with a long commentary on Chaucer's storytelling, especially on the legends already written, or projected, of Cupid's saints. The commentary includes a brief excursus, possibly intended by Chaucer as a playful (sooth pley, quaad pley?) reference to Gower, on the stories that Chaucer wouldn't think of repeating because they deal with incest.[11] At the end of the commentary, the Man of Law disclaims any intention of competing with the poet: "I speke in prose, and lat him rymes make" (B 96). The surprise of a rhyme royal prologue and tale, the story of Constance, follows. Was there a prose tale for the Man of Law originally? Many scholars have followed the lead of Tatlock and accepted the suggestion that the *Melibeus* was originally the *Man of Law's Tale*, referred to with some contempt in the epilogue as involving "philosophie," "phislyas"(?), and "termes queinte of lawe."[12] In the epilogue, the Parson's readiness to "snib" the Host for swearing—"What eyleth the man, so synfully to swere?" (B 1171)— effectually loses him his turn at storytelling. The Host apparently avoids him until the last possible moment, paying no heed to his feelings about swearing. Only when everyone else has told his tale and the Host's control over proceedings is coming to an end, does the Parson get his second chance.[13]

The connections between the Man of Law's links and the Parson's Prologue include not only the dramatic relationship of Host and Parson but also the method of telling time and the preparation for a prose tale. The shadows have proportion of eleven to six with the height of the person causing them; it is four o'clock. The pilgrims are "entryng at a thropes ende," and the Host gives repeated emphasis to the sense of finality:

> Lordynges everichoon,
> Now lakketh us no tales mo than oon.
> Fulfilled is my sentence and my decree;
> I trowe that we han herd of ech degree;
> Almoost fulfild is al myn ordinaunce.
> I pray to God, so yeve hym right good chaunce,
> That telleth this tale to us lustily. (I 21)

No reference here to the Host's authority as judge and reporter (only as monitor), to the prize-awarding final supper at the Tabard, or even to the approaching reunion with his spouse and the danger that his remarks on the journey will be reported to her. Either Chaucer had abandoned these elements of his plan or he had not yet invented them when he wrote the Parson's Prologue.

The animus against the Parson, first triggered by his rebuke of the Host for swearing, finds nourishment no doubt in a silent antipathy and in the sense each man has that the storytelling presided over by the Host has superseded religious purpose, especially on the way back to Southwark. The tone of triumph with which in the end the Host calls on his defeated rival is unmistakable:

> "Sire preest," quod he, "artow a vicary?
> Or arte a person? sey sooth, by thy fey!
> Be what thou be, ne breke thou nat oure pley;
> For every man, save thou, hath toold his tale.
> Unbokele, and shewe us what is in thy male;
> For, trewely, me thynketh by thy cheere
> Thou sholdest knytte up wel a greet mateere.
> Telle us a fable anon, for cokkes bones!" (I 29)

There is a symphony of effect in these lines. Suffice it to note the familiar "thou" throughout; the questioning of the Parson's status; the minor climax of implication in "sey sooth," as if the Parson might not; the reference to his silence, "unbokele"; and the major climax, an anticlimax consisting of the fable for the "greet matteere" and the innocuous "cokkes bones" for the crashing oath the Parson (and we) are waiting for. This time the Parson gives him the answer direct and, as Chaucer puts it, "al atones": "Thou getest fable noon ytoold for me" (I 31). But this is the only "thou." By six lines, a Bible reference, and a proverb later, the Parson has turned to the pilgrims and is addressing his proposal to them—"yow . . . ye . . . yow." It is the pilgrims that accede and bid the Host say "That alle we to telle his tale hym preye" (I 66). The Host, realizing that the occasion has a certain solemnity, and perhaps appreciating, too, the quality of his critic, addresses him respectfully for the first time—"yow . . . youre . . . yow"—with a blessing replacing the customary oath.

The Host with his respectful address is perforce acknowledging what the Parson has accomplished in his brief outline of what he plans to do. He will confine himself to "moralitee and vertuous mateere," and do the pilgrims "plesaunce leefful."

> But trusteth wel, I am a Southren man,
> I kan nat geeste "rum, ram, ruf," by lettre,
> Ne, God woot, rym holde I but litel bettre;
> And therfore, if yow list—I wol not glose—
> I wol yow telle a myrie tale in prose
> To knytte up al this feeste, and make an ende.
> And Jhesu, for his grace, wit me sende
> To shewe yow the wey, in this viage,
> Of thilke parfit glorious pilgrymage
> That highte Jerusalem celestial. (I 51)

The Parson will turn the storytelling, the device by which the Host has led the pilgrims away from their religious commitment, into a devotional exercise. The feast will be a communion. The pilgrimage, long since past its physical destination in Canterbury, will be subsumed, through the miraculous transformation of motive that makes the Parson the last of the narrators, into a figure of the greater journey, the conventional but powerful image of life as a pilgrimage, its destination an afterlife that offers the possibility of salvation. The pilgrims sense the appropriateness:

> For, as it seemed, it was for to doone,
> To enden in som vertuous sentence.   (I 63)

The Host assents, urging the setting sun as a reason for brevity: "Beth fructuous, and that in litel space" (I 71).

Has the storytelling contest been abandoned, along with the plan for four stories from each pilgrim? Or are they later inventions? Is the present *Parson's Tale* with the Retraction intended as an ending for the *Canterbury Tales*? Or were we to have as an ending a return to the Tabard and a double role for the Host as husband and literary critic? In short, which finally won the day in Chaucer's imagination, pilgrimage or storytelling?[14]

About one of these questions there can be little doubt. The only evidence that points to the Retraction as a part of the *Canterbury Tales* is in the rubrics. The "I" in the Retraction is clearly Chaucer, not the Parson. He refers to the "tale" as "this litel tretys," and when he comes to the works he is revoking, he includes the *Canterbury Tales* as one of many, not set off from the others, with nothing to indicate that it is the work he is bringing to a close:

> and namely ... my translacions and enditynges of worldly vanitees, the whiche I revoke in my retracciouns: as is the book of Troilus; the book also of Fame; the book of the xxv. Ladies; the book of the Duchesse; the book of Seint Valentynes day of the Parlement of Briddes; the tales of Caunterbury, thilke that sownen into synne; the book of the Leoun; and many another book, if they were in my remembrance, and many a song and many a leccherous lay. (I 1087)

If he had been trying to eliminate the possibility of regarding this passage as the conclusion of the *Canterbury Tales*, he could hardly have been more explicit.[15] The question of the "treatise" as *Parson's Tale* is more nearly moot. The reference at the beginning to penitence as "the right wey of Jerusalem celestial" bears out part of the promise that the Parson makes in his prologue. However, the treatise hardly qualifies as "a myrie tale in prose" nor as a "meditacioun." It is conceivable, but unlikely, that Chaucer intended the treatise as the *Parson's Tale*. If he did, it belongs, with its prologue, to an early stage of development. For the echoes of it in many of the tales in the Wife of Bath's group would date it as clearly in existence before her original tale became the *Shipman's Tale*, and before the work that resulted in the B², D, C, and E-F fragments.

Certain conclusions are inevitable. The retraction and the *Parson's Tale* are more closely linked to each other than either is to the *Canterbury Tales*. The Retraction, by the language in which it refers to the *Canterbury Tales*, not only eliminates itself as a conclusion for the work, but indicates a period when Chaucer rejected and abandoned his masterpiece—a period, incidentally, before the one in which the Wife of Bath exerted her hold over the poet's imagination and her influence over the pilgrims.

The fact that Chaucer wrote sometime between 1386 and 1394 a translation of the *De Contemptu Mundi*, by Pope Innocent III, and that he also wrote the *Treatise on the Astrolabe* in 1391 (probably also the *Equatorie of the Planetis* in 1392) strengthens this indication,[16] which receives further reinforcement from two lyrics dated by most critics in these same years:[17]

> For elde, that in my spirit dulleth me,
> Hath of endyting al the subtilte
> Wel nygh bereft out of my remembraunce. ("Venus" 78)

> . . . in no rym, dowteles,
> Ne thynke I never of slep to wake my muse,
> That rusteth in my shethe stille in pees.
> While I was yong, I put hir forth in prees;
> But al shal passe that men prose or ryme;
> Take every man hys turn, as for his tyme. ("Scogan" 42)

The element of self-contradiction—the poet is, after all, writing in the very medium he is rejecting—does not outweigh the aura of conviction the lines convey. Taken along with the implications of the Retraction and the literary relationships of the *Parson's Tale*, they force us to confront the question, largely ignored by critics, When did Chaucer retract the Canterbury tales that "sownen into synne"? Was there a period before 1394 when he wrote the treatise on penitence called the *Parson's Tale*, as well as the "Wretched Engendrynge of Mankynde," and then a later period, just before his death, when he added the Retraction to the treatise? Or does the Retraction belong to that same period of religious commitment? "Now preye I to hem alle that herkne this litel tretys or rede" are the opening words of the Retraction. After listing the works that he retracts and those he thanks God for having written, Chaucer prays for the "grace to biwayle my giltes, and to studie to the salvacioun of my soule," and specifically for the "grace of verray penitence, confessioun and satisfaccioun to doon in this present lyf . . . so that I may been oon of hem at the day of doom that shulle be saved." This is the language and the spirit of the treatise. An interval of time between the *Parson's Tale* and the Retraction seems unlikely.

The late Professor Carleton Brown surmised that in the Man of Law's head-link (to line 98) we have the passage originally intended to introduce the first tale of the series.[18] He pointed to the mention of the date (appropriate to the start of the pilgrimage), the Host's formal exhortation against the waste of time (a topic treated by other poets of Chaucer's day at the beginning of ambitious undertakings), the catalogue of the author's works, the comparatively undeveloped character of the Host, and the paralleling of many of the elements of the passage in the General Prologue following line 826. In addition, there is the Man of Law's difficulty in thinking of a tale, more understandable if he is the first pilgrim to be called on. If we accept Professor Brown's theory, we can discern an artistic purpose more solemn and more restricted in scope than that represented by the *Canterbury Tales* as we know them. The series of stories was to start with the Man of Law telling the prose *Melibeus* and to end with the Parson's "vertuous sentence." The Host, after the *Melibeus*, would call upon the Parson, smell a Lollard in the wind at his comment on swearing, and trigger the intervention of the Wife of Bath, who after a part of her prologue would tell the *Shipman's Tale*.

The general resemblance of this sequence of events to what happens in the first part of Fragment A suggests that Chaucer retained the idea, throughout his work on the *Canterbury Tales*, of a striking contrast for the first two stories as well as the mechanism for bringing it about, that is, the intervention of a pilgrim not called on by the Host. Between the two moral tales in prose, the *Melibeus* and the perhaps unwritten *Parson's Tale*, would occur the poetry—the romances, the fables, the saints' legends, and the fabliaux, each in accordance with the degree of the speaker. The disagreement of Parson and Host was invented to reinforce this early design. But Chaucer had probably not yet determined the order in which the other pilgrims were to tell their stories, and either left the name of the pilgrim who had preceded the Parson blank or changed his mind several times. Hence the evident confusion of the manuscripts as to the reading in the first line of the Parson's Prologue.

Whether we accept the Man of Law's links as the original framework for the start of the storytelling, and whether we accept the evidence of the *Parson's Tale* and the Retraction as indicating a period in the early 1390's when Chaucer abandoned the *Canterbury Tales*, we must still see the Host-Parson quarrel as introducing the more conventional and the earlier of the two endings envisaged by Chaucer for the work. Chaucer would perhaps have retained the Parson as the final storyteller. We would still have experienced his effort to bring the pilgrimage to its proper goal in "Jerusalem celestial." His vision would have remained a part of the total design. The fiction would have continued beyond the Parson's vision to the concluding supper at the Tabard, where the comedy of literary judgment and of human interaction would have reaffirmed men's freedom to choose for themselves and the inevitable meaning their choices inadvertently create. What is the evidence for this view of the development of the *Canterbury Tales*? It rests on the general direction that Chaucer's imagination took, which we considered at the beginning of this chapter. It rests on the specific changes that involve the *Shipman's Tale*, the Wife of Bath, and the Parson-Host relationship. It rests on what we have still to consider— the number of tales each pilgrim would tell and the storytelling contest itself.

4. Beginnings—"Turne over the leef"

The A fragment of the *Canterbury Tales*, which includes the General Prologue, the *Knight's Tale*, and the three contrasting fabliaux, sets forth a plan for the whole work different in two very important respects from that envisaged in all the other parts. Only here do we find any mention of a storytelling contest with a prize-awarding final supper at the Tabard, the prize to be a free dinner at the other contestants' expense, the judge to be the Host. The Knight alone among the storytellers refers to the competition:

> I wol nat letten eek noon of this route;
> Lat every felawe telle his tale aboute,
> And lat se now who shal the soper wynne.   (A 891)

In the Parson's Prologue such a conclusion seems explicitly ruled out. The Host reiterates that they are approaching the end of their association together:

> Fulfilled is my sentence and my decree;   (I 17)
> . . . .
> Almoost fulfild is al myn ordinaunce.   (I 19)

The Parson echoes the Host's comment, expressing his intention "To knytte up al this feeste, and make an ende" (I 47). And the narrator voices a general consensus that "it was for to doone,/To enden in som vertuous sentence" (I 63).

The other special feature of the plan in the A fragment is the number of tales each pilgrim is to tell. The Host, in outlining his idea for entertainment on the road, says:

> This is the poynt, to speken short and pleyn,
> That ech of yow, to shorte with oure weye,
> In this viage shal telle tales tweye
> To Caunterbury-ward, I mene it so,
> And homward he shal tellen othere two.   (A 794)

The ordinary way to handle this discrepancy is to assume that Chaucer found this number of tales unmanageable and quickly abandoned it in favor of a single tale from each pilgrim. Certainly the B^2 fragment, with its interruptions and the shift of a tale from Wife of Bath to Shipman, strongly implies a single tale as the plan. The Parson's Prologue makes the situation explicit, as the Host calls on the Parson:

> Now lakketh us no tales mo than oon.   (I 16)

. . . .
For every man, save thou, hath toold his tale.   (I 25)

The Cook alone, and that in the A fragment, acts on the assumption
that he will have more than one turn in the storytelling. Roger Knight
of Ware finds the Host's satiric comment on the food he serves anything
but amusing and threatens to pay him off by exposing the innkeeper's
feet of clay:

> And therfore, Herry Bailly, by thy feith,
> Be thou nat wrooth, er we departen heer,
> Though that my tale be of a hostileer.
> But nathelees I wol nat telle it yit;
> But er we parte, ywis, thou shalt be quit.   (A 4362)

Unfortunately for the ordinary way of handling the discrepancy,
evidence of a number of different kinds points in the opposite direction,
namely that the plan for four tales per pilgrim is the later one, that it
in fact marks a change made at the very end of Chaucer's work on the
Canterbury Tales. We have already seen that the dynamics of storytelling, as opposed to a mere collection of tales, proved the energizing
principle in the group of tales connected with the Wife of Bath; that
the unconventional "soper at oure aller cost" was to supplant as ending
the Parson's use of his long-delayed turn to show the pilgrims the way
"Of thilke parfit glorious pilgrymage/That highte Jerusalem celestial"
(I 51); and that, in general, Chaucer's imagination was moving in
the direction of implicit meaning and experienced value, rather than
of the overt morality popular in his day. The storytelling contest and
the prize-awarding supper are associated with the larger plan in the A
fragment. To say that Chaucer dropped the idea of a contest in favor
of having the pilgrims merely amuse each other with stories would be
to say that he chose the less complicated and interesting of two alternatives, and that he made the choice, not in any weakening state of health
as a way of bringing to an end what he could never bring to completion,
but at the very beginning of his work on the tales. The association of
the contest and the larger number of tales in the A fragment, and the
fact that neither is mentioned or acted on in any other part of the
Canterbury Tales, argue strongly for regarding both as late changes
in Chaucer's plan.

33

Yet their coming at the very start of the *Canterbury Tales* militates against acceptance of this theory of the change. Every reader of Chaucer starts with the A fragment and recognizes that at the end the plan of the work is different. The obvious way to see this change as having occurred is from four tales to one, from the "soper at oure aller cost" to "Jerusalem celestial." How could Chaucer have come to write the first part of his work after he had written everything else? How could he have planned to change to four tales per pilgrim when he was so far from having completed a single round of stories?

The answer to both these questions is to be found in part in the *Shipman's Tale*. There we saw Chaucer rushing ahead with his inspiration for a connected series of tales before he had removed the inconsistencies from the first, or even written a proper introduction to it. The General Prologue is not only inconsistent in the number of pilgrims and of priests; it is also incomplete in not yet having portraits of the Nun's Priest and the Second Nun. The inspiration of his developing fiction, with its interacting parts, had him working on the end (the Parson's Prologue) before he had decided on a penultimate speaker (see the confusion in I 1), on the outward and homeward journeys almost simultaneously, on the pilgrims in the Blee Forest before they have reached Dartford (where presumably they spend a night). We can only glimpse his purposes in multiplying the size of his work by four. The Cook would pay back the Host later; he would first tell the "jape that fil in oure citee" and complete the profane triptych of fabliaux that balances the Knight's chivalric idealism. Multiple relationships among the pilgrims—the Cook's delight with the Reeve, his annoyance at the Host, his reconciliation with the Manciple—were to contribute to the impression of a social microcosm composed of many-faceted individuals, whose motives helped to create a providential design. Meanwhile, the stories of the guildsmen, the Yeoman, and the Plowman could wait, with the portraits of the Nun's Priest and the Nun, on time and inspiration.

The other question is easier. Chaucer came to write the first part of his work after he had written everything else, because he was not attacking the early part of the storytelling for the first time. The *Shipman's Tale* as Wife of Bath's connected to a part of her prologue and to the Man of Law's Epilogue, which prepared the way for the

34

Parson as final narrator and followed the Man of Law telling a prose tale, probably the *Melibeus*—this sequence was either an earlier beginning than A or was attached to an earlier beginning. This early sequence was changed when the *Constance* became the *Man of Law's Tale* and the Wife of Bath, with her developing prologue and her new tale, was detached to serve as stimulus for so much on the homeward journey. After the five tales were attached to the *Shipman's Tale* and after the tales connected to the Wife of Bath were written and joined, after the adventures of the Canon's Yeoman and the Manciple in the Blee Forest were depicted, Chaucer turned back to the beginning, which the erratic course of his invention had for some time neglected. At this moment a series of new ideas and modifications of old came to him—the *Palamon and Arcite* as *Knight's Tale*; the three churls as balance; the variety of motives producing pattern, meaning, and value; the four stories for each pilgrim; the telling of stories, which had already superseded the mere collection of stories, becoming a storytelling contest; and the pilgrimage ending, not with the Parson's overt morality, but with the irony of the Host as judge and literary critic; the use within the stories of the kind of portraits developed in the Prologue; heroes with epithets in fabliaux, "hende" Nicholas, "deynous" Symkin, and Perkyn "revelour"; frequent references to time and place as a means, not just of keeping the stages of the pilgrimage distinct, but of giving as many dimensions as possible to the literal existence of the pilgrims.

The other evidence for regarding A as late in its present form is both external and internal. The external involves the mention of *Palamon and Arcite* as a separate work in the prologues to the *Legend of Good Women*. The *Knight's Tale* shares this distinction with the *Second Nun's Tale*. A suggestive indication in the fragment that starts off with the *Second Nun's Tale* occurs when the Host welcomes the Canon's Yeoman and his master to the company of pilgrims and asks,

> Can he oght telle a myrie tale or tweye,
> With which he glade may this compaignye? (G 598)

Here we see one of the two instances outside of A where the possibility of more than a single tale is mooted. The association of this wavering about the number of tales with the incorporation of an earlier written saint's legend into the *Canterbury Tales*, and the emphasis on entertainment without any mention of the storytelling contest suggest the order in which some of the ideas already noted as present in the A fragment came to Chaucer. The use of *Palamon and Arcite* as the *Knight's Tale* stands out as by far the most important of these new ideas. It solved the problem of an appropriate opening to the storytelling. It gave within the opening story a pattern Chaucer had been creating in his account of the pilgrimage:

> For certeinly, oure appetites heer,
> Be it of werre, or pees, or hate, or love,
> Al is this reuled by the sighte above.   (A 1672)

It provided a far firmer expression of idealism than the *Melibeus* or the *Constance*, as a ground for contrast with the ensuing fabliau material. It marked a startling conjunction of already composed materials—the portrait of the Knight and the chivalric romance—a conjunction that Chaucer celebrated by actually adapting the beginning of the story to the Knight's position as pilgrim and competitor in the Host's game. The late dating of these changes receives some confirmation from the fact that the list of Chaucer's works in the Prologue to the *Legend of Good Women*, though altered in the second, post-1394 version to include the translation of Pope Innocent III's *De Contemptu Mundi* (G 414–15), retains the easily removed couplet that names *Palamon and Arcite* as a separate work:

> And al the love of Palamon and Arcite
> Of Thebes, thogh the storye is knowen lite. (G 409)

The internal evidence for regarding A in its present form as late includes the other mention of the "tale or two," in the words of the "Host to the Franklin" as he calls on him for his story:

> What, Frankeleyn! pardee, sire, wel thou woost
> That ech of yow moot tellen atte leste
> A tale or two, or breken his biheste.   (F 698)

This mention of a "tale or two" at the end of the series of stories connected with the Wife of Bath, often called the marriage group, implies that the change was in the direction of enlargement and that it came towards the end of the period when Chaucer was working on the two big groups of stories, those that are concluded with the *Frank-*

lin's Tale and those assembled in the B² fragment. Chaucer himself gives us additional evidence, the more striking for its obliquity, when in apologizing to his readers for the churlishness of the tales he is about to "reherce," he advises them:

> . . . whoso list it nat yheere,
> Turne over the leef and chese another tale;
> For he shal fynde ynowe, grete and smale,
> Of storial thyng that toucheth gentillesse,
> And eek moralitee and hoolynesse.
> Blameth nat me if that ye chese amys. (A 3181)

The evidence that the author gives, while at work on the beginning of the storytelling, that much exists already to which the reader may turn is unmistakable.

The diagram of the road to Canterbury has grown more complex as a result of our discussion of beginnings and endings. It now includes all the fragments and three distinct plans for arranging them.

Below is a résumé of the development of the *Canterbury Tales*, including not only the three plans but also a period when Chaucer had ceased to work on his masterpiece:

I. 1387–1390?: Period of the first conception of the *Canterbury Tales*, to which belongs the sequence Man of Law (*Melibeus*), Wife of Bath (Prologue, to line 168, *Shipman's Tale*), . . . Parson's Prologue (as introduction to the final tale). Perhaps ended with composition of the *Constance.*

1391–1393?: Period when Chaucer, having abandoned the *Canterbury Tales*, devoted himself to translating *De Contemptu Mundi* and writing the treatise on penitence (*Parson's Tale*), with the Retraction. Also the *Astrolabe* and the *Equatorie*. Ended with the revision of the Prologue to the *Legend of Good Women*, in 1394.

II. 1394?–1398?: Resumption of the *Canterbury Tales*. Expansion of Wife of Bath's Prologue. Conception of the marriage group. Formation of Fragments D, C, E-F, B², G, and probably H. Replacement of the *Melibeus* by the *Constance* as the *Man of Law's Tale* (still the first story, but now detached from any other). Suggestion that drama of reunion between the Host and his wife would follow the (perhaps still unwritten) *Parson's Tale.*

37

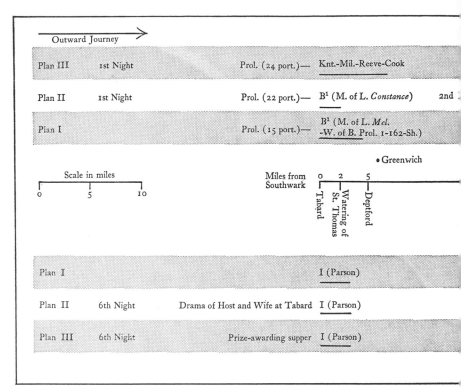

III. 1399–1400: Expansion of the plan to four tales per pilgrim, with the storytelling now a contest. The new start with Fragment A, with the Knight displacing the Man of Law as the first storyteller. The work to end with the prize-awarding supper.

Whether the first plan involved any attention to the road or to the days of the pilgrimage can no longer be determined. When Chaucer returned to the *Canterbury Tales*, presumably after revising the Prologue to the *Legend of Good Women*, he included a number of references to the road—enough, though barely enough, to indicate a five-day journey, as follows:

First day. The Man of Law telling the *Constance* (replaced in the final period by Fragment A as we have it; the *Knight's Tale* with the three churls as contrast). The pilgrims spend the night at Dartford.

Second day. Fragment B[2]: The pilgrims pass Rochester.

Third day. Fragment G: The pilgrims leave their inn at Ospring

38

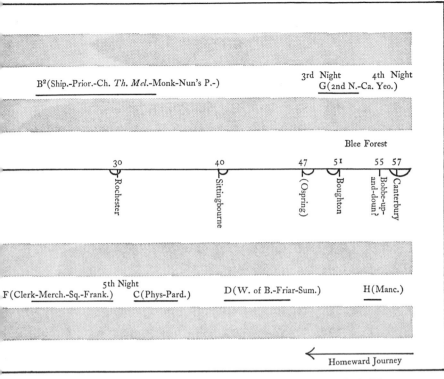

B²(Ship.-Prior.-Ch. *Th. Mel.*-Monk-Nun's P.-)

3rd Night   4th Night
G(2nd N.-Ca. Yeo.)

Blee Forest

30   40   47 51   55 57

Rochester   Sittingbourne   (Ospring) Boughton Bobbe-up-and-doun? Canterbury

5th Night
F(Clerk-Merch.-Sq.-Frank.)   C(Phys-Pard.)   D(W. of B.-Friar-Sum.)   H(Manc.)

← Homeward Journey

early in the morning, are overtaken by the Canon and his Yeoman at Boughton under Blee, and enter Canterbury.

FOURTH DAY. Fragment H: Bobbe-up-and-doun (Harbledown?) Fragment D: Sittingbourne. Fragment C. The night at Rochester.

FIFTH DAY. Fragment E-F. The Parson's Prologue as introduction for an unwritten final tale. The supper at the Tabard with the award of the prize.

The contrast between the first period and Chaucer's later work on the *Canterbury Tales* is both striking and paradoxical. The portraits of the Prologue had at first an inert relationship with the tales; the frame served simply to accommodate a wide range of stories. The stories themselves had women as central figures, most of them good in a sense less limited than in the *Seintes Legende of Cupide*. Prudence, Griselda, Virginia, and Constance belong almost without question to this early period from 1387 through 1390.[19] They should probably be joined by

39

Canace, Dorigen, and the Prioress's widow.[20] Whether Chaucer intended it or not, the *Canterbury Tales* started out a more varied "Legend of Good Women."

Only the Wife of Bath's original tale breaks the pattern. Here the woman still dominates, but her conduct turns upside down the moral standards of her sister-heroines. The Wife of Bath's freedom to express moral sentiments not shared by her creator sets her apart from the other early storytellers. Her frankness about sex motivates Chaucer's apology in the Prologue, suggests the freedom of all the pilgrims in the poet's disclaimer of responsibility for what they say, and prepares the way for the more dynamic relationship between the portraits of the Prologue and the pilgrims' behavior on their journey. This greater freedom not only originates in the Wife of Bath but continues to find stimulus in her capacity for development, a capacity reflected in the expansion of her confession and the assignment to her of a new tale. Paradoxically, the focus shifts in the story she herself tells and in the stories she inspires. Men replace women as protagonists. Her own rapist-knight sets the style, and Chauntecleer, the unnamed hero-victims of Friar and Summoner, the Pardoner's revelers, January, Sir Thopas, the alchemical conman of the Canon's Yeoman, "hende" Nicholas, Aleyn and John, and Perkyn "revelour" carry on the pattern.[21]

Two things call for special comment in the way the *Canterbury Tales* developed. The energies come from the deepest levels of human motivation—from sex, from the lust for power, from the quest for love and happiness. These energies find release when the emphasis falls on the *telling* of stories, not just on the gathering of them in a frame. The game the Host devised freed both the pilgrims and their creator.

The use that Chaucer made of religious material in the final six years of his life suggests that his return to a secular and mundane point of view was as complete as had been his earlier rejection of it in the Retraction. The development of the Wife of Bath and the Pardoner, the transformation of the Griselda story, the creation of the Merchant and January, and the contrast of Nun and Canon's Yeoman, of Knight and churls, reveal an artistic absorption, a creative fecundity, a firmness of comic spirit, a commitment to "game" and the "ernest" that game reveals, which promises as a conclusion not a retraction of his best work but the "soper at oure aller cost" awarded by that subtle judge and

40

reporter Harrie Baillie to his choice as the best spinner of yarns among the pilgrims. The period of overt religious feeling was succeeded by one of subtle indirection, where morality is experienced rather than expressed. That this period of intellectual vigor continued to Chaucer's death or to a totally incapacitating final illness is suggested by the fragmentary and uncertain state in which the *Canterbury Tales* was left. If he had had even a short period of respite before death, Chaucer could hardly have failed to devote some effort to the arrangement and clearer definition of what had drawn from him so much in invention and artistry.

5. Prologue—"And preestes three"

The discussion of the development of the *Canterbury Tales*, starting as it did with the sexual ambiguity of the narrator of the *Shipman's Tale*, has left to the last the Prologue. We have seen that two elements in the Prologue, the storytelling contest and the four tales for each pilgrim, came probably at the very end. Other elements—the keeping of the sea between Orwell and Middelburg, the twenty-year-old Squire's "chyvachie" in Flanders, Artois, and Picardy, and the Knight's pilgrimage without so much as a change of his "gypon," armor-stained from a campaign in Prussia—point to the earliest years of the Canterbury period, 1387 and 1388.[22] Further evidence of the way Chaucer worked comes with the lines:

> Another Nonne with hire hadde she
> That was hir chapeleyne, and preestes thre.   (A 164)

The priests become the single "Nonnes Preest" named Sir John (B 3999) when the Host calls on him; and though the Second Nun and the Nun's Priest both tell tales, neither has the portrait one might expect from the narrator's assurance that he will tell "al the condicioun / Of ech of hem" (A 37–38). The "wel nyne and twenty" Chaucer tells us he met at the Tabard work out to be thirty or thirty-one, depending on whether we count in Chaucer or not.[23] The Prologue belongs thus to the whole period of Chaucer's work on the *Canterbury Tales*, has a number of inconsistencies, and shows evidence of being incomplete.

The possibility of reconciling at a stroke two of the inconsistencies lies in a study of the grouping of the pilgrims. The Knight's group of three, representing among the pilgrims the military life, contrasts with the Prioress's group of five, representing the religious.

> A Yeman hadde he and servantz namo
> At that tyme, for hym liste ride so. (A 102)

The lines not only stress the austerity of the Knight but lay the ground for the pretentiousness of the Nun, whose retinue is so much larger. This element of characterization Chaucer apparently abandoned when he came to assign a tale to the Nun's Priest at the end of his work on the biggest group of tales, B^2. The importance of keeping his fictional narrators distinct drew more of Chaucer's attention as the frame story evolved. He was the more willing, perhaps, to make the sacrifice of so telling a detail if he was adding at the same time the Monk and the Friar to the number of pilgrims. The religious group then would still consist of five, the greater variety would help to distinguish the narrators from one another, and the total of pilgrims would still add up to twenty-nine, if we include Chaucer in the number.

Chaucer realized the advantages of grouping the pilgrims and used considerable variety in the rationale behind the groups. Only five of the pilgrims, in series of two and three, are treated as entirely separate from the others. The groups themselves come in pairs, at the beginning, in the middle, and at the end. At the same time, he seems to have realized that groups of more than five would be difficult to remember and so would defeat the purpose for which they were formed. Hence his final arrangement of the pilgrims as follows:

> 3 Knight, Squire, Yeoman (father, son, and retainer)
> 3+2 Prioress, Nun, Priest (Prioress and attendants) and Monk, Friar (the five forming a religious group)
> 1; 1 Merchant; Clerk
> 2 Man of Law, Franklin (traveling companions, a law and land group)
> 5+1 Guildsmen and Cook
> 1; 1; 1 Shipman; Physician; Wife of Bath
> 2 Parson, Plowman (brothers, villagers)
> 5+1 Churls and Chaucer (within this group, Summoner and Pardoner paired as traveling companions).

A study of the rhymes that link some of the portraits would appear to dispose of a theory so speciously convenient. It is true that the portraits of the pilgrims substituted for the two priests, the Monk and the Friar, are joined by rhyme. But if these portraits were added, how to account for the rhyme linking the final line of the Friar's to the first line of the Merchant's? The portrait of the Merchant contains the reference to the sea route between Orwell and Middelburg, a reference that marks it as belonging to the earliest years of the Canterbury period. The rhyme Huberd-berd would seem to eliminate any possibility of viewing the Monk and the Friar as late additions to the company. Only the name Huberd gives pause, coming at the end of the long portrait, setting off the Friar from all the other pilgrims except Madame Eglentyne, its singularity reflected in the closing lines of the next portrait—the three lines sharing an ironical use of "worthy" and the distinction of being among the flattest Chaucer ever wrote:

> This worthy lymytour was cleped Huberd   (A 269)
> . . . .
> For sothe he was a worthy man with alle,
> But, sooth to seyn, I noot how men hym calle.   (A 284)

That the Friar does not need his name, that Chaucer never mentions it again, that in contrast three priests would very much need to be distinguished from one another—these considerations suggest that the introduction to Huberd, after we have come to know him so well, survives from an earlier line naming the three priests, a line that almost writes itself if we remember that the Host calls the Monk Sir Piers:

> Another Nonne with hire hadde she,
> That was hir chapeleyne, and preestes thre   (A 164)
> [Cleped Sir John, Sir Piers, and Sir Huberd.]
> A Merchant was ther with a forked berd,
> In mottelee. . . .   (A 271)

Other considerations lend support to the theory of the replacement of the two priests by the Monk and the Friar. We have already seen the close relationship between the B² fragment and the tales connected with the Wife of Bath. When the Nun's Priest was being assigned his tale, the Monk in B² and the Friar in D were being similarly provided.

The strong attack on corruption associated with the Church, indirectly made in the description of the Parson, is carried home directly in the tales of the Friar and the Summoner, in the confession of the Pardoner (associated by its echoes of the *Parson's Tale* with the Wife of Bath and the Merchant), and in the portraits of the Monk, the Friar, the Summoner, and the Pardoner (for the last two we shall see below some reason to assign a late composition). Finally, the portraits of the Monk and the Friar, linked as they are by rhyme and hence probably composed at the same time, are among the most complex of the descriptions in the Prologue, especially in the use of indirect discourse to catch and expose the very accent of the casuistry with which these pilgrims justify their misconduct.

If this explanation is correct, and the three priests were once named and joined by rhyme to the portrait of the Merchant, it would indicate that Chaucer did not originally intend to include descriptions of all the pilgrims in the Prologue. Such a conclusion inevitably directs attention to another list, joined by rhyme to the Plowman's portrait and ending with a degree of finality that makes the following portraits something of a surprise:

> Ther was also a Reve, and a Millere,
> A Somnour, and a Pardoner also,
> A Maunciple, and myself—ther were namo. (A 544)

Chaucer's original plan for the Prologue involved perhaps the shorter series of fifteen portraits, with some of the pilgrims described fully, the five guildsmen drawn in a group picture, and some simply named.[24] With the substitution of the Monk and the Friar for two of the priests, Chaucer decided to furnish portraits of all of the pilgrims. He left the list of churls because he didn't complete all the descriptions at once, because the list provided the rhyme for the final line of the Plowman's portrait, and because, as Professor Malone suggested, the list performed the function of telling his readers, when they had long since lost count, that there were only five to go. Chaucer also left the line with the three priests unchanged because he realized that he would be altering it anyway when he composed the descriptions of the Second Nun and the Nun's Priest. The motivation for the addition of nine portraits to a "clause" (A 715) already long was at least twofold—Chaucer's recognition of the interaction between character and tale as the energizing principle of his general scheme, and his growing interest in the lower orders as he worked on the fabliaux and the confessions of the Wife of Bath and the Pardoner.

This theory for the development of the Prologue, which dovetails neatly with what we have seen of the development of the *Canterbury Tales* as a whole, can be summarized as follows:

I. 1387?–1388: Portraits of fourteen of the pilgrims and the joint portrait of the five guildsmen were composed; the Nun, the three priests, and the five churls were simply listed without being described, the priests being differentiated from one another by name. Rhymes connected the Yeoman and the Prioress, the names of the priests and the Merchant, the Cook and the Shipman, and the Plowman and the list of churls.

II. Ca. 1396: Chaucer substituted the Monk and the Friar for two of the priests, composed their portraits (linked by rhyme), and inserted them in the appropriate place, using the name of the third priest for the Friar in order to preserve the rhyme Huberd-berd, but leaving the line mentioning the three priests to be altered when he composed portraits of the Nun and the Nun's Priest. During this period he was also writing the descriptions of the five churls. It was probably in this period that composed the introductory lines for the portraits (A35–42), in which he says he is going to tell us about each of the pilgrims.

If correct, the theory as outlined reveals a considerable change in attitude toward the society depicted in the Prologue. Originally the portraits were to start with the Knight and end with the Parson and his brother the Plowman. A selfless dedication to their roles would thus characterize the far-traveled and energetic Knight, protecting Christendom on every one of its borders, and the no less energetic pair, clerical and lay, giving vital service within the constricted limits of the village. Protected from external foes and strong at the source of its livelihood, the society could afford the moderate range of characters in between (including the scholarly Clerk and the generous Franklin), many of them self-seeking, one or two given to vice, but none of them living off the corruption of their fellows. With the insertion of Monk and Friar and the spelling out of character in the portraits of the five churls, the picture undergoes a distinct change. The general impression given by the community of pilgrims is lighter, more gamey and more gamesome. Decorum and middle-class respectability have been diluted by trickery, dishonesty, and license. But if the pilgrims promise livelier and more varied activity, the society is far less firmly established. If Knight, Parson, and Plowman still lead their admirable lives, we no longer have as our final impression of the society a village secure in the ministrations of its brave priest and the energetic labor of its sturdy peasant. Instead, the Summoner as counselor of the young and his companion the Pardoner, preaching to win silver for himself, close out the portraits. The Church not only harbors unspiritual and vicious men but allows its great power to be used by them for the subversion of the community's moral life. The society now depicted by Chaucer is distinctly threatened, not by marauders the Knight can ward off, but by the corruption of the very institution whose function it is to give spiritual and moral leadership.

The sense of risk, of issues not easily resolved, of an outcome that might go against the establishment, accompanies the increased emphasis on the telling of stories, the game of the contest, the distancing of the narrator from the didacticism of the pilgrims. Chaucer's experience with the elements of his fiction freed him from the anxieties of imposed morality, showed him the advantage of giving full play to the oppositions he found in himself and in society. His growing confidence in his art as a delicate gauge of value found a reflection in his own tendency to withdraw from overt moral judgment. The pilgrims spoke for themselves. The pilgrimage became a model for the world, the more complex for the variety of forces let loose in it. To a limited vision, these forces threatened anarchy. What they really threatened was an outcome not predetermined. In this respect, the product resembled the process that brought it into being. Chaucer himself did not foresee the end product when he invented the game of the storytelling. As his experience with the elements of his fiction developed, he realized that, within the limits of his game, events had significance in the same ways they did in the world—that predisposition to form and inevitability of meaning were characteristics that his art at its best shared both as process and product with his world.

We have recovered as much as we could of the process. We have seen the extent to which the indeterminacies of game superseded the certainties of pilgrimage. It remains to explore the art of the product, to see how the elements in the fictional world the poet was evolving relate to one another and attain meaning. The exploration will fall into four parts: first, the great Prologue, with its emphasis on character as the ground for action; then the three main groups of stories—the Knight's and the three churls' on the first day, followed by the longest sequence, beginning with the Shipman's and ending with the Nun's Priest's and finally the stories connected with the Wife of Bath, which were intended, if our reconstruction of the process is correct, for the homeward journey.

the meaning of
chaucer's prologue and its art

"The condicioun/Of ech of hem"

THE Prologue to the *Canterbury Tales* opens with a description of nature; it proceeds with the perfectly casual concurrence of pilgrims at the Tabard—"Bifil that in that seson on a day" (A 19)—and then, while the pilgrims sleep and Chaucer has, as he so reasonably puts it, time and space, it plunges into a series of twenty-four portraits.[1] The casual and reasonable quality of the introduction should not conceal from us the presumption of the poet, the challenge he was setting to his skill, and the significance of these portraits for the stories that were to follow. He will tell us, he says,

> al the condicioun
> Of ech of hem, so as it semed me,
> And whiche they weren, and of what degree,
> And eek in what array that they were inne. (A 41)

This exhaustive program for each of the portraits makes by implication a considerable claim for the poet's observation and insight, relieved by the modesty of the limitation, "so as it semed me," but only superficially. For the phrase keeps before us the fiction of the narrator's presence at the inn and on the pilgrimage. He is telling us what he experienced, what he learned of the pilgrims by observation and contact. Furthermore, this program implies the detailed and systematic description of each pilgrim, such as he has given us of the Duchess Blanche. Standing too much alone, even for the *Book of the Duchess*, the ponderously complete portrait, multiplied as it threatens to be by twenty-nine,

48

would have destroyed the reader's interest before he reached the stories in the *Canterbury Tales.*

With the portraits themselves, we discover that the modest "so as it semed me" takes precedence over the promise of a complete description for each pilgrim. The poet is at once more ingenious and more skillful than to depend on system to imitate life. What he does finally is to rely, in the fiction he has set up, on his own impressions to determine what he will tell us of each of the pilgrims. The presumption of such a decision is mitigated for us by the mildness and apparent simplicity of Chaucer the pilgrim as he complies, for instance, with the Monk's and the Friar's self-justifications, and by the withdrawal from overt criticism of Chaucer the narrator. It is justified by the sharpness of his observation and by the constantly varied strategies he employs to project the observation. The shifting interplay in the portraits between detail and generalization, between the fact and its implications, between the explicit and the omitted, between the naive and the witty, between the ordered and the random, keeps the reader's expectations constantly alert. The several scales of value by which the pilgrims reveal their worth suggest the complex standards of a living society. They include not only the moral, the social, the financial, but also the extent to which each pilgrim emerges as an individual.[2]

The time-and-space relationships are also complicated. We are simultaneously at the Tabard as Chaucer talks to the Pardoner, on the road to Canterbury as he observes the pilgrims' horses and the relative positions of the Miller and the Reeve in the caravan, and omnipresent as he tells us what only the Merchant knew of his own net worth: "Ther wiste no wight that he was in dette" (A 280). The final effect of the portraits is paradoxically one of movement, movement not only of the pilgrims but of the observer. Chaucer seems to have realized, in meeting the challenge he had set himself, that life cannot be caught standing still. The fiction that he created of himself as one of the pilgrims, and the fact that it was a fiction, gave him opportunities to move about as he observed now this facet, now that, of the life he was imitating; as he noted down at once the sudden insight rather than wait for its logical place in the portrait and risk losing it entirely.[3]

The long series of portraits provides the key to the meaning of the *Canterbury Tales.* The fact that, coming at the beginning, they are so

49

numerous and loom so large compels attention from the reader. Their impact is given direction, when the series is finished, by what seems another example of the poet's simplicity, his apology for plain speaking:

> But first I pray yow, of youre curteisye,
> That ye n'arette it nat my vileynye,
> Thogh that I pleynly speke in this mateere,
> To telle yow hir wordes and her cheere,
> Ne thogh I speke hir wordes proprely.
> For this ye knowen al so well as I,
> Whoso shal telle a tale after a man,
> He moot reherce as ny as evere he kan
> Everich a word, if it be in his charge,
> Al speke he never so rudeliche and large,
> Or ellis he moot telle his tale untrewe,
> Or feyne thyng, or fynde wordes newe.   (A 736)

While seeming to apologize for the vulgarity of some of his pilgrims, Chaucer is really asserting the autonomy of all of them. They are the basic reality. What the poet is about to write he has simply heard them say. By dissociating himself from any responsibility except to the truth, Chaucer implies an identity for each of his pilgrims capable of being misrepresented; he alerts us to the importance of the smallest details ("everich a word"); he prepares us to accept the stories as utterances of the pilgrims, as further revelations of their characters.

The sense of simultaneous realities—of a poet telling us his experiences, of a group of miscellaneous people on pilgrimage, of the extension of actuality through the inner world of each pilgrim's imagination—does not wait for the stories to impress itself on our awareness. We get it from the portraits. Each of the pilgrims carries with him his previous experience, his habits, his learning, his knowledge of the world, as well as his clothes and his physical appearance. Chaucer does not hesitate to define his characters in terms of their past, as well as what he could see and hear in the moments of his contact with them. Three things result. First of all, there is a far wider range of possibilities in each portrait and at each moment of each portrait. Secondly, the opportunities of presenting character through specific detail are greatly extended. And finally, the quality of the detail becomes a sign of the direction and a measure of the extent of the pilgrim's vision. What we see is occasionally not the pilgrim at all, but what it has meant most to him to do in his life.[4]

The group of the first three pilgrims shows some but by no means all of the possibilties that Chaucer was to exploit in the long series of portraits. The contrast of what one might best call the inner life in the three men finds expression not only in the quality of the details but in their organization and in the stance from which Chaucer views them. The Knight is of course the dominant figure, and his character defines itself in the chosen companions of his pilgrimage as well as in his own qualities and attainments—his gentleness, in the freedom given his son in matters of dress and action; his effectivness as a soldier, in the neat competence of his yeoman-retainer; his dignity and sincerity, in the very absence of further retinue.

The portrait of the Knight emphasizes the devotion of a lifetime to the ideals of chivalry. The greater part of the portrait is seen from the point of view of omniscience, and when Chaucer moves in to tell us of "his array," the details of his dress confirm our impression that no boasting of battles fought or honors conferred could come from this quiet-spoken man. At the very beginning Chaucer stresses the constancy of his conduct. He is a "worthy" man,

> That fro the tyme that he first bigan
> To riden out, he loved chivalrie,
> Trouthe and honour, fredom and curteisie. (A 46)

And later we learn that

> He nevere yet no vileynye ne sayde
> In al his lyf unto no maner wight. (A 71)

This later passage would create no surprise, were it not for the intervening list of battles. But in that list the space of romance is canceled, and the Knight finds an actuality that sets him off from the Gawains and Bevises of medieval literature. Each of the names has resonance as a site of battle. Collectively they confirm the lifetime devoted to chivalry, representing forty years at least of intermittent campaigning. They do more. They define the kind of fighting the Knight has engaged in. Each of the battles was on the borders of christendom. From Alexandria to Prussia to Spain to North Africa and back to the Holy Land, they represent every frontier with "hethenesse," and with the single exception of the expedition "Agayn another hethen in Turkye," an exception that lends the whole list an air of probity, they were "for the faith." Thus they reinforce the life of dedication outlined in general terms at the beginning of the portrait at the same time that they localize and actualize it.

The meekness of a maid comes then as a surprise attributed to a man who has spent his life in the army, who has taken part in fifteen mortal battles and slain his man three times in single combat. This meekness serves also to differentiate him further from the medieval stereotype. The "curteisie" which the knight has loved all his life has nothing to do with the passion of the courtly lover. Rather it represents a purity of manner that has resisted the crudities of camp life and that eschews the outward display of dress. Rules of conduct have become nature for the Knight. He carries about with him a far-traveled and well tested devotion to high principle: "He was a verray, parfit gentil knyght" (A 72).

The portrait of the Knight depends for its main effect on the interaction of ideal and actual. The initial statement of the ideal has a refreshing directness, mingling with such value words as the thrice used "worthy" and the repeated "honour," the simplicity of expressions like "fro the tyme that he first bigan / To riden out" and "no man ferre," and preparing us for the meaning of the list of battles with the single line "As wel in cristendom as in hethenesse" (A 49). The list of battles starts with the most famous (Alexandria, 1365), continues with the most recent (Lettow, Ruce, Pruce, where the Knight was so signally honored), and goes on to the first (Algeciras, 1344). Geographical considerations then dictate the return via Algeria (Belmarye) to the Holy Land (Lyeys, 1367, and Satalye, 1361). A summary then suggests that most of the Knight's fifteen mortal battles had been in the Mediterranean region, and the battles suggest the other kind of fighting, the single combat at Tramyssene, the whole list ending with the exceptional aid to a heathen against another heathen. The order here, linear and impressionistic rather than strictly logical, establishes firmly the conversational tone, yet performs its function in the larger whole by giving the Knight's idealism a specified and largely consistent part in the contemporary world.

The couplet that follows the list,

> And everemoore he hadde a sovereyn prys;
> And though that he were worthy, he was wys,   (A 68)

points beyond the portrait at meanings of "worthy" less stringent than those the Knight fulfills—at knighthood as rank and at substance as wealth that in actuality are too generally divorced from wisdom and devotion to high principle. The concessive "though" strikes a radical note and suggests that the poet, however unassuming in manner, however ready to accept the social order, is not deceived on questions of "worth."[5] But Chaucer leaves comparisons aside as he turns briefly and effectively to the everyday manners of the Knight, to the quality of his relationship with other men, where the ideal plays against the expectations aroused in the audience both by the hard campaigning of the battles and by the romantic aura of chivalry. The single line of summary, one of the two grammatically distinct lines in the portrait, gains further emphasis from the rhyme and from the recall in "verray," "parfit," and "gentil" of what has gone before.

Chaucer introduces his own observations as pilgrim by drawing closer to his audience as well as to the Knight: "But, for to tellen yow of his array . . ." (A 73). The horses, as befitted a man of the Knight's eminence, were good, but the single item of dress described, the "gypon" of fustian, bears on it stains of armor, which authenticate the career as soldier, the sincerity as pilgrim, and the quality as man, of its bearer.

The sobriety of the Knight serves as background for the multifarious colors and abilities of his son the Squire. The note is struck at the very beginning with the word "lovyere." The details of physical appearance, of dress, of military experience, of talents, tumbling out pell-mell, have reference either implicit or explicit to his "hope to stonden in his lady grace"; they culminate in the humorous hyperbole of the couplet

> So hoote he lovede that by nyghtertale
> He sleep namoore than dooth a nyghtyngale   (A 98)

where the chiming of "nyght," in addition to the rhyme, climaxes the exaggeration of sentiment and expression. The poet has little need for the wider range of omniscience; the squire is *there* physically. He is all attractive surfaces, and Chaucer finds it appropriate to give the rhyme

53

the decorative prominence throughout that comes from avoidance of run-on lines. The summarizing line, which had come almost at the end of the Knight's description, breaks from the poet in mid-portrait, as if in irresistible response to the Squire's own exuberance. But it is important to see the line in its setting, for the language, in contrast to the directness of the Knight's portrait, has certain obliquities, as we noticed earlier in the couplet about the Squire's sleeplessness:

> Embrouded was he, as it were a meede
> Al ful of fresshe floures, whyte and reede.
> Syngynge he was, or floytynge, al the day;
> He was as fressh as is the month of May.   (A 92)

The beginnings here—"Embrouded was he," "Syngynge he was," and "He was—" suggest the progression from clothing to activity to essence. But the alliteration of *f*'s and *m*'s, the repetition of "fressh," and the image used for essence, picked off the embroidery, as it were, give the four lines a reciprocating effect. If the squire's essence is spring freshness, it is also embroidery. *He* was "embrouded," as well as his garment.

While the Squire is less serious than his father at the same age, he is perhaps more gifted. The unusual list of accomplishments—

> He koude songes make and wel endite,
> Juste and eek daunce, and weel purtreye and write   (A 96)

—added to his physical strength and his prowess in skirmishes across the channel, depicts the potentialities of youth unlimited by the choices, the commitments that time will enforce. The juxtaposition of modishness and firmer promise—the "lokkes crulle" and the "wonderly delyvere," the "born hym weel, as of so litel space," and the lover's nightlong revelry, the "justing" and the "dauncing—" continues to the final couplet, and represents the impressions and the data gathered by the poet of this youngest of his companions throughout the pilgrimage: "Wel koude he sitte on hors and faire ryde" (A 94). But the final line tips the balance in favor of promise as Chaucer recalls the first glimpse of father and son at the Tabard:

> Curteis he was, lowely, and servysable,
> And carf biforn his fader at the table.   (A 100)

Here the general traits are followed by what appears at first to be just another trivial detail, but the anticlimax is only apparent. The qualities that, after the nightingale couplet, we expect to be directed to the Squire's lady gain an unexpected depth in the image of the single action that directs them instead to his father.

After the extraordinary confrontation of experience and youthful energy in the portraits of Knight and Squire, the description of the Yeoman has a neutral, almost perfunctory tone. The details add up to neatness, spruceness, competence—nothing more. The weapons don't mean belligerence. The Christopher doesn't mean unusual piety. Even more than in the case of the Squire, we learn of the Yeoman in terms of physical detail, and the poet has far less need of insight into motive or knowledge of past exploits to set him before us. We see him not as he appeared at the inn but as a pilgrim accoutred for travel. For he belongs to the outdoor world—"Of wodecraft wel koude he al the usage" (A 110)—and it is the condition of his weapons that stands out:

> Wel koude he dresse his takel yemanly:
> His arwes drouped noght with fetheres lowe.　　　(A 107)

Behind the glitter of these weapons, which are variously "bright and kene," "myghty," "gay" (twice), and "sharp," the man himself is almost obscured: "A not heed hadde he, with a broun visage" (A 109). The Yeoman carries around with him the disciplined competence, the readiness for practical exigencies, that makes him the ideal servant for the Knight. Within the narrow range of his influence reigns a perfect propriety, and he is no doubt invaluable to his master. But he is hardly unique. Along with a number of other pilgrims, he makes nonsense of the critical opinion that Chaucer's characters are a company of non-pareils.[6] The poet himself, after striving to take pleasure (the repeated "gay" reveals the effort) in the Yeoman's zeal for his equipment, gets no closer to the man than the casual observation, "A forster was he, soothly, as I gesse" (A 117).

The first three pilgrims, then, help to define each other. The poet, having expressed an unequivocal admiration for the Knight and an amused and delighted sympathy for the Squire, approaches the Yeoman through his unusually spruce arrows, finds little else of interest save similarly maintained hardware, and ends up at a certain distance from his subject. No critical note has sounded in any of the portraits, but the distinctions in quality reveal themselves clearly, not only in the details of career, dress, and appearance that Chaucer carefully selects, but also in the tone of the comment, even in its rhythm. The grammatically distinct line, rare in the Knight's portrait, is common in the other two. But the meaning of its prominence is conditioned in the two portraits by other factors. The Squire's portrait abounds in details and finally presents us with a plethora of verbs. We get the sense of a man so active and varied that observation must express itself in the short cadence. The Yeoman's portrait, in contrast, has little variety and finally runs out of adjectives to describe the things he bears about him. The effect of the short cadences here is of observation labored and at last running down completely. The chief distinction between the three men is not moral; they are all three admirable in their way. Nor is it even social, despite the distance between Knight and Yeoman. Rather it is in the realm of their vividness as people. And here the greatest distance is between the Squire and the Yeoman. After the brilliance of the Squire's portrait, Chaucer can depend on the interest of contrast to carry him through the next description. And for those concerned enough to observe carefully, the Yeoman's portrait has its own subtleties of treatment. One further point. The grouping of characters helps in keeping them distinct. Not only are the contrasts and the parallels more pointed. But one group of pilgrims can be set against another.[7]

The next group, incomplete though it is, offers a superb contrast to the one led by the Knight. In one respect, however, the two are alike. Chaucer manages to convey the distinctions between the Prioress, the Monk, and the Friar, and between the representatives of religion and those of the military life, without a word of overt criticism. In fact, his enthusiasm seems to mount as he descends the moral scale, reaching a crescendo in the triple negative of praise for the Friar: "Ther nas no man nowher so vertuous" (A 251).

At the same time, the ideal against which the pilgrim is measured and found wanting finds stronger expression in each succeeding portrait. The result is to load those least able to sustain it with a burden of praise which exposes their shortcomings. Standards merely implied in the description of the Prioress emerge directly in the efforts of the Monk and the Friar to justify themselves. Chaucer permits us to witness a drama with deliciously comic overtones. The two clerics, pleased to find such a mild and complaisant listener, bask in his apparent approval and cannot resist the impulse to show off. We hear in their tones a complete satisfaction with the effect they are producing; and at the same time we recognize how clear an atmosphere for observation Chaucer's acquiescence has created, how gratuitous, and even perhaps distorting, direct criticism would be. Chaucer's praise, far from obscuring the moral issues involved, stimulates the reader by leaving to his judgment the measure of the apparent disparity. Chaucer's art has strong tendencies to the dramatic; in the portraits of the Monk and the Friar, description slips imperceptibly through indirect discourse into drama, and we are suddenly hearing the accent of the pilgrim as an element of characterization.

The strong moral issues which the Monk and the Friar raise are muted in the portrait of the first of the religious group, the Prioress. No possibility of self-defense arises, for the Prioress has no conception of the standards by which she might be criticized. She indulges no serious vices. On the contrary, she strives for a perfect propriety of conduct. The poet approaches her, as it were, uncertainly, noting her predisposition to smile, paying tribute to her goodwill in the adjective "simple," but recording also the self-consciousness of "coy." The mildness and delicacy of her oaths bring her closer to us but continue the ambiguity; then we are formally introduced, as if in deference, this once, to the amenities: "And she was cleped madame Eglentyne" (A 121).

The indiscretion of the name drives the poet back to omniscience for the assurance, amusingly linked to the name by rhyme: "Ful weel she soong the service dyvyne" (A 122). But "weel" means manner, not spirit, the poet hastens to point out, making certain that we understand by repeating the "ful" with "semely," and by linking divine service with the French which she speaks "ful faire and fetisly"—as well, that is, as she could have learned it in an English provincial convent. The deference of Chaucer's movements as he introduces us to the Prioress is qualified by the delightful juxtapositions—Eglentyne–service dyvyne–Frenssh, and especially Stratford atte Bowe–Parys. The modifiers, weel, fair, semely, fetys (note the later echo in tretys), have already established themselves, invariably reinforced by "ful."

Having set the tone with amusing delicacy, the poet can settle down to the thing he first saw and still remembers best—the Prioress's table manners. Details of her skill in eating run right through the line of summary: "In curteisie was set ful muchel hir lest" (A 132). The Prioress fully intends her table manners to be noticed, an unmistakable sign that, like her French, they are not quite the best. In the final summary of this first movement of the portrait, we find the same excess; the sentence runs through at least three full stops, as if in imitation of the Prioress, before resting satisfied at the effect created:

> And sikerly she was of greet desport,
> And ful plesaunt, and amyable of port,
> And peyned hire to countrefete cheere
> Of court, and to been estatlish of manere,
> And to ben holden digne of reverence.   (A 141)

Complaisance, good manners, and conduct that will win deference from others—these are the things it means most to the Prioress to practice. The poet, no stranger himself to "cheere of court," suggests that the effort shows through the attempted perfection.

The next section of the portrait, the poet warns us, will not present surfaces, but the inner woman:

> But, for to speken of hire conscience,
> She was so charitable and so pitous ...   (A 143)

A most hopeful beginning—but "pitous" rhymes with "mous," and tears for the casual rodent caught in a trap give way to those shed over the misfortunes of her own little dogs, fed with no leftovers but with the best convent fare. This time there is no need to insist. Her heart goes out to the small and the totally dependent, "And al was conscience and tendre herte" (A 150). But the words cannot help suggesting other and more fitting objects of solicitude for a prioress.

The final section of the portrait returns to the surfaces, to dress and appearance. We are not surprised at the carefully pleated wimple, but the adjectives used of her features have the aura of romance.[8] "Hir mouth ful smal, and therto softe and reed" (A 153). And the size of the woman comes as something of a shock after the emphasis on delicacy and sensibility—then we remember that nothing quite fits, that her courtliness is too cultivated and her charity out of proportion to its objects. The clothing brings us a third reference to religion, but this time we learn in advance of the decorative intention:

> Of smal coral aboute hire arm she bar
> A peire of bedes, gauded al with grene. (A 159)

The prayer life represented by the beads is further compromised by the "brooch of gold ful sheene" with the motto that has caused so much comment, *Amor vincit omnia*.[9] To the Prioress, I think, the bangle is simply a handsome piece of jewelry; she has long since forgotten the motto, if she ever read it. The carelessness in attaching to her beads what the "crowned A" proves to have been originally a love token, exists, however, in the larger context of God's all-conquering love. This love transforms the motto and may transform the Prioress.

The portrait of the Prioress represents the triumph of Chaucer's technique. The interest of her character is not at all obvious. She has neither the outstanding worth of the Knight nor the engaging and multifarious talents of the Squire. From research in contemporary records, we learn how common in the convents of the period were her failings, and how far from the notoriety earned by some of her sister-nuns.[10] Yet she stands before us in the portrait with the vividness of a living woman. The patience of Chaucer's observation, his willingness to try to catch the minutest quality rather than rest in the exaggeration of caricature, his skill in telling us more than he says but without obvious irony—the extent to which the qualities emerge from visual, auditory, even tactile imagery:

> She leet no morsel from hir lippes falle,
> Ne wette hir fyngres in hir sauce depe (A 129)

—the sense we get, as with Criseyde, of a social and a sentient being, whose tears flow despite the proprieties, despite the possible damage to the lustre of those "eyen greye as glas"—the contrast of her care in drinking:

> Hir over-lippe wyped she so clene

That in hir coppe ther was no ferthyng sene
Of grece, . . .   (A 135)

where the run-on and assonance and crudeness of "grece" imitate the
lady's fastidious avoidance—the discretion with which the poet reminds
us of the nun when we have almost lost sight of her, first, with the single
word "charitable" in describing her manners, then with the line "Ful
semyly hir wympul pynched was" (A 151), where the labials and close
front vowels, in contrast to the preceding "And al was conscience and
tendre herte," return us from emotional life to the prim surfaces—the
delicacy with which the incongruities are suggested, and the way in
which the coral beads and the golden, mottoed brooch reflect in their
varied implications so much of the Prioress's character and finally suggest the claims to power of the religion she is so superficially living—
these qualities, these effects, this art make the portrait effective and the
Prioress memorable.

That she originally had with her a retinue of a nun and three priests,
and that two of the priests gave way to the Monk and the Friar, is a
possible explanation of the discrepancy later when the Host calls on *the*
Nun's Priest for a story. It would mean that Chaucer kept constant
the number of five for the religious group, and that he also kept constant
the number of pilgrims at twenty-nine.

The fact that the next two portraits were among the last to be
written would help to account for their developed drama and their
decided anticlericalism. The Monk and the Friar, to an extent not
matched in any of the other descriptions, are constantly breaking into
speech themselves. Chaucer never quite lets them escape his control, and
yet catches their accent in the mimicry always on the verge of becoming
direct quotation. Here, for instance, is the Monk:

Ther as this lord was kepere of the celle,
The reule of seint Maure or of seint Beneit,
By cause that it was old and somdel streit
This ilke Monk leet olde thynges pace,
And heeld after the newe world the space.
He yaf nat of that text a pulled hen,
That seith that hunters ben nat hooly men,
Ne that a monk, whan he is recchelees,

Is likned til a fissh that is waterlees,—
This is to seyn, a monk out of his cloystre.
But thilke text heeld he nat worth an oystre;
And I seyde his opinion was good.
What sholde he studie and make hymselven wood,
Upon a book in cloystre alwey to poure,
Or swynken with his handes, and laboure,
As Austyn bit? How shal the world be served?
Lat Austyn have his swynk to hym reserved!   (A 188)

With occasional interpolations and with changes of pronouns and
tenses, the words are practically all the Monk's. They bear out the
manliness, the executive ability that has already marked the speaker for
advancement in the Church. They start out mildly enough, with an
endorsement of new methods in place of the rule that "was old and
somdel streit." But as the Monk warms to the subject and meets with
what he takes to be agreement, he drops the judicious tone and shows
his contempt for the regulations that get in the way of his activities, and
especially for the idea that monks should devote themselves to scholarship and manual labor. What he is really criticizing, of course, is the
monastic ideal, and in the image of the fish out of water he catches the
incongruity of his own career as a monk.

But the portrait cuts two ways. Though he has no use for the religious
life, and a real passion for fine clothes, good food, and hunting, a full-
bloodedness reflected in the words of possible sexual import—venerie,
manly, prikyng, lust—he is on the way up in his order. His own appearance reflects the prosperity of the cell he runs. And that in turn
reflects his ability to handle serfs and underlings and look out for the
worldly interests of the order. He is "A manly man, to been an abbot
able" (A 167). And if we are amused at the repetitions of sound, and
the rhyming of able with stable—if we are struck by hearing the bridle

Gynglen in a whistlynge wynd als cleere
And eek as loude as dooth the chapel belle   (A 171)

—we recognize in the image, not a literal meaning, but the way the
Monk dominates his surroundings and impresses men with his mere
presence: "Now certeinly he was a fair prelaat" (A 204). The word

"prelaat" surprises us. The line, coming almost at the end, brings to a focus the relationship between the Monk's abilities and, not just his order, but the Church. The prelacy of such a man measures the extent to which ideals have been swallowed in institutionalism. At the end, though, his portrait seems to run down. Having imposed himself on his order, on Chaucer, and on us, he has little to offer but the reiteration of his presence, a note that will sound later on the pilgrimage when he is cut off after only sixteen tragedies:

> He was nat pale as a forpyned goost.
> A fat swan loved he best of any roost.
> His palfrey was as broun as is a berye. (A 207)

The Friar's accent, on the other hand, is one of insinuation. A thorough scoundrel, the first we meet in the company of pilgrims, he is gifted, physically attractive, thoroughly equipped to entice others down the primrose path with him. The portrait, after opening with some shocking claims for the Friar and for all four orders of friars—their proficiency in "daliaunce and fair langage"—presents us with the first example in the Prologue of the innocent statement that will not yield an innocent meaning:

> He hadde maad ful many a mariage
> Of yonge wommen at his owene cost. (A 213)

The puzzling generosity stimulates conjecture as to motive, and if most readers arrive at an unsavory conclusion, they find confirmation in the phallic innuendo of the next line: "Unto his ordre he was a noble post" (A 214).

The Friar's voice keeps breaking into the description, but it has none of the Monk's assertiveness. His note is rather one of bland equivocation that makes religion attractive to others and profitable to himself:

> For he hadde power of confessioun,
> As seyde hymself, moore than a curat,
> For of his ordre he was licenciat.
> Ful swetely herde he confessioun,
> And plesaunt was his absolucioun:
> He was an esy man to yeve penaunce,

62

Ther as he wiste to have a good pitaunce.
For unto a povre ordre for to yive
Is signe that a man is wel yshryve;
For if he yaf, he dorste make avaunt,
He wiste that a man was repentaunt;
For many a man so hard is of his herte,
He may nat wepe, althogh hym soore smerte.
Therfore in stede of wepynge and preyeres
Men moote yeve silver to the povre freres.   (A 232)

The passage is a far cry from the Monk's contemptuous "nat worth an oystre" and "yaf nat . . . a pulled hen." The semblance of sweet reason sounds in the five introductory "For's" that lead up to the climactic "Therfore." All the rhymes but one (herte-smerte) involve religious terms and emphasize the Friar's use of sound to corrupt sense. Words like "repentaunt" and "confessioun" roll off his tongue as adornments; reinforced by pins, knives, gay music, a clean neck, and a good physique, they part "faire wyves" from their coin and their virtue. Piety and zeal in begging serve the most vicious purposes. His conduct is not, like the Monk's, a denial, but a perversion of the ideals of his order.

In a passage that does not quite reach indirect discourse, Chaucer mimics his attitude and manner of speech, wrenching word meanings with a suave indifference that matches the Friar's:

He knew the tavernes wel in every toun
And everich hostiler and tappestere
Bet than a lazar or a beggestere;
For unto swich a worthy man as he
Acorded nat, as by his facultee,
To have with sike lazars aqueyntaunce.
It is nat honest, it may nat avaunce,
For to deelen with no swich poraille,
But al with riche and selleres of vitaille.
And over al, ther as profit sholde arise,
Curteis he was and lowely of servyse.
Ther nas no man nowher so vertuous.   (A 251)

Words such as worthy, honest, curteis, lowely, and vertuous sharpen

themselves on the context of the Friar's activities. The idealistic connotations of these words, so often weakly invoked, find an unwonted
strength in the effort to suppress them. They help to remind us, along
with the Friar's cynical avoidance of the poor and the sick, of the ideals
of his order and of his religion. The passage presents, however, a
further contrast to the Monk's portrait, in addition to the distinction in
tone. The Friar, like the Knight, can be thoroughly depicted only from
the stance of omniscience. He does not actually say these things; in fact,
his outward appearance and manner are convincing enough to deceive
both the poor widow and the affluent love-day litigants. Only from
Chaucer's insight into motive and his knowledge of the concealed
activities of the man, can this mimicry of basic attitude emerge.

The strategy of the portrait presents us first with the inner corruption
of the Friar and of the orders he represents. Against the background of
corruption appear the details that point to his success, to his gaiety, to his
adaptability, to his popularity. These details would seem trivial, were
they not so shocking to our sense of justice, and were they not so vivid—
the quality of worsted, for instance, in his semicope, "That rounded as
a belle out of the presse" (A 263), where the shape and the sheen and
the newness find expression in the image. Then, lest our imagination
rush beyond the expression and strike from the bell unintended res-
onances (those of "rounded" and "presse" are acceptable), Chaucer
describes in the next two lines the way the Friar *sounds*—

> Somwhat he lipsed, for his wantownesse,
> To make his Englissh sweete upon his tonge   (A 265)

—reminding us that we have already heard that cloying voice, and
recalling the "wantowne" of the very first line of the portrait. Though
the organization is not so firm as in the description of the Knight, the
tendency is to move from omniscience to observation, from internal
reality to external detail, and the lisp, like the Knight's gypon, serves
as an epitomizing image. But it is not our final impression of this beau
ideal of friarly conduct. That comes in the twinkling eyes.

The contrast between the military and the religious groups is a
startling one. Had we portraits of the Second Nun and the Nun's Priest,
it might be somewhat less so. But, even then, the effect would be height-
ened by our expectations of the two sets of pilgrims. From those

dedicated to war we could hardly expect as high a standard of conduct as from those who devote their lives to the Church and religion. The contrast of course stimulates interest, and it may also reflect a tendency in Chaucer's art throughout the Canterbury period, a tendency to set out extremes as a framework for what is to follow. This pattern is to be found not only in the stories of Fragment A, where the *Knight's Tale* is followed by the fabliaux of the three churls, but also in the marriage group where, though not so closely juxtaposed, the extremes of Wife of Bath and Griselda are used by the Clerk to imply his own attitude, and then serve to stimulate the Merchant and the Franklin into tales on the same subject. A third instance of such a pattern occurs on the day of arrival in Canterbury, initiated in the two stories of the Second Nun and the Canon's Yeoman but never carried further—a contrast, in this instance, of the genuine piety appropriate to the shrine the pilgrims are approaching, and of the casual worldly concerns that intervene and divert attention from worship. A fourth possibility is the suggested earlier plan for the opening of the storytelling, the contrast between the Man of Law telling the *Melibeus* and the Wife of Bath telling the *Shipman's Tale*.[11] The first two groups of pilgrims present, it is true, a more complicated pattern. But the first and the last of the portraits, the Knight's and the Friar's, set a framework of moral excellence that easily includes not only the intervening pilgrims but all the ones who follow until the contrast is repeated in the two final groups, the Parson and his brother and the five churls.

That the moral import emerges from detail and over-all pattern, rather than from the author's comment, establishes at the outset one of the fundamentals of Chaucer's art in the *Canterbury Tales*. Just as the storytelling will supersede pilgrimage in projecting the deepest levels of insight in the poem, just as the enjoyment of fiction will replace didacticism, so here the ernest in game exposes the simplicities of overt morality, the element of play underlines what the detail and the patterns suggest. Rhymes, moral absurdity, the puzzle of seeming innocence, and the poet's sheer love of his craft and his creatures, all contribute to the sense of play, to the ernest in game. The Prioress's conscience and tender heart, her tears and her pity, deflate in the rhyme word mouse. The poet's agreement with the Monk's aggressive self-justification satisfies the Monk and simultaneously exposes him to us as it pushes to absurdity what the pulled hen and the oyster-cloister rhyme have already implied. We must believe the blunt assertion, "And I *seyde* his opinion was good" (A 183; italics mine). The "everich a word" claims of the narrator compel us to. But we do not for a moment accept the evaluation. Nor do we finally believe that the narrator accepts it. What Chaucer establishes here is an obliquity of relationship between narrator and pilgrim and between narrator and reader. He challenges us to understand his meaning. He prepares us for the puzzle of the Friar's generosity, which rhymes with his "daliaunce and fair langage":

> He hadde maad ful many a mariage
> Of yonge wommen at his owne cost.   (A 213)

He prepares us for the parody of sweet reason and confessional unction and for the shocking single line on the Friar's virtue. He gives us no easy definition of his own moral position. If we would find Chaucer in his work, nothing less than the whole work will serve. Meanwhile the values emerge from the detail and the design rather than the assertions. They do not suffer from the narrator's enjoyment of the pilgrims, or from the games he plays with us or with them. On the contrary, these elements add an unwonted freshness to the values and express confidence in an ordering providence.

The next series of portraits begins with two single pilgrims, continues with a government group of two traveling companions, and ends with the portrait of the five guildsmen and that of their accompanying cook. This arrangement has more coherence than at first appears. For one thing, it progresses from the isolation of the two single pilgrims to the total conformity of the guildsmen. It also presents a series of three minor contrasts, in which the first elements—namely, the Merchant, the Sergeant of the Law, and the guildsmen—have in common a pretentious pushing for worldly advancement. The tonalities in this series tend to be muted. The interest intensifies somewhat with the Clerk, the Sergeant of the Law, and the Franklin. But the Merchant at the beginning and the guildsmen and the Cook at the end make small impact on the poet. He finds it possible to dismiss them with perfunctory notice.

The contrast between the Merchant and the Clerk is emphasized by the repetition of "sownynge" applied to their manners of speech:

> His resons he spak ful solempnely,
> Sownynge alwey th'encrees of his wynnyng.
> He wolde the see were kept for any thyng
> Bitwixe Middelburgh and Orewelle.   (A 277)

This of the Merchant, who speaks the language of big deals and protectionism. But of the Clerk we learn:

> Noght o word spak he moore than was neede,
> And that was seyd in forme and reverence,
> And short and quyk and ful of hy sentence;
> Sownynge in moral vertu was his speche,
> And gladly wolde he lerne and gladly teche.   (A 308)

Both portraits start with appearance; they present an initial contrast between affluence and threadbare poverty. But as the poet probes beneath the surface, the values are reversed. The Merchant has his illegal dealings in currency and his credit rating as his central concerns in life; and the adjective "worthy," which Chaucer twice uses of him, must shed even its implications of substance and mean in his case "appearing substantial." So restricted in literal meaning, the word radiates connotations which expose the man's essential emptiness. The poet ends the portrait by telling us that he didn't bother to catch the Merchant's name. The Clerk, on the other hand, reveals beneath his shabby surface not only a dedication to his scholarly activities but a gratitude, a sense of obligation, to those who make his studies possible. The poet can joke about the external poverty of learning:

> But al be that he was a philosophre,
> Yet hadde he but litel gold in cofre.   (A 298)

But then, as if ashamed of the attitude implicit in the joke, he hastens to explain that the Clerk spent all that he could get on books and learning, and ends with the warm tribute to the Clerk's speech and his enthusiasm for acquiring and imparting knowledge.

The perfectly balanced couplet that, appearing for the first time in the *Canterbury Tales,* concludes with such warmth of tribute the Clerk's portrait—

> Sownynge in moral vertu was his speche,
> And gladly wolde he lerne and gladly teche   (A 308)

—punctures the pretensions of the Man of Law:

> Nowher so bisy a man as he ther nas,
> And yet he semed bisier than he was.   (A 322)

The Sergeant of the Law and his riding companion the Franklin represent the landed gentry and the courts, but of course with important distinctions. The former is a lawyer by profession, knowing, diligent, and hard working, while the latter, born to his position, devotes himself to good living and a generous hospitality, serving in the local courts and representing his shire in Parliament simply out of duty. The epicurean, not the hard-driving professional, wins the poet's approval. For the Man of Law seeks power and status; he uses his skill and his position to establish his own fortune. Though he engages in no shady dealings, he acquires land, not to enjoy the use of it, but with a dry and finicky legalism, beautifully expressed in the line "Al was fee symple to hym in effect" (A 319), and again later, with what was very likely a pun on an actual Sergeant's name (Thomas Pynchbek):[12] "Ther koude no wight pynche at his writyng" (A 326). Though his speech has none of the stereotyped bluster of the Merchant's, he yet suffers from an implied comparison with the Clerk—he is too ready to dispense wisdom and claim the attention due to reverence of mien and voice:

> Discreet he was and of greet reverence—
> He semed swich, his wordes weren so wise.   (A 313)

The Franklin, who derives from his land, not a sense of possession and status, but a fruitful abundance for himself and others, wins like the Squire a sympathetic response from the poet. We learn first of his appearance, beard white as a daisy and ruddy complexion; then of his epicurean taste. He is the thorough gourmet, discriminating in his pleasures; but before we learn of the careful arrangements he has made for gratifying them, we experience in a remarkable image his generosity, his intent to share with others the good things his wealth provides:

> It snewed in his hous of mete and drynke,
> Of alle deyntees that men koude thynke.   (A 346)

The Franklin has earlier been called both "Epicurus owene sone" and "Seint Julian"; there is a similar disparity between the daisy and snow images and the sauce that must be "poynaunt and sharp" or woe to the cook. But the dominant impression is one of natural abundance and innocent pleasure—an impression confirmed by the respect in which he is held, the duties he performs, the "morne milk" to which the whiteness of his dagger and pouch is compared, and the way in which "worthy" recovers its richness of literal meaning in the final line of the portrait: "Was nowher swich a worthy vavasour" (A 360).

With the guildsmen we return to the concern for worldly advancement evinced by the Merchant and the Man of Law, and we reach at the same time the nadir of individuality among the pilgrims. Here we have five men dressed alike, with identical aspirations, probably even married alike. Chaucer implies an aloofness on their part, an exclusive preference for each other's company, that repulsed his efforts to get acquainted and that excuses him from trying to differentiate them. They prefer to be seen as members "Of a solempne and a greet fraternitee" (A 364). The security of the group induces them to forego the association with the other pilgrims that might have defined them as individuals. We see no physical features; we only catch a glimpse in a single word (*shaply*; my italics) of the general portliness that, along with their possessions, qualifies them for aldermen:

> Everich, for the wisdom that he kan,
> Was *shaply* for to been an alderman.   (A 372)

We hear no voices; and at the end we lose sight of the men in what Chaucer assumes would be their wives' delight in precedence. The poet subtly protects himself from a charge of snobbery in dealing with these proud burgesses. They have with them, he tells us, a Cook

> To boille the chiknes with the marybones,
> And poudre-marchant tart and galyngale.   (A 381)

The specially prepared meals imply a dining apart from the others and a desire to avoid as much as possible the upsets and casual intimacies inherent in travel. The Cook, of course, helps to define the guildsmen's pretensions. Chaucer emphasizes his skill in cooking, but also drops a hint about his interest in London ale and is himself shocked at the unappetizing sore on his shin. The guildsmen reveal in their choice of cook a strictly limited refinement.

The portraits of the next three pilgrims are strongly individualized. Like the Merchant and the Clerk, these pilgrims belong to no group. In fact, we are surprised at first to find them on the pilgrimage. The description of the Shipman starts innocently enough. He is from far in the West, from Dartmouth, Chaucer guesses; and he rides a nag as best he can. His appearance, though, has a striking detail:

> A daggere hangynge on a laas hadde he
> Aboute his nekke, under his arm adoun.   (A 393)

The naked dagger has no immediate significance as Chaucer tells us of his weathered hue, his easy fellowship, the toll he levies on the wine cargoes from Bordeaux, "whil that the chapman sleep. Of nyce conscience took he no keep" (A398). Then quite calmly, in a conditional sentence that minimizes violence and will not quite yield an innocent meaning, we get it, as it were, between the eyes:

> If that he faught, and hadde the hyer hond,
> By water he sente hem hoom to every lond.   (A 400)

Almost before the meaning sinks in—"nyce conscience" indeed—the poet changes the subject—"But of his craft"—and hastens to immerse us in the technical terms of expert seamanship. The kind of summary we have gotten earlier in the line about conscience interrupts the account of the shipman's skill. This time the summary drops the tone of understatement, recognizing the qualities needed for survival in the ruthless world of an unpoliced sea, and catching in concrete terms the feel of the sailor's struggle with the elements:

> Hardy he was and wys to undertake;
> With many a tempest hadde his berd been shake.   (A 406)

Again, as in the line about conscience, the summary looks both ways. What appears to be further praise of the Shipman's skill actually throws light on his undertakings. They have carried him into every haven from Wisby on the Baltic to the westernmost point on the Atlantic coast, "And every cryke in Britaigne and in Spayne" (A 409). The understatement and obliquity of the portrait are not so much critical of the Shipman as imitative of his world. What is shocking to a landsman is everyday on the sea. The casual menace of the naked dagger strikes a lawless note among the pilgrims. But there is nothing devious about it, and the image of the Shipman, shaken but undaunted by tempests, has an epic quality, matched among the pilgrims only by the Knight.

The interest in the Physician's portrait is on a somewhat lower plane. The emphasis through the first twenty-four lines is on his skill and knowledge. What promises to be an obliquity at the beginning—

> In al this world ne was ther noon hym lik,
> To speke of phisik and of surgerye   (A 413)

—turns out to be simply the necessary concomitant, then as now, of real knowledge: the ability to win the confidence of a patient through his explanation of what he is doing. For Chaucer leaves us in no doubt that the Physician has all the current theory and practice at his finger tips: "He was a verray, parfit praktisour" (A 422). The one critical note, and that as yet a minor one, comes in the implication that he allies himself with the apothecaries to overcharge his patients for drugs. The exhaustive list of authorities, ancient and modern, completes the impression of deeply learned skill.

The final ten lines show the interaction between the professional and the personal sides of his character. The tone becomes lighter, and our impression of the man too, as we learn in witty terms of his dependence on diet rather than the Bible for his well-being:

> Of his diete mesurable was he,
> For it was of no superfluitee,
> But of great norissyng and digestible.
> His studie was but litel on the Bible.   (A 438)

The interplay between the rhyme word Bible (with its internal near rhyme "but litel") and the terms used of diet—"no superfluitee," "greet norissyng," "digestible"—gives subtle impact to a line that at first seems a gratuitous non sequitur. The doctor has come to believe in the sufficiency of the physical remedies he dispenses to others. Two lines devoted to his expensive clothing, the only two in the portrait that deal with appearance, bring us back to the more serious charge of greed:

> And yet he was but esy of dispence;
> He kepte that he wan in pestilence.
> For gold in phisik is a cordial,
> Therefore he lovede gold in special. (A 444)

The playful ambiguity of the word "esy," clarified in the next line, and the bland speciousness of the connection between the practice of medicine and the love of gold dismiss the Physician on a humorous note and prevent us from weighing too heavily the man or his failings.

The third of the single pilgrims is even more surprising than the piratical Shipman or the skeptical Physician—an unattended woman, the good Wife of "beside Bath." To meet her for the first time in the Prologue without associating with her portrait the remarkable revelations she later makes of herself provides a test of human forbearance. For the seeds of her later development are evident throughout. Yet the portrait, though lively, is by no means the most striking in the Prologue. We do not, for instance, hear her voice, as we do that of the Parson who follows her in the series. And the strategy Chaucer uses in his description of her does not provide quite the same sense of aesthetic fulfillment to be found in some of the others, those of the Squire and of the Prioress, for instance. The fact is that her character is too pronounced in all of its manifestations to permit of much subtlety.

After noting her deafness and her skill in clothmaking—"She passed hem of Ypres and of Gaunt" (A 448)—the poet presents a little scene in the parish church, where her efforts to "pass" show in the richly ironical context of "charitee."

> In al the parisshe wif ne was ther noon
> That to the offrynge bifore hire sholde goon;
> And if ther dide, certeyn so wrooth was she,
> That she was out of alle charitee. (A 452)

Her extravagance in always trying to be first is further illustrated by the amazing weight of fine headgear she manages to carry on the Sabbath. Chaucer then drops the confining atmosphere of the parish and tells of her clothing—scarlet stockings "ful streite yteyd" and moist new shoes—and her face, bold, fair, and red of hue.

By this time it is apparent that the Wife of Bath, though unattended, can take care of herself at least as well as the Shipman. In attempting to define the senses in which "She was a worthy womman al hir lyve" (A 459), the poet details five husbands, loses the train of thought ("worthy") in the other lovers that the husbands suggest, then picks it up again in the series of pilgrimages which make her, with the Knight, the most traveled of the company. The line of summary, "She koude muchel of wandrynge by the weye" (A 467), though it yields a possibly innocent literal meaning, recalls also the digression on lovers and associates it with the journeys. With the journey to Canterbury, too; and Chaucer gives us a picture of the Wife, "gat-tothed," sitting astride her horse with a huge hat which suggests a buckler, a footmantle about her large hips, and sharp spurs on her feet:

> In felaweshipe wel koude she laughe and carpe.
> Of remedies of love she knew per chaunce,
> For she koude of that art the olde daunce.   (A 476)

From clothmaking and precedence at the offering to the old dance of the art of love, the portrait suggests by its organization the release from parish confinement that the Wife finds on the pilgrimage.

With the Parson we come to the still center of the turning wheel. He and his brother the Plowman in strong contrast to the Wife of Bath, find within the limits of the parish a sufficient field for their activity. If, as many scholars believe, these two portraits were originally intended to bring the series of formal descriptions to a close, the first plan of the Prologue would have provided a strong affirmation of the values of medieval society. The Knight at the top, the Plowman at the bottom, the one on the beleaguered frontiers, the other at the village heart, both actively living the ideals of their religion in their respective spheres—as first and last of the pilgrims described, they would have suggested a framework of moral strength for the whole society. As Chaucer worked on the drama of the journey itself, he apparently found his own interest increasingly engaged by the less noble in human

73

activity, and returned to the Prologue to give it a different frame and a different emphasis. He was probably also motivated by a development in his perception of the world around him, by a new sensitivity to the forces of corruption in Church and State, and by a desire to give a more accurate if less idealistic picture of his society. Chaucer was not, like his friend Gower, primarily interested in the social and political issues of his time. But he explored in his writings an ever greater range of contemporary life. With the range came an awareness of social evil.

The portrait of the Parson has several distinctive features. It contains no reference to the physical appearance or dress of the pilgrim. It is written throughout from the standpoint of omniscience. And it has both a unifying theme in the Parson's living what he teaches and a central image in the good shepherd. Though it portrays the parson at his work in the parish, it is entirely free of the unctuous religious terms that are so marked a feature of the description of the Friar. At the same time, it avoids a pallid do-goodism by a wealth of concrete detail.

Only after telling of the Parson's reluctance to collect tithes, his readiness, on the contrary, to share his own substance with poorer parishioners, and after showing us the Parson visiting afoot in all weathers the farthest in his parish, does Chaucer make explicit the unifying theme:

> This noble ensample to his sheep he yaf,
> That first he wroghte, and afterward he taughte.   (A 497)

We hear the Parson's voice in the immediately ensuing indirect quotation:

> Out of the gospel he tho wordes caughte,
> And this figure he added eek therto,
> That if gold ruste, what shal iren do?
> For if a preest be foul, on whom we truste,
> No wonder is a lewed man to ruste;
> And shame it is, if a prest take keep,
> A shiten shepherde and a clene sheep.   (A 504)

We experience directly the vigor of his speech, and learn that though he is not hard on sinful men, he will not hesitate to "snybben" the

74

obstinate, whatever their rank; only after experiencing the details are we told in more general terms,

> He waited after no pompe and reverence,
> Ne maked him a spiced conscience. (A 526)

Similarly, the shepherd and the sheep appear figuratively through a passage of nineteen lines before the Parson is explicitly identified as the good shepherd: "He was a shepherde and noght a mercenarie" (A 514).

A few lines of the portrait, foreshadowing the priest who is the victim in the *Canon's Yeoman's Tale*, are negative and satirical:

> He sette nat his benefice to hyre
> And leet his sheep encombred in the myre
> And ran to Londoun unto Seinte Poules
> To seken hym a chaunterie for soules,
> Or with a bretherhed to been withholde. (A 511)

But the portrait as a whole is forthright and positive; it throws emphasis on the life lived in imitation of Christ as the best of sermons; it concludes by reiterating the unifying theme:

> But Cristes loore and his apostles twelve
> He taughte, but first he folwed it hymselve. (A 528)

The fellowship of the Parson and his brother the Plowman reflects the Gospel world of simple people living close to the soil. The two portraits support each other in spelling out the Christian paradox in practical and worldly terms—the potential wealth in poverty, the abundance of life in self-sacrifice. As a result, Chaucer can devote a mere thirteen lines to the Plowman without appearing perfunctory. Some of the generalizations in the Parson's portrait apply equally to his brother—"But riche he was of hooly thoght and werk" (A 479), for instance; the line on patience in adversity; and the line "He koude in litel thyng have suffisaunce" (A 490). The Parson's reference to the "shiten shepherde" and his rejection of a "spiced conscience" are recalled in the first thing we learn of the Plowman, "That hadde ylad of dong ful many a fother" (A 530). The emphasis is equally on work and on the spirit in which the work is done, and the pronounced

Bible echoes include a reflection of Job as well as Christ's summary of the law:

> God loved he best with al his hoole herte
> At alle tymes, thogh him gamed or smerte,
> And thanne his neighebor right as hymselve.   (A 535)

The explicit action of the Plowman's work for others, the "thresshe" and "dyke" and "delve," add the muscle of real effort to sympathy; and the care in meeting his own obligations, paying tithes not only on his income but on his property as well, shows him as not impractical in his own affairs. The final line brings him and his brother into the company of pilgrims with the only reference to clothing or physical appearance in either portrait: "In a tabard he rood upon a mere" (A 541).

The Miller, separated from the Plowman and his brother by the list of the last five pilgrims, represents the first movement in a rapid descent to the moral level of the Summoner and the Pardoner, who as traveling companions form a group within this final set of churls and bring the portraits to a close on a note of thorough corruption and degradation. The Miller's portrait, only a little longer than the Plowman's, concentrates, as no previous one, on appearance, and matches with a vigor of language the crude vitality of the man. Chaucer keeps returning, as if fascinated, to the grossness of the physical features, and only in a two-line section near the end does he squeeze in some information about the man's conduct as a miller. Chaucer starts by describing his size and his strength, which win him the ram at every wrestling match. The next few lines make it clear that the Miller is a kind of ram himself:

> He was short-sholdred, brood, a thikke knarre;
> Ther was no dore that he nolde heve of harre,
> Or breke it at a rennyng with his heed.   (A 551)

As if the implicit likeness suggested a technique, the portrait returns to the Miller's appearance with a series of animal and metal images. His beard's redness resembles a sow or a fox, and its breadth a spade. The wart on his nose nourishes a tuft of hairs, "Reed as the brustles of a sowes erys" (A 556). The "nosethirles" black and wide help to suggest, across an intervening line about his sword and buckler, the "greet forneys" of his mouth, which leads in turn to the bawdy vulgarity of his talk. The cheating of his clients takes up only a single line, and is discounted by the playful reference in the next line to the proverbial "An honest miller has a golden thumb." The white coat and blue hood, insisted on rhythmically, add a touch of incongruity, despite their appropriateness for a miller, to the dominant blacks and reds of his physique. But his blowing on a bagpipe to lead the pilgrims out of town broadcasts the noisy vigor of his presence.

The language imitates the Miller's quality, not only in the implications of the imagery—sow, fox, spade, furnace—but also, with discretion, in the sound and rhythm. The juxtaposed accents of "stout carl" in the first line are picked up again in "short-sholdred," and the sound of "carl" is echoed and roughened at the end of the same line in "thikke knarre." The line "Or breke it at a rennyng with his heed" (A 551) catches some of the swiftness and shock of the action with its muting of all but the three main accents and the withholding of any clue (such as rhyme) until the final word. "Upon the cop right of his nose he hade / A werte" repeats again the juxtaposed accents and throws the wart into relief by the combination of run-on and caesura. "Brustles" stiffens with both sound and sense the "toft of herys," and "nosethirles" (in place of "nostrilles") gives proper weight and a back-country archaism to what were no ordinary features.

In contrast to the Miller, the "gentil" Manciple disappears from sight and almost from awareness in the quiet satisfaction he takes over the shrewdness of his financial dealings, "Of which achatours myghte take exemple" (A 568). After the Miller's noisy bagpiping, the hush of silent caution is almost audible:

> Algate he wayted so in his achaat
> That he was ay biforn and in good staat.   (A 572)

The absurdity of Chaucer's full-throated comment practically demolishes this buyer of victuals:

> Now is nat that of God a ful fair grace
> That swich a lewed mannes wit shal pace
> The wisdom of an heep of lerned men?   (A 575)

And for the next ten lines we hear no more of the Manciple, but only of the wisdom of his thirty and more masters, expert in the law and capable, a dozen of them, of managing vast estates or even the affairs of a country; "And yet this Manciple sette hir aller cappe" (A 586). The portrait projects the awe in which the Manciple holds his employers and, in the qualifying word "duszeyne," the concern with which he watches them in the hope of covering up his petty pilfering. Only the exclusive guildsmen receive quite such a complete dismissal from the poet.

The Reeve, who has in common with the Manciple a shrewdness in handling his superiors, receives in his portrait a longer and much more detailed consideration from the poet. The description, like the Miller's, starts with physical appearance, brings in near the end his clothing and accoutrements, and concludes with his contrasting position in the cavalcade of pilgrims. But vocation, which in the Miller's case is dismissed in two lines, occupies for the Reeve fully half of a reasonably long portrait. The impression created is of a secretive and unpleasant nature, only gradually unfolded from the point of view of omniscience. His physical makeup, choleric and lean, is rendered intentially humble and unobtrusive by the Reeve's clean-shaven face and priestlike tonsure. An unusual feature he cannot conceal draws the poet's attention:

> Ful longe were his legges and ful lene,
> Ylyk a staf, ther was no calf ysene. (A 592)

The Reeve's abilities in his office, however, are outstanding. He has learned to estimate crop yield by weather conditions and so has a sure test for the honesty of his underlings. Unlike most reeves, he has dealt directly with his lord for years and has complete charge of the activities in his manor. Not unnaturally, his talents have created a superstitious awe in those under him:

> Ther nas baillif, ne hierde, nor oother hyne,
> That he ne knew his sleighte and his covyne;
> They were adrad of hym as of the deeth. (A 605)

What seems a new subject, the description of his dwelling, confirms a growing impression of isolation from his fellows, and introduces a section on his own prosperity. The house "ful faire upon an heeth" and the privy wealth stored up in the shadow of green trees are founded on dealings so shrewd that his lord, though cheated of his own substance, is constantly rewarding him in gratitude for his seeming generosity. The carpentry, learned in youth and still skillfully practiced, represents the one guileless activity of a life otherwise spent in calculation and deception. His horse and his clothing are suitably neutral; the rusty blade and the tucking up of his gown like a friar suggest once again an affected humility and an intention of seeming harmless; and his riding ever "hyndreste of oure route" expresses both instinct and conscious choice in this most cautious and antisocial of the pilgrims.

The specific information Chaucer gives us of the Reeve, including even the name of his town in Norfolk, makes it at least possible, as in several other of the portraits, that Chaucer had in mind an actual person. But Chaucer understood the advantage of mingling the general and the specific in his art and may well have combined suggestions from a number of actual models. It should surprise no one that Oswald the Reeve, of Heath Place, juxta Bawdeswelle, Norfolk, has an established identity only in the *Canterbury Tales*.

After the withdrawn and sapless cunning of the Reeve, the flagrant depravity of the Summoner strikes with considerable impact. The personal and professional aspects of his character are hardly distinguishable, and the portrait proceeds by imperceptible steps from appearance to personal habits to conduct in his office. But while the horrors of his appearance receive a vivid projection, the corrupting influence he wields over others reveals itself largely in terms of riotous good fellowship and professional reassurances to his companions that a bribe will clear them of all consequences. Men's inurement to such ugly and flagrant immorality is strikingly presented in two lines. At the beginning we learn that "Of his visage children were aferd" (A 628). But later, after describing his empty-headed drunkenness, the poet tells us: "A bettre felawe sholde men noght fynde" (A 648). The Summoner, despite his appearance, has no trouble finding companions and disciples; far from evading men's scrutiny, he even affects a playful extravagance in the garland he wears and the huge cake he carries.

Chaucer shows in the course of this portrait what he has not permitted himself in any of the others—an overt antagonism towards his subject. His contempt for the Summoner breaks through the naive objectivity of his usual attitude twice, first in his description of the Latin tags the man gives voice to when in his cups, and again in his revulsion against the doctrine of penitence which the Summoner proclaims to his companions in vice. The second instance is the more complex. After a forthright statement of disagreement, "But wel I woot he lyed right in dede" (A 659), Chaucer asserts the Church's spiritual power in the strongest terms, only to undercut his position in the final line, "And also war hym of a *Significavit*" (A 662). To bring in as climax to the Church's power over men's souls its authority to imprison their bodies suggests inability to distinguish between the vital and the merely important and represents, on the surface, a naive conformity with popular standards. But it also points to the source of the Summoner's own influence. The power to imprison that is embodied in the significavit enables him to carry on his sinister blackmail against the "yonge girles of the diocise." Chaucer's seemingly innocent comment carries a bitter undertone of satire against the Church which permits its temporal powers to be so viciously abused. The Summoner's doctrine is actually no worse than the Friar's. What arouses the poet's indignation is the element of force which the Summoner employs in his corruption of others—the distinction, as it were, between seduction and rape.

Undertones of a judgment less easily evaded than that which the Summoner, through his office, helps to pervert are created by the language of the portrait.[18] They start with the second line, where the Summoner is said to have a "fyr-reed cherubynnes face," and are picked up again in the remedies with which he vainly strives to rub off the symptoms of his disease:

> Ther nas quyk-silver, lytarge, ne brymstoon,
> Boras, ceruce, ne oille of tartre noon;
> Ne oynement that wolde clense and byte,
> That hym myghte helpen of his whelkes white,
> Nor of the knobbes sittynge on his chekes.   (A 633)

The white sores, irritated by strong chemicals, and the rich foods and "strong wyn, reed as blood," that aggravate the disease, project an image of torment—fire without and fire within—torment that the suggestions of "brymstoon," or "tartre," of "oynement" and "clense" confirm as a mere foretaste of what is to come. The suspension of meaning through almost four lines, with the tolling of accented negatives from *nas* to *n'oil-* to *noon* to *n'oyn-*, and the quickening of rhythm from the stress-heavy first line to the three-stress fifth, reinforce the inexorability of the last two lines, with the negative "helpen" echoed in "whelkes" and given further emphasis by the double alliteration.

Later the Summoner's *Questio quid iuris* resounds through the tavern, where nobody, least of all the speaker, cares about the meaning of the question or its answer. Finally, we hear his own voice as he makes light of the consequences of sin:

> And if he foond owher a good felawe,
> He wolde techen him to have noon awe
> In swich caas of the ercedekenes curs,
> But if a mannes soule were in his purs;
> For in his purs he sholde ypunysshed be.
> "Purs is the ercedekenes helle," seyde he. (A 658)

And, under the foolish levity, sounds three lines later the poet's "For curs wol slee right as assoillyng savith" (A 661). The Summoner's joke brings into relation with the undertone of judgment and doom another recurrent motif of the portrait—the light-witted improvidence of the man. His lechery is like a sparrow's, his Latin like a jaybird's English. He is so "gentil" and "kynde" that a quart of wine will buy from him a year's immunity for a good "felawe" and his concubine. The word "felawe" occurs three times in six lines and suggests the empty-headed jocosity that serves for fellowship in his life, as the lame joke about the archdeacon's hell suggests what passes for wit. But the Summoner is by no means harmless. Though the portrait ends on the extravagance of the garland and the huge cake, we learn, just before, of his hold over the young people of the diocese, who confide in him and seek his advice.

The fellowship of the Summoner and the Pardoner, more fully described than that of any of the other pilgrims, occupies most of the first six lines of the latter's portrait. Their singing the song "Com hider, love, to me" may simply reflect the undaunted exuberance of the two rascals and give vocal emphasis to the dissonance their missions and their characters set up, a dissonance that sounds so clearly the corruption of the Church. But followed as the song is by the long description of the Pardoner's appearance, especially the climactic and explicit "I trowe he were a geldyng or a mare" (A 691), it insinuates the possibility of a homosexual attraction. The figurative language that Chaucer uses to describe the Pardoner suggests at first an artificial lifelessness. His hair resembles in its color wax, in its texture flax; and it is carefully arranged in "colpons" (a word used of things cut off from their source of growth). A later series of images involving small animals—glaring hare's eyes, small goat's voice—implies the deeply physical nature of his effeminacy, and the absence of beard brings the poet to the supposition that he is a "geldyng" or a "mare." The effort that the Pardoner makes to appear both informal and modish strengthens the impression. Like many of his kind, he only half-wills the concealment of his peculiarities. With a part of his being he wants to be noticed; hence the hoodlessness that calls attention to the sparse hair arranged so carefully over his shoulders; hence his singing with the Summoner, whose trumpet bass exposes by contrast his own high treble. For a man whose success depends so entirely on a public performance, his physical makeup, described in the first half of the portrait, provides a considerable handicap.

Chaucer introduces the second half of the portrait, which takes up his activities as a Pardoner, with the words "But of his craft." The ostensible office of the Pardoner is to dispense indulgences in return for charitable offerings to the Hospital of St. Mary Rouncivale at Charing Cross. But the only mention of pardons comes in the description of his appearance when we learn that his wallet is "bretful" of them, "comen from Rome al hoot." He goes to some trouble to look authentic, having sewed to his cap a "vernycle," popularly associated with the Papal City. But he makes no effort to appear clerical, an indication, I think, that major orders are no necessary part of his performance.[14] The authenticity of the pardons gains him the credence of his ignorant victims. It is not difficult for a man so provided to overawe a parson and get leave to preach. Once he has the ear of a congregation, it is clearly the relics he emphasizes. They have the advantage over pardons of suffering no depletion through use. To the poet's eye, they are transparently not what they purport to be:

> For in his male he hadde a pilwe-beer,
> Which that he seyde was Oure Lady veyl:
> He seyde he hadde a gobet of the seyl
> That Seint Peter hadde, whan that he wente

Upon the see, til Jhesu Crist hym hente.
He hadde a croys of latoun ful of stones,
And in a glas he hadde pigges bones.   (A 700)

But the Pardoner is eloquent enough to convince the parson and his flock, even against the evidence of their senses, for they, if anyone, would recognize pig's bones. With his "feyned flaterye and japes," he transforms his collection of trash into precious relics and takes his victims for all he can squeeze out of them. The climax of the portrait, however, is not the relics, amusing as the disparity is between the actuality and the claims their owner makes for them; it is the Pardoner himself as "noble ecclesiaste" in the church, tuning up on the offertory for his opportunity to win silver in the sermon: "Therefore he song the murierly and loude" (A 714). Part of his delight is in the role itself, the opportunity it affords him to escape the ambiguities of his nature, his complexity as a person, and become, as the words "wel affile his tonge" suggest, the instrument of his own avarice.

The Pardoner is a much shrewder villain than the Summoner. No indulgence in good fellowship distracts him from his aim; he gets as much out of his victims as he can. But though he preys on the superstitions and weaknesses of ignorant villagers, and though his role demands of him a far greater talent and a complete hypocrisy, he does not depend for success on the corruption of others. It is their purses rather than their morals that he attacks. Furthermore the distasteful aspects of his physical makeup do not result, as do the Summoner's, from his own misconduct. The misuse of his talents, the absorption of his energies in avarice, has the effect of isolating him from his fellows. The satisfaction he takes in his appearance—"Hym thoughte he rood al of the newe jet" (A 682)— and his pride in his ill-earned income emerge clearly in Chaucer's description and prevent the kind of sympathy a fuller awareness of his position would inspire.[15] They keep him well within the world of comedy. But they do not arouse the kind of contempt Chaucer reveals for the Summoner, both in the portrait and later in the closely related quarrel with the Friar.

The portraits of the Pardoner, the Summoner, and the Friar bear a closer relationship to the performance of the three on the journey than do those of any of the other pilgrims. Not only do the Friar and the

Summoner flesh out each other's portraits with the closest illustrative material, but the Friar, in his story, and the Summoner, in the anecdote with which he responds before launching into his story, bring up the very subject—damnation—that forms an undertone throughout the description of the Summoner. The Pardoner, in his confession and his sample sermon, gives us a demonstration of his techniques in making "the person and the peple his apes," fully justifying the shocking term "noble ecclesiaste" by the effectiveness of his tale. And at the end he responds to the Host's rebuke with an anger which the Host cannot understand, but which the poet's insight into the Pardoner's physical makeup helps to explain. This unusually close relationship between the portraits and the events of the pilgrimage suggests that they may well have been produced during the same period of Chaucer's work on the *Canterbury Tales*; it lends some support to the theory that the final five portraits and those of the Monk and the Friar were added to the series, and were not a part of the original plan.

The effect of giving two rogues such as the Pardoner and the Summoner the final positions, instead of the Parson and the Plowman, has already been pointed out. The vision of the Summoner counseling the "yonge girles of the diocise" and of the Pardoner taking over from the "povre person dwellynge upon lond" gives a vivid emphasis to the forces of corruption in society and to the weakness and ignorance on which they prey. It more than balances the impression earlier created by the portraits of the good shepherd and his brother the Christian plowman.

Chaucer worked with the problems inherent in this long series of portraits because he wanted to throw the emphasis from the very beginning on the basic reality of his fiction. The portraits create the groundwork of character that transforms the *Canterbury Tales* from a mere collection of stories into a drama of conflicting visions. By introducing his pilgrims at the start, Chaucer gives us a sense not just of a succession of single pilgrims telling stories—he could have done that more effectively by describing each pilgrim as the Host calls on him— rather he gives us a sense of the potential for action and response represented by the whole society of pilgrims. The pilgrims are not confined to simply telling stories. They talk about themselves; they quarrel; they even break into one another's stories. The physical movement of the journey is occasionally made manifest, but the dynamics of character are always in the foreground; the progressive revelation of character and the action of character against character make for constant interest. The relationship between the portrait and the tale that the pilgrim tells varies in each instance. A few of the pilgrims fail to make an impact in the stories they tell. But so well have the portraits prepared us for self-expression that when the Canon's Yeoman joins the group and tells a story, we read it as a revelation of his character. All the stories have this potential of an extra dimension, a meaning beyond their interest as stories. Utterances of the pilgrims, they extend our knowledge of the narrators as all creative effort must.

The game that Chaucer has the Host invent expands the stage of the pilgrimage from the Canterbury Way to the known world of medieval man. The pilgrims expose more than their personalities; they show us a society rich in distinctions, with the high and the low, the crude and the delicate, the spiritual and the cynical, hearing one another out; they give us a sense of the varied possibilities in the life of fourteenth-century England, of the freedom to live and to envision life, and, at the same time, a sense of the forces that restrict the possibilities and the freedom; they give us, in short, a paradigm of society.

The interaction of portrait and story has a further effect. It simplifies the problem of belief. We are never asked to believe that the events of a story are plausible, but only that a particular one of the pilgrims could plausibly have told it. So absorbed do we become in the revelation and interaction of character, that few readers question Chaucer's conception of thirty pilgrims telling each other stories that all can hear as they ride along a narrow road.[16] Indeed the impression of actuality has been so marked that many readers have assumed a real pilgrimage and people that Chaucer knew as models for his fiction.[17]

The art of the Prologue makes possible all that follows. It establishes the groundwork of character, the sense of a community, the impression of a literal actuality, and the potential of polysemous meaning that the game of storytelling may release. The autonomy of the pilgrims, confirmed by Chaucer's denial of his own responsibility for what they say, was already subtly suggested by their refusal to stand still under his scrutiny. Their movement and his compel an avoidance of system; they stimulate alertness in both the narrator and the reader; they contribute to the lifelikeness of the imitation. That the judgments of the narrator are sometimes outrageous, that at other times the meanings are to be ferreted out from ambiguity or apparent nonsense, draw the reader into the game of evaluation. The pilgrims will tell stories. The Host will judge them. As in the Prologue, this overt judgment will have validity only if it is confirmed by the literal details, the patterns they form, and the meanings the patterns imply. The ultimate values will not be verbally imposed. They will emerge from the interplay and the development of the elements that the Prologue sets in motion. The enjoyment that the narrator so clearly takes in his companions will extend to the stories they tell, and will communicate itself to us as one of the most important implicit values in the story he tells.

IV

the first day's storytelling

"Oure appetites heer"

C HAUCER has hardly ended his apology for the language he will have
to use if he is to describe accurately the events of the pilgrimage,
indicating the autonomy of the pilgrims he has been at such pains to
set before us, when we hear the Host offering the company his plan for
their diversion—a storytelling contest with a prize for the winner, the
one "that telleth in this caas / Tales of best sentence and moost solaas"
(A 798). Two things are worth noting about the Host's proposal. The
contest will continue over the whole journey, on the way to Canterbury
and back, and will reach its climax with the award of the supper "at
oure aller cost" in the Tabard dining room. It will thus have a structure
at variance with that of the pilgrimage itself, which will presumably
reach its climax when the pilgrims visit the shrine of St. Thomas.[1] The
second point about the Host's proposal is the power over the pilgrims it
gives the Host. He will ride with them and be their guide "right at
myn owene cost," but "whoso wole my juggement withseye / Shal
paye al that we spenden by the weye" (A 806). The pilgrims in assenting to the plan make the Host's control over them even more absolute—
he is to be both judge and reporter of their tales, their governor "in
heigh and lough," with the single exception of the price of the supper
for the winner of the contest. That is set as a part of the agreement.
Their careful handling of money casts some doubt on their submission
to the Host's authority; it also throws ironic light on the deeper issues.
   Some of the implicit areas of conflict in the plans for the pilgrimage
have the potential of comedy—the Host versus Chaucer as reporter of

87

what happened, the taste of an innkeeper as literary critic, the impossible size of the single penalty for disobedience in this traveling common-wealth set up as an absolute monarchy in pursuit of happiness. Some of the others have a more serious import—the "sentence" and "solaas" of the stories, the religious meanings of the pilgrimage versus the pleasure-seeking release of the springtime journey, the small likelihood that a group so diverse can organize the future meaningfully.

Having gained title to such power, the Host wisely refrains from an early test and leaves to chance the choice of the first storyteller. To everyone's delight, the lot falls to the Knight, and he responds in a more dignified and gracious way than did the original first storyteller (the Man of Law) in an earlier version of the first day's stories.[2] Chaucer calls the Knight "this goode man" and remarks on his faith-fulness "To kepe his foreward by his free assent" (A 852)—a line that makes implicit distinction between the obligations that are undertaken freely and those that are forced on us. The Knight begins what he calls the "game" with some enthusiasm. He even calls attention, after a few lines of introduction and summary, to the prize-supper to be awarded for the best tale.

These beginnings are all auspicious. The Knight should tell the first tale, but the Host should not be the one to choose him. Chaucer had recognized the proprieties in having the Host originally call on the Man of Law. Then he thought of the expedient of drawing cuts for the first position. This way the choice emerges from an order not man made, not even rationally testable. The Host, in asking the Knight to draw a cut, is not so much ordering him as giving him the precedence; he calls him "my mayster and my lord." The two other pilgrims singled out by the Host are the Prioress and the Clerk. The first is getting a foretaste of the deference the Host will later pay her in asking her to tell a tale. The Clerk, on the other hand, receives not courtesy but the admonition to overcome his shyness. The Knight supports the temporary order set up by the Host and will even come to his aid when his authority is challenged; he never himself needs direction from others. It is appropriate that in his tale he shows some real understanding of the sources of power.

The opening of the *Knight's Tale*[3] presents us with Theseus the Conqueror. We see him returning in triumph from Scythia married to

the queen he has conquered, with her sister Emily in attendance. We
see him responding to the distress of the kneeling women by abandoning
his own plans in order to right their wrongs. He takes immediate and
decisive action, killing Creon, capturing Thebes by storm, dismantling
the city, and restoring to the ladies the bones of their husbands. The
action suggests an establishment, energetic, dedicated to justice, confident in the leadership of its lord and governor. If there is a hint of the
excessive throughout—in the emphasis on Theseus' pride as he rides
to Athens (A 895)—in his immediate response to the weeping ladies:

> "What folk been ye, that at myn hom-comynge
> Perturben so my feste with criynge?"
> Quod Theseus. "Have ye so greet envye
> Of myn honour . . . ?" (A 908)

—in his expectation "That al the peple of Grece sholde speke / How
Creon was of Theseus yserved" (A 963)—in the punishment meted
out to the Thebans for the crime committed by their king, and especially
in the perpetual imprisonment adjudged Palamon and Arcite because
of their royal blood—if all of this seems excessive, Theseus clearly sees
himself as the agent of power on earth, responsible that no unnecessary
risks be run to his ability to order his world. The final picture is an
impressive one:

> And whan this worthy duc hath thus ydon,
> He took his hoost, and hoom he rit anon
> With laurer crowned as a conquerour;
> And ther he lyveth in joye and in honour
> Terme of his lyf; what nedeth wordes mo?
> And in a tour, in angwissh and in wo,
> This Palamon and his felawe Arcite
> For everemoore; ther may no gold hem quite. (A 1032)

And so the story would end if, as some have opined, Theseus were the
representative and executor of divine power on earth.[4] Clearly he is
not. Later in the tale, the Knight (and Chaucer) tell us so explicitly:

> The destinee, ministre general,
> That executeth in the world over al

89

> The purveiaunce that God hath seyn biforn,
> So strong it is that, though the world had sworn
> The contrarie of a thyng by ye or nay,
> Yet somtyme it shal fallen on a day
> That falleth nat eft withinne a thousand yeer.
> For certeinly, oure appetites heer,
> Be it of werre, or pees, or hate, or love,
> Al is this reuled by the sighte above.
>   This mene I now by myghty Theseus. . . .   (A 1673)

In fact, the things that Theseus wills rarely come to pass exactly in accordance with his intentions. Imprisonment for Palamon and Arcite, yes. But not perpetual. And while in prison, the sight of Emily, singing and gathering flowers in the garden "To make a subtil gerland for hire hede" (A 1054).

The relationship between Palamon and Arcite, cousins, blood brothers, rivals in love, becomes during the rest of the story the center of interest for the conqueror Theseus as well as for the reader. That this relationship is enigmatic, a series of articles attests.[5] Here, as earlier with the conqueror Theseus, the surfaces are apt to be deceptive. For instance, most criticism has tended to award the primacy to Palamon as lover of Emily. Yet it is clear from his own words that though he first thinks of her as a lady, he changes his opinion and prays to her as Venus:

> And therwithal on knees doun he fil,
> And seyde: "Venus, if it be thy wil
> Yow in this gardyn thus to transfigure
> Bifore me, sorweful, wrecched creature,
> Out of this prisoun help that we may scapen.
> And if so be my destynee be shapen
> By eterne word to dyen in prisoun,
> Of oure lynage have som compassioun,
> That is so lowe ybroght by tirannye."   (A 1111)

The contrast of Arcite's response is striking:

> "The fresshe beautee sleeth me sodeynly
> Of hire that rometh in the yonder place,

And but I have hir mercy and hir grace,
That I may seen hire atte leeste weye,
I nam but deed. . . ."   (A 1122)

Palamon clearly allows his impatience with imprisonment to persuade
him that divine help is at hand, while Arcite's consistently more realistic
view of the world makes prison less irksome and Emily's humanity
immediately apparent. Arcite's refusal to press the justice of his claim,
and his recognition that persuasion will have no effect on his love or
Palamon's and that in any case they are both in prison with Emily
beyond reach, confirm for us his tendency to see things as they are and
to be less active in seeking to change them. The two men have equal
claims to Emily, distinct characters, and a common respect for the
ideals of chivalry.

Their qualities emerge when Arcite gets both release from prison and
banishment from Athens, and the two lovers indulge in twin laments,
each thinking the other's situation the more favorable. Here the parallelism, so prominent in the story, is for the first time explicit and formal.
Arcite and Palamon, cousins and sworn brothers, are separated first by
their love for Emily and now by Arcite's release from prison. But they
are alike in their grief and envy. Each devotes the first part of his lament
to an envious comparison of his own situation with his cousin's.

"O deere cosyn Palamon," quod he,
"Thyn is the victorie of this aventure."   (A 1235)

Thus Arcite, as, in retrospect, he finds prison and the contemplation of
Emily's beauty a paradise compared to his own freedom to be anywhere
but in Athens. And Palamon, chafing at confinement and his cousin's
opportunities to act:

"Allas," quod he, "Arcita, cosyn myn,
Of al oure strif, God woot, the fruyt is thyn."   (A 1282)

Each reveals the subtly differentiated character noted by Marckwardt,
and at the same time foresees for his cousin his own fate. In the end,
victory is Arcite's, and the fruit of all the strife Palamon's. That the
outcome assigns victory to the thoughtful and reward to the impetuous
is a further twist to the irony.

Both men proceed to derive a general conclusion from their predicament. Arcite's theme is the limitation of man's vision, which often makes him work for his own misfortune:

> Allas, why pleynen folk so in commune
> On purveiaunce of God, or of Fortune,
> That yeveth hem ful ofte in many a gyse
> Wel bettre than they kan hemself devyse?
> Som man desireth for to han richesse,
> That cause is of his mordre or greet siknesse;
> And som man wolde out of his prisoun fayn,
> That in his hous is of his meynee slayn.
> Infinite harmes been in this mateere.
> We witen nat what thing we preyen heere.   (A 1260)

As in the earlier part of the lament, the sentiment is appropriate to the more rational and restrained of the two heroes, but now his own fate, not Palamon's, is the one foreshadowed: Arcite's prayer for victory will be granted to his infinite harm, and he will again be "exiled" from his "wele," this time "in his colde grave / Allone, withouten any compaignye" (A 2779).

Palamon, on the other hand, is impatient of the injustices men suffer from the gods, and of the responsibilities their rational nature entails: "O cruel goddes," he addresses them,

> What is mankynde moore unto you holde
> Than is the sheep that rouketh in the folde?
> For slayn is man right as another beest,
> And dwelleth eek in prison and arreest,
> And hath siknesse and greet adversitee,
> And ofte tymes giltelees, pardee.
>   What governance is in this prescience,
> That giltelees tormenteth innocence?   (A 1314)

Man is different from the beasts, Palamon continues, only in having to control himself in this life, and in suffering punishment after death. The injustice that Palamon complains of will first bring about his defeat, which Chaucer is careful to ascribe to no defect of Palamon's strength or valor, as "by the force of twenty is he take / Unyolden, and ydrawe unto the stake" (A 2642). But finally injustice will work in his favor. Saturn, whom he blames later in his lament for his confinement, will slay his guiltless rival "right as another beest," and so make possible his marriage to Emily.

The equilibrium between the two heroes, set up by the parallel laments, is further emphasized by the Knight's question:

> Yow loveres axe I now this questioun:
> Who hath the worse, Arcite or Palamoun?
> That oon may seen his lady day by day,
> But in prison he moot dwelle alway;
> That oother wher hym list may ride or go,
> But seen his lady shal he nevere mo.   (A 1352)

This equilibrium recurs at every crisis of the story and constitutes Chaucer's principal contribution to it. Equal in grief at the end of Part I, the two knights are equally happy at the end of Part II; for a second time their equivalence is rhetorically underlined, and the contrast with the end of Part I, the contrast between joy and despair, is emphasized:

> Who looketh lightly now but Palamoun?
> Who spryngeth up for joye but Arcite?
> Who kouthe telle, or who kouthe it endite,
> The joye that is maked in the place
> Whan Theseus hath doon so fair a grace?   (A 1874)

Part III of the tale consists almost entirely of parallel elements— the three temples, the two armies and the two heroes, the three visits, the three prayers, and the three omens. It ends with the two heroes equally confident, though the intervention of Saturn on the celestial plane tips the balance in favor of Venus and Palamon. But the good fortune of Palamon, which would be so pronounced with his marriage to Emily at the end, does not occur until after Theseus has spoken. Theseus, who has their lives in his hand both at the beginning of the tale and in the middle, intervenes at the end not only to order the marriage but also to interpret in his long Boethian speech the outcome of the heroes' rivalry: their fates are still equivalent. Viewed in the light of the chivalric ideal, Arcite's death at the height of his glory and Palamon's attainment of love and happiness are equally desirable.

Parallelism and paradox are thus at the heart of the story. They are inherent in plot and structure, from the ironical laments at the end of Part I, through the apparently contradictory but granted prayers, to the opposite but paradoxically equivalent fates which the heroes meet. Delineation of character is also parallel and paradoxical. Palamon and Arcite respond in turn to the same or similar stimuli throughout the story. But Palamon's impetuosity results in a prayer to the less violent deity, and a delayed victory, while Arcite's reasoning leads him to pray to Mars for an immediate but, as it turns out, short-lived triumph.

Similarly, Theseus the Conqueror, who seems all-powerful throughout the tale, has even his foreign policy shaped in the end by events that happen quite apart from his will. The man whom in the beginning he has imprisoned perpetually to insure against the possibility of Theban revenge marries his sister-in-law as part of the arrangements by which he will "have fully of Thebans obeisaunce" (A 2974). The interval of "certeyn yeres" between the death of Arcite and the final parlement lends emphasis to the limits of Theseus' power. He thinks to settle the troublesome problem of Palamon and Arcite, first, by imprisonment; then, at the intervention of Perotheus, by exiling Arcite and keeping Palamon in prison; then when he finds them fighting in his territory, the one returned, the other escaped, by execution. The impassioned pleas of Ypolita and Emily cause him to have gentler thoughts. He begins to understand his obligations as a ruler:

Fy
Upon a lord that wol have no mercy,
But been a leon, bothe in word and dede. (A 1775)

He recognizes his common humanity with the two lovers. He devises the expedient of the tournament as a way of determining who shall have Emily to wife. But an event happens that will not occur again in a thousand years, and Arcite's death nullifies the results of the tournament. Theseus's earlier decision that the jousting will have limits has preserved the defeated Palamon, as well as the two hundred other participants; and after a suitable interval it occurs to the wise ruler that the "sighte above" has indeed worked things out for mortals in the "foule prisoun" of this life "Wel bettre than they kan hemself devyse" (A 1254), and all that he need do is will it himself. The paradoxical nature of power, which Theseus comes perhaps dimly to understand, is one of the thematic elements in the story.

Even more significant is what happens at Arcite's death. As Arcite feels the inexorable approach of his end, he calls Emily and Palamon to him and dwells at first on the bitterness of his experience. The lines most frequently quoted express the soul-shaking contrast, the triumph and disaster that Arcite has gone through. But he sees, beyond his suffering, the values that both he and Palamon have aspired to. It is these values that he gives in his final instructions to Emily:

> I have heer with my cosyn Palamon
> Had strif and rancour many a day agon
> For love of yow, and for my jalousye.
> And Juppiter so wys my soule gye,
> To speken of a servaunt proprely,
> With alle circumstances trewely—
> That is to seyen, trouthe, honour, knyghthede,
> Wysdom, humblesse, estaat, and heigh kynrede,
> Fredom, and al that longeth to that art—
> So Juppiter have of my soule part,
> As in this world right now ne knowe I non
> So worthy to ben loved as Palamon,
> That serveth yow, and wol doon al his lyf.
> And if that evere ye shul ben a wyf,
> Foryet nat Palamon, the gentil man.   (A 2797)

The long conflict comes to an end in this act of generosity and reconciliation. The uncertain quicksand of accident, particularized in the descriptions of Mars's influence and Saturn's, referred to obliquely in Egeus' "thurghfare ful of wo" (A 2847) and Theseus' "foule prisoun," may cause the death of Arcite. Courage and devotion to an ideal are valuable, not for the results they bring about, but precisely because they make the results irrelevant.

The conviction implicit in the thematic elements is what makes *Palamon and Arcite* finally so appropriate to the Knight.[6] His gentle nature—

> He nevere yet no vileynye ne sayde
> In al his lyf unto no maner wight   (A 71)

—finds its reflection in Arcite's last moments. The equivalence of
Arcite's and Palamon's fates, which the structure of the tale does so
much to emphasize, is also relevant. For a man like the Knight, whose
life has been spent advancing the Christian cause in combat with the
heathen, life and death are constant alternatives, but there is no alternative to honor. In each of his many combats, he has faced the fates of
Palamon and Arcite and has regarded them as equally desirable. That
this conviction was Chaucer's before it became the Knight's is evident
from the history of the poem. Chaucer tells us, in the Prologue to the
Legend of Good Women, that it was an independent poem. The happy
conjunction of an already composed Knight's portrait with an already
written *Knight's Tale* is a paradox to match the ones in Chaucer's version of the story.[7]

The end of the *Knight's Tale*, the first of the stories, is a most important juncture in the *Canterbury Tales*. In rapid succession and without
any sense of strain, a number of significant things happen. Everyone
thinks the story a "noble" one, especially the gentlefolk. The Host is
delighted that his "game" is working so well, and calls on another of the
prominent and presumably respectable pilgrims, the Monk, for a tale "to
quite with the Knyghtes tale." Two words (my italics, below) in the
colloquy penetrate the thick skull of the Miller and, with the drink that
makes riding his horse difficult and insulting the other pilgrims easy,
move him to cry out "in Pilates voys":

> By armes, and by blood and bones,
> I kan a *noble* tale for the nones,
> With which I wol now *quite* the Knyghtes tale.   (A 3127)

We recognize at once the "janglere" and "goliardeys" that breaks
doors down with his head; we recognize also the challenge that he poses
to the good order of the traveling community. The Host's request that
he wait while "som bettre man" tells a tale incites the Miller to open
rebellion:

> "By Goddes soule," quod he, "that wol nat I;

For I wol speke, or elles go my wey."
Oure Hoost answerde, "Tel on, a devel wey!
Thou art a fool; thy wit is overcome."   (A 3135)

Somewhat mollified by his success, the Miller acknowledges but does
not apologize for his drunkenness and tells the pilgrims truculently to
blame it on the ale of Southwark if he says anything amiss:

"For I wol telle a legende and a lyf
Bothe of a carpenter and of his wyf,
How that a clerk hath set the wrightes cappe."
    The Reve answerde and seyde, "Stynt thy clappe!
Lat be thy lewed dronken harlotrye.
It is a synne and eek a greet folye
To apeyren any man, or hym defame,
And eek to bryngen wyves in swich fame.
Thou mayst ynogh of othere thynges seyn."   (A 3149)

The suddenness of the Reeve's injection of himself, given some
emphasis by the rhyme in the third syllable of his utterance, underlines
how surprising his effort to stop the Miller is. His assumptions about the
story, his setting himself up as a defender of morality, his abandonment
of his habitual unobtrusiveness—all are, at least for the time, incomprehensible. Yet it is curiosity rather than disbelief that the passage inspires.
This transition between stories, with three people speaking and two
others involved, has the aura of authenticity. It shows us the pilgrims
indeed spontaneous, free of control by the Host as well as by the author,
who will remind us again that he accepts no responsibility for the
conduct of his companions.

Chaucer introduces the Miller's reply by again referring to him as
drunk, but the Reeve's challenge has sobered him. He picks up the
Reeve's reference to wives as the chink in his pose of moral indignation,
and silences his opponent with a series of incisive remarks on suspicious
husbands, revealing at the same time that the two men have previous
acquaintance, and laying the ground for some subtle implications in the
narrator's speech that follows. The Miller starts off rhyming the
Reeve's name, Oswald, or Osewold, with "cokewold," insinuates by
the clever positioning of the three-times-repeated "oon" that if Oswald's

wife is indeed bad, she is one in a thousand and one, admits his own vulnerability in being also with wife, but asserts his reluctance, when it comes to horned animals (or cuckolds),

> As demen of myself that I were oon;
> I wol bileve wel that I am noon. (A 3162)

He concludes with a statement of general principles, the last couplet providing the rhyme sound for the first four lines of the narrator's speech:

> An housbonde shal nat been inquisityf
> Of Goddes pryvetee, nor of his wyf.
> So he may fynde Goddes foyson there,
> Of the remenant nedeth nat enquere."
>   What sholde I moore seyn, but this Millere
> He nolde his wordes for no man forbere,
> But tolde his cherles tale in his manere.
> M'athynketh that I shal reherce it heere. (A 3170)

Having thus associated himself with the Miller both by the unprecedented repetition of rhyme and by their mutual intention to tell the story, and having raised, through the Miller, the suggestive issues of "Goddes foyson" and of God's privities and of a wife's, Chaucer proceeds to use from the end of the last line quoted *shal* (in internal rhyme with *tale*), *reherce*, and *heere* as the rhyme sounds in three successive couplets in the passage that follows (italics mine):

> *And therfore* every gentil wight I preye,
> For Goddes love, demeth nat that I seye
> Of yvel entente, but for I moot reherce
> Hir tales alle, be they bettre or werse,
> Or elles falsen som of my mateere.
> *And therfore*, whoso list it nat yheere,
> Turne over the leef and chese another tale;
> For he shal fynde ynowe, grete and smale,
> Of storial thyng that toucheth gentillesse,
> And eek moralitee and hoolynesse.
> *Blameth* nat me if that ye chese amys.

The Millere is a cherl, ye knowe wel this;
So was the Reve eek and othere mo,
And harlotrie they tolden bothe two.
Avyseth yow, and put me out of blame;
And eek men shal nat maken ernest of game.   (A 3186)

The careful positioning of the two *therfore*'s and the *blameth* (all three involved in the rhyme sounds) lends formality and the aura of reason to what everyone recognizes as an ambiguous warning. How many, I wonder, have been deceived into turning the leaf and missing not only God's "foyson" but privities of several kinds as well? The passage implies again the freedom of Chaucer's pilgrims. And this time the "game" that we should not be too solemn about means something more general than the Host's game of storytelling, which it certainly includes—the spirit of play, the delight that comes from form, wherever experienced, an imitation, perhaps, of God's pleasure as he contemplates his creation.

The parallelism set up in the *Knight's Tale* is carried forward on two levels—in the *Miller's Tale*, where Nicholas and Absolon vie for Alisoun's favors, and in the world of the pilgrimage, where the Miller and the Reeve fling stories rather than challenges at each other. The Miller's intention of mocking the Knight's views shows itself in two verbal echoes, the first one taken from Arcite's bitter anticipation of the grave—"Allone, withouten any compaignye" (A 2779, 3204)—and applied to Nicholas' situation as lodger at John the Carpenter's; the second taken from the description of Palamon's final happiness—

And thus with alle blisse and melodye
Hath Palamon ywedded Emelye   (A 3098)

—and developed from an innocent description of Nicholas' solitary nocturnal music (A 3214) into a euphemism for the joys of illicit passion (A 3306, 3652). The Miller shows himself indeed a "goliardeys" by eschewing any pretense that love ennobles and by showing us a set of characters driven by instinct to a deliciously comic denouement. If goliard, then the best of goliards. For the Miller carries on the impression made by his brilliant reply to the Reeve. Characters and plot interact. Each element functions effectively. The narrator keeps the timing of the two plots under control, concentrating attention now on the flood, now on the misplaced kiss, preparing for the cry of "Water!" that brings the two miraculously together. Yet there is also room for background, time for the detail that suggests life. Scenes are permitted dramatic fullness. Dialogue and action present repeatedly the surprisingly characteristic facet of character, as when Nicholas springs his trap on John the Carpenter—

> And atte laste this hende Nicholas
> Gan for to sik soore, and seyde, "Allas!
> Shal al the world be lost eftsoones now?"
> This carpenter answerde, "What seystow?
> What! thynk on God, as we doon, men that swynke."
> This Nicholas answerde, "Fecche me drynke"   (A 3492)

—or when Absolon turns away from Alisoun's titter and the "clapte" window to find vengeance, but first,

> Who rubbeth now, who froteth now his lippes
> With dust, with sond, with straw, with clooth, with chippes,
> But Absolon, that seith ful ofte, "Allas!"   (A 3749)

In short, we find in the goliard's tale a pleasure in "Goddes foyson," quite apart from the ulterior motives being served.[8]

The Miller places Alisoun in the center of his tale, aware that in doing so he is implicitly criticizing the great weakness of the *Knight's Tale*. It is not just that Emily has so little to do in the story but that what she does do is either ludicrous to the Miller, as when she prays for virginity, or purely conventional, and indeed denigrated by the Knight, as when she mourns Arcite's death. By giving Alisoun the longest and the central one of three formal portraits, the Miller shows his sense of her importance. The eighteen-year-old wife of the aged carpenter is not a complicated woman, and the portrait catches the freshness, the bloom, the appeal to every sense that makes her a magnet to men. Animals with soft fur, good things to eat and smell, bright things to look at, the swallow's song are all invoked in the effort to project her quality. Two other important elements qualify the impression. One is her clothing, neat, modest, and, in the case of the brooch on her collar, suggesting a protective function: "As brood as is the boos of a bokeler"

(A 3266). But no amount of care with her clothing can conceal that she is very much alive under it: "Hir shoes were laced on hir legges hye" (A 3267). Nor prevent men's thoughts from running beyond aesthetic enjoyment:

> She was a prymerole, a piggesnye,
> For any lord to leggen in his bedde,
> Or yet for any good yeman to wedde. (A 3270)

All three of these elements—the attractive and vibrant physical being, the effort to control it, the effect on men—figure in the first scene with Nicholas. Her first response to his crude advances is to reject them:

> And she sproong as a colt dooth in the trave,
> And with hir heed she wryed faste awey,
> And seyde, "I wol nat kisse thee, by my fey!
> Why, lat be," quod she, "lat be, Nicholas,
> Or I wol crie 'out, harrow' and 'allas'!
> Do wey youre handes, for youre curteisye!" (A 3287)

But if she can resist a crude physical attack, she gives in to pleas for mercy and fair proffers, permitting him the liberties that before she has repulsed:

> Whan Nicholas had doon thus everideel,
> And thakked hire aboute the lendes weel,
> He kiste hire sweete and taketh his sawtrie,
> And pleyeth faste, and maketh melodie. (A 3306)

Alisoun is very much more a presence in the *Miller's Tale* than Emily is in the Knight's. The Miller's description imitates in its form the troubling impact she has on men, as it allows itself to veer repeatedly from the proper description of what she wears to suggestions of the senses she stimulates and to the indecent thoughts she arouses.[9]

The Miller's two lovers are, like the Knight's, paradoxically differentiated, but instead of the Knight's subtle distinction, here the contrast is blatant. On the one hand we have Nicholas, quiet, orderly, studious, and devout, given to solitary concerts in his room for entertainment:

> And al above ther lay a gay sautrie,
> On which he made a-nyghtes melodie
> So swetely that all the chambre rong;
> And *Angelus ad virginem* he song;
> And after that he song the Kynges Noote.
> Ful often blessed was his myrie throte. (A 3218)

But *his* innocence is on the surface only. Expert in astrology and "deerne love," "sleigh and ful privee," he is the operator par excellence, the more effectual for his appearance, "lyk a mayden meke for to see." On the other hand, Absolon, basically innocent, flaunts his flamboyant hairdo, his modish shoes, his gay clothing in public. Even his talents are public—barbering, law, dancing. The music he makes is not solitary, not devout. He could

> . . . pleyen songs on a smal rubible;
> Therto he song som tyme a loud quynyble;
> And as wel koude he pleye on a giterne.
> In al the toun nas brewhous ne taverne
> That he ne visited with his solas,
> Ther any gaylard tappestere was. (A 3336)

The fates of these contrasted lovers are strikingly foreshadowed in the descriptions which the Miller gives us of them. "Hende" Nicholas, expert in "deerne love" and devious arts, carefully and quietly works out his plot, which involves the foretelling of a flood and the imposition on John's household of a pattern similar to the one in his own room. The tubs in the rafters, like the "augrym stones" on the shelves at his bed's head, are "faire apart." And though Nicholas takes down with him on the fateful night no psaltery, still,

> Ther as the carpenter is wont to lye,
> Ther was the revel and the melodye;
> And thus lith Alison and Nicholas,
> In bisynesse of myrthe and of solas,
> Til that the belle of laudes gan to rynge,
> And freres in the chauncel gonne synge. (A 3656)

Not only has Nicholas successfully arranged the elements in his own world; but the Miller has mockingly echoed the Knight's description of Palamon's marital bliss, brought to a climax his own rich use of musical elements in general and "melodye" as a rhyme word in particular, and set a standard for the comic use of religious terms to mean sex, unlikely to be equaled (or even understood by those who worry about the proper time for "lauds").

With the arrival of Absolon, however, Nicholas overreaches himself. Then the burning need for water, which he has not foreseen, for all his skill in foretelling "Whan that men sholde have droghte or elles shoures" (A 3196), draws from his "myrie throte" no *Angelus ad virginem*. His careful arrangements come tumbling about his ears, and the "deerne love" ends in a public altercation before the neighbors.

Absolon's fate also matches his character. His basic innocence and his effeminacy, implicit, as Father Beichner has shown, in his name and hairdo, condition his lovemaking.[10] He is as inept and public as Nicholas is skilled and secret. His inexperience leads him to try everything; first, a serenade under the lady's window, which effectually warns the husband; then intermediaries, gifts, money, histrionics—"He pleyeth Herodes upon a scaffold hye" (A 3384). His squeamishness about farting is complemented by his interest in sweet smells, his censing of the ladies in church, and his preparations for the previsioned "feeste" with chewing of "greyn and lycorys" and holding "trewe-love" under his tongue. His love call to Alisoun at her window on the fateful night epitomizes the quality of his wooing. Was ever such a sound heard before in the literature or the art of lovemaking?

> What do ye, hony-comb, sweete Alisoun,
> My faire bryd, my sweete cynamome?
> Awaketh, lemman myn, and speketh to me!
> Wel litel thynken ye upon my wo,
> That for youre love I swete ther I go.
> No wonder is thogh that I swelte and swete;
> I moorne as dooth a lamb after the tete.
> Ywis, lemman, I have swich love-longynge,
> That lik a turtel trewe is my moornynge.
> I may nat ete na moore than a mayde.   (A 3707)

Absolon's airy notions of love are effectually shattered by experience.

His first contact with his mistress is so crude as to cure him of any taste for paramours for the rest of his life. In his physical revulsion, he seizes on an instrument for vengeance against his mistress which is at least as cruel as the shock his delicate nature has suffered from the misplaced kiss. The hot coulter has a double relevance. It measures by its cruelty, intended as it is for Alisoun, the intensity of his anger and revulsion. At the same time it ironically symbolizes—hot and used in ploughing—his sexual inadequacy.[11] Wielding this symbolically ironic but literally effective weapon in his accidental combat with Nicholas, he is met with a weapon only to him as lethal.

The Miller opposes to the idealism of the *Knight's Tale* a crude realism. His picture of two rival lovers is an effective contrast to Palamon and Arcite and indicates an impatience on the teller's part with the exalted conduct of knights and their ladies.[12] As Palamon and Arcite meet equivalent fates in the ideal world of chivalry, Nicholas and Absolon ignobly and unwittingly fight each other in a crudely realistic world and receive in their moment of contact equivalent checks.

The mere mention of the Miller's subject, before he has told his tale, draws, as we have seen, a protest from the Reeve; and Robin shows in his reply that he is not at all reluctant if his tale serves a double purpose. The annoyance of the Reeve is an unearned increment, and the quarrel that results stems more from Oswald's choleric disposition than from intentional insult in the *Miller's Tale*. The aggressive Miller knows the Reeve, perhaps as a result of business dealings, and clearly enjoys offending him; but the offense could be taken only by a hypersensitive and vindictive man, since the gullible John, victim of the tale, has only his carpentry in common with the shrewd Oswald of the pilgrimage.

Oswald in fact talks himself into taking offense at the *Miller's Tale* and replying in kind. His initial impulse is to grouse a little about the story and to dissociate himself from revenge, not from lack of ability to retaliate, but out of a distaste for descending to the Miller's level and because of his age. The mention of his age releases a set of maudlin reflections—images of lost youth, of senility, of desire without capability—suggesting that his mind dwells on the obscenity he has just sought to shun. He ends his discourse with an image that recalls those spindleshanks, "Ylyk a staf, ther was no calf ysene" (A 592). He has always a colt's tooth, he tells us, despite the years

> Syn that my tappe of lif bigan to renne.
> For sikerly, whan I was bore, anon
> Deeth drough the tappe of lyf and leet it gon;
> And ever sithe hath so the tappe yronne
> Til that almoost al empty is the tonne.
> The streem of lyf now droppeth on the chymbe.   (A 3895)

The image expresses vividly his character, conserving and miserly of life as of substance.

The Host finds the "sermonyng" a pure waste of time—"The devel made a reve for to preche" (A 3903)—and in a voice as "lordly as a kyng," orders him to tell his tale. Stung perhaps by the Host's contemptuous comments, the Reeve decides to go on the offensive, since it is, as he says, permissible "with force force of-showve." As he warms to the task, his vindictiveness shows itself, causing him to take as personally directed at him what the carpenter among the guildsmen might have more reasonably found abusive:

> Right in his cherles termes wol I speke.
> I pray to God his nekke mote to-breke;
> He kan wel in myn eye seen a stalke,
> But in his owene he kan nat seen a balke.   (A3920)

The quarrel between the two men reflects a natural antipathy in their characters, and forms an unconscious extension of the parallelism set up in the *Knight's Tale* and consciously imitated in the Miller's. Two passages, one in each of their tales, point up the parallelism by foreshadowing ironically the outcomes of the tales and at the same time reflecting the distinction in character of the two men. They are both comments on learning.

In the *Miller's Tale*, John the Carpenter finds in the news that his lodger Nicholas has fallen into a trance a confirmation of his own attitudes—belief in the safety of ignorance, superstitious dread of the unknown, and the feeling that scholars are incapable in practical matters. He illustrates his attitude toward learning with an exemplum:

So ferde another clerk with astromye;
He walked in the feeldes, for to prye
Upon the sterres, what ther sholde bifalle,
Til he was in a marle-pit yfalle;
He saugh nat that. . . . (A 3461)

In the end, of course, it is John the Carpenter who, through his belief in an astrological prediction, fails to see what is before his eyes and at the cry of "Water!" assumes "Nowelis" flood, cuts the cord, and comes crashing down. His very pride in handling practical details—in buying the tubs and making the ladders with his own hands—makes it easy for Nicholas to brand him as the mad instigator of the precautions against flood.

In the *Reeve's Tale*, the triumphant miller, having outwitted the clerks and stolen their grain, taunts them with their learning in granting their request for shelter and food.

Myn hous is streit, but ye han lerned art;
Ye konne by argumentes make a place
A myle brood of twenty foot of space.
Lat se now if this place may suffise,
Or make it rowm with speche, as is youre gise. (A 4126)

Symkin's house with its one room will, after all, suffice the clerks without speech or argument. The "streitness" will give them not only room for revenge but the means of annulling the miller's early triumph. The miller's pride, mistaken in the tainted blood with which he is allied, is equally mistaken in his assumption of superiority over the clerks, and is given the final blow by his confused wife, who strikes unwittingly the head she has unwittingly horned.

The two comments on learning, John's from a posture of superstitious ignorance, Oswald's from a knowledge intimate enough to understand how learning can be misused, help to point up the contrast between the two pilgrims. The bluff, sensual Miller lives in a world whose highest intellectual attainment is the practical joke; hence his tale with its lip-smacking portrait of Alisoun, its emphasis on the bodily functions, its mockery of delicacy and squeamishness in the picture and fate of Absolon.[13] The Reeve, on the other hand, presents in his tale the world of spiritual corruption and economic maneuver in which he himself lives. His choleric and vindictive nature finds expression in the bitterly satirical portraits of the miller and his family; his own chicanery gives him sharp eyes for the deception practiced by others, whether scholars, or priests, or his own underlings. To the frank sensuality of the Miller, he opposes a sapless and efficient hypocrisy.[14]

There is a further and more important contrast in the two passages— the contrast in the attitudes of the two ultimate victims, John and Symkin. John is here solicitous about the welfare of Nicholas, just as later, when he hears about the flood, he is to think first and almost exclusively of his wife's safety. For the Miller, doubtless, John's solicitude for Nicholas and his genuine love for his wife made even funnier his eventual downfall and the multiplication of his injuries. The cruel humiliation and injury of the only character in the tale with any claim to goodness does not disturb Robin the Miller. Rather he is delighted to bring all of the characters whom he despises or cannot understand to ignominious or painful fates. Only Alisoun, whose distinctions are physical and whose responses are uncomplicated—who represents, in effect, the feminine ideal in the Miller's world—is at the end unscathed.[15]

Symkin, on the other hand, gives no occasion for divided feelings. An ignorantly presumptuous bully and the aggressor throughout the tale, he is expressing in his comment on learning his contempt for the clerks his victims. The passage not only is the connecting link between the two parts of the tale but epitomizes its poetic justice. As an expression of Symkin's disdain, it looks back on the beguiler beguiling. In its emphasis on the "streitness" of Symkin's lodging, it foreshadows the beguiler beguiled.

But if the *Miller's Tale* is cruel in its outcome, the *Reeve's Tale* is vindictive in its poetic justice.[16] The Reeve understands what the Miller does not, the attractiveness of virtue to others. He is careful to make the ultimate victim of his tale the aggressor and the villain. But he is also careful to make him similar in appearance and character to the Robin of the pilgrimage. The greater the skill with which he castigates his victim, the clearer his own angry sensitivity to insult. The verbal combat between the two pilgrims is paradoxical in its outcome. The Miller's faults are patent and he makes no effort to conceal them. But the Reeve, in accepting what he imagines to be a challenge, ranges himself by the vulgarity of his tale with the "cherles" of the pilgrimage. The skill with which he exploits his advantages over the Miller is a trap. Not only does he expose himself—which is to the hypocrite the ultimate defeat—but he has also unconsciously chosen a tale in which the young win out, with their resilience and gay opportunism, over their shrewd, calculating, avaricious elders—a pattern given point by the Reeve's discourse on his own old age in the prologue to the tale.

The young, including not only the clerks but the miller's daughter Malyne, along with the clerks' horse Bayard, give the *Reeve's Tale* the animation and the verve associated with the fabliau as a genre. The series of comic explosions at the end gets its impetus from Aleyn's and John's initiatives. It starts rather quietly with the aubade that expresses Malyne's love for her clerk and her betrayal of her father's theft. John's displacement of the cradle that has brought the miller's wife to an unwonted fulfillment in bed now sends Aleyn to Symkin with his vaunt:

> "For by that lord that called is seint Jame,
> As I have thries in this shorte nyght
> Swyved the milleres doghter bolt upright,
> Whil thow hast, as a coward, been agast."
> "Ye, false harlot," quod the millere, "hast?"   (A 4268)

The fight between Aleyn and Symkin, their fall on the other bed, the mistaken assumptions of the miller's awakened wife, her more knowing and successful search for a staff than John's, her knockout blow administered the bald miller, the clerks' beating of their opponent and their retrieval, as they depart, of the grain he has stolen from them—all follow in rapid succession, each event unexpected until it happens, but then seen as the inevitable and comic outcome of all that has gone before.

The northern dialect of the clerks throughout and Bayard's equine "Wehee" as he heads for the mares in the fen provide an additional source of amusement. The clerks use a sufficient number of northernisms to mark their speech as odd but not obscure; their unexpected departures from the norm in grammar and vocabulary have vivid, bucolic, and humorous impact. John's

> "Oure manciple, I hope he wil be deed,
> Swa werkes ay the wanges in his heed;"   (A 4030)

his

"Step on thy feet! Com of, man, al atanes!" (A 4074)

and Aleyn's

"Herdestow evere slyk a sang er now?
Lo, swilk a complyn is ymel hem alle," (A 4171)

and John's

"I is thyn awen clerk, swa have I seel!" (A 4239)

are still alive with the effect they had almost six centuries ago.[17]

The clerks as heroes throw unintended reflections on their putative creator the Reeve. They satisfy him by winning a total victory over his victim the miller. They no doubt also give him pleasure in the "colt's tooth" part of his mind, where "Oure wyl desireth folie evere in oon" (A 3880). But vicariously gratifying as their sexual prowess may be, it suffers in comparison with what happens in the *Miller's Tale*. Casual fornication with whatever woman is available represents a distinctly lower moral plane than Nicholas' passion for Alisoun. The clerks' sexual activities in the *Reeve's Tale* are not even casual. They are carried out in reprisal and as compensation for their failure to match the miller in their business dealings with him. The Reeve imagines a world where sex is not so important as economics, and where the young, indistinguishable from one another except by name, run roughshod over their elders. He has perhaps more in common with Symkin than he realizes.

If the Reeve is offended by the *Miller's Tale*, the Cook is delighted with the Reeve's: "For joye him thoughte he clawed him on the bak" (A 4326). "Herbergage," as the Cook sees it, is the argument, the danger of admitting someone to "his pryvetee," and he cannot allow the theme to be dropped here. He has himself a tale he would like to be permitted to tell, "A litel jape that fil in our citee" (A 4343). The Host accedes, implying that the tale had better be fresher than the food that the Cook sells, but begging him not to be angry—"A man may seye ful sooth in game and pley" (A 4355). "Only too true," says Roger the Cook, quoting the Flemish proverb "sooth pley, quaad pley," and threatening to make his second tale about a "hostileer":

But nathelees I wol nat telle it yit;
But er we parte, ywis, thou shalt be quit." (A 4362)

Hogge of Ware then starts in on the third fabliau in succession, with portraits like those in the Prologue, and Perkyn "revelour" to match epithets with "deynous" Symkin and "hende" Nicholas, and an argument of "herbergage" not only like the *Reeve's Tale* but like the Miller's as well. The parallelism and paradox of the *Knight's Tale* are reflected on two levels—in the rivalry of Nicholas and Absolon for Alisoun within a tale, and in the verbal combat of two pilgrims, the Miller and the Reeve. The unfinished *Cook's Tale* shows another pattern simultaneously coming into being—the chivalry of the *Knight's Tale* with its abstract idealism, balanced by a realistic triptych of life in the town, life in the country, and life in the city, giving threefold and intensifying reiteration to the themes of betrayal and deception. Perkyn "revelour" is tripping a criminal path to the everlasting bonfire and has gone to live with

> . . . a compeer of his owene sort,
> That lovede dys, and revel, and disport,
> And hadde a wyf that heeld for contenance
> A shoppe, and swyved for hir sustenance. (A 4422)

The casual fornication of the *Reeve's Tale* has become professional—to add one more thread to the pattern that is evolving.

In the events of the first day, broken off though they are, we have some of the limits of Chaucer's theme for the whole work sketched in. This is the meaning of the startling conjunctions with which the work opens. The strong trumpet call of the Knight's chivalric idealism is matched by the equally strong earthiness of the Miller, Reeve, and Cook. The patterns are there as support to character. They are no more rigid than the patterns of decorum and control which the Host fails to maintain at the end of the decorous and rigidly controlled *Knight's Tale*. Where the patterns *are* broken, they are significantly broken. The unreality of Emily in the *Knight's Tale*, as contrasted to the fully realized Alisoun of the Miller's, emphasizes the incompleteness of the Knight's experience. The fact that John has no resemblance to the Reeve other than the latter's carpentering as a young man, while

Symkin's personality is a caricature of Robin the Miller's, points up the sensitivity and vindictiveness of the Reeve. The dominance of character over accident in the *Knight's Tale*, as opposed to the reverse pattern in the other tales, is only one side of the paradox. For the Knight is superior to the circumstances of his life through a specialization of interest and vision which leads him to overlook many things not only seen but enjoyed by the Miller and his ilk.

In addition to the light thrown on character, the stories of the first fragment help to carry out one of the basic thematic emphases in the *Knight's Tale*. The succession of tales does not result from the Host's decision, nor does Chaucer seem to force the patterns that have emerged. Rather they come into being from the self-centered purposes of a number of men—from the Host's love of fellowship, power, and money, from the Knight's love of chivalry and his gentle manners, from the Miller's raucous bravado and his dislike of courtly love, from the Reeve's choleric anger and the Cook's delight in bawdry. The clash and contrast of motive thus becomes another pattern, and the extent to which the purpose finds fulfillment, an indication of the relative value of the motive. The suggestion of a moral element is not, however, obtrusive. The preponderance of the patterns is aesthetic; the pleasure they give, unthreatened by the taint of hypocrisy and self-satisfaction.

This predisposition to form in the universe of Chaucer's art reflects the universe that the poet lives in if we take at real value his amusing disclaimers of responsibility. Thus in the *Knight's Tale*, in the *Canterbury Tales*, and in the England that the poem claims to reflect accurately, the forms that make experience comprehensible are willed, not by Theseus, not by the Host, not even by Chaucer. The *Knight's Tale* attributes these forms to the "sighte above," and though they have there a more moral import than in the first fragment of the *Canterbury Tales* as a whole, there is an implication in Chaucer's repeated disclaimers that in the latter they have the same source. In the warning "And yet men shal nat maken ernest of game," Chaucer suggests that the divine "purveiaunce" has a comic bias.

on the road past rochester

"Taketh the moralite"

THE longest fragment of the *Canterbury Tales*, the one labeled by the Chaucer Society B², takes the pilgrims past Rochester on what must have been the second day of the pilgrimage. For they spent a night at Ospring before the *Second Nun's Tale*, and they could not have traveled the forty-six miles from Southwark past Rochester to Ospring in a single day.[1] The fragment itself seems to have been more casually assembled than any of the others. Two of the stories were probably originally assigned to other pilgrims and to positions in the storytelling different from the ones they now occupy. A third, the series of tragedies called the *Monk's Tale*, was conceived as an independent work and written, with the exception of some of the "modern instances," soon after Chaucer's return from Italy in 1373.[2] Chaucer gives the Monk motivation for telling the tragedies by having the Host affect a rather insolent familiarity in addressing him. They represent a dignified rebuke by the "abbotable" prelate rather than a reflection of his interests. The relationship generally between the portraits of the Prologue and the tales of the fragment has little importance, with three of the stories being told by pilgrims for whom no portrait exists and only one of the six, the Prioress's, reflecting the personality as described in the Prologue. To an unusual degree, then, for the *Canterbury Tales*, these stories are self-contained.

Yet interesting relationships develop and events occur that influence the significance of the narratives. The latent rivalry between the Host and Chaucer flares up as the Host calls on Chaucer for a "tale of

myrthe," dislikes the *Thopas* so much that he stops it, offers Chaucer
another chance, and finds in the *Melibeus* the inspiration for an autobiographical account of his subservience to his wife. Later he boasts:

> And wel I woot the substance is in me,
> If any thyng shal wel reported be. (B 3994)

In fact, the Host behaves more confidently and more foolishly than in
any of the other fragments. He supports the Knight in his interruption
of the Monk's tragedies, pays an exaggerated deference to the Prioress
in calling on her for a tale, and treats both the Monk and the Nun's
Priest to tasteless remarks on their sexual prowess. His critical comments
on the stories are invariably and unwittingly comic. Also striking, in this
fragment, is the variety of genres. Fabliau, miracle of the Virgin, parody
of popular romance, didactic allegory, a series of short tragedies, and
mock-heroic beast fable succeed one another, each one distinct in
genre, and only the first and the last in the same verse form.[3]

The literary interest represented by the Monk's definition of tragedy,
by the Nun's Priest's mock-heroics and Chaucer's parody, by the variety
of genres, by the interrupted tales, and by the Host's critical comments,
though providing a unifying element to the fragment, does not include
reference to the contest which the Host proposes in the General Prologue. The interruptions especially afford repeated opportunities for
mention of the prize, but the only consequences the Host cites, as he
comments on the interrupted tales, are annoying the company and, in
almost putting him to sleep, forfeiting a good report of the tale. The
Host regards himself as audience and reporter of the tales, but not yet
as their judge in any but the most generalized sense. He has a stake in
the pleasure of the company and admonishes the Monk: "Ryde forth,
myn owene lord, brek nat oure game" (B 3117). In supporting the
Knight's interruption of the tragedies, he shows his concern for the
quality of the entertainment:

> Swich talkyng is nat worth a boterflye,
> For therinne is ther no desport ne game. (B 3981)

After blessing the Nun's Priest for his story and appreciating his physique, he concludes, "Now, sire, faire falle yow for youre tale!" (B
4650). The addition to the game of a contest and the conclusion of the

pilgrimage with a prize-awarding supper developed in part perhaps as an extension of the literary interest in this fragment, and especially from the role Chaucer found himself playing as pilgrim.

The two central stories that Chaucer tells not only show the poet dealing with the inevitable problem of comparative excellence, but provide an enigmatic clue to further meaning. Will Chaucer, whose great fiction is that he is not writing fiction, give himself what he considers the best story? Or will he carry the modesty *topos* to the absurd extreme of assigning himself one of the worst? Chaucer's solution plausibly avoids either of these alternatives, maintaining the suspension of disbelief by a dazzling display of professional skill in the amusing parody, *Sir Thopas*, and at the same time reaping a dramatic dividend with the Host's crude and misconceived interruption. His second story, the *Melibeus*, again reveals the professional, but this time in a less entertaining guise. Its systematically didactic literal level discourages attention to the subtle and distinct allegorical meanings, and again wins a naive if less violent response from the Host. The make-believe is enhanced by the poet's incognito. He is both there to report accurately, and not there in any way that feeds *amour propre* or disturbs the equanimity of those he imitates. The suggestion of the artist's predicament points to the subtlest thematic element in the fragment—the art of storytelling itself and the kinds of disguise an audience may force an author's interests to wear.

Disguises, of course, are a part of the sport the pilgrims are regaling themselves with. The Prioress, whose portrait in the Prologue throws light on her performance, does not present the most interesting facet of this problem; her disguises are all inadvertent. The Monk's, on the other hand, are too clearly motivated. Rather it is the Prioress's presence in the audience for the teller of the final tale in the series that makes the most interesting aspects of the problem manifest. The Nun's Priest, who might well be, in Chaucer's mind as well as for the majority of readers, the real winner in the storytelling contest that finally eventuates, does not quite succeed in remaining out of sight behind his fiction. His struggle to resume his disguise, to regain objectivity, to recover the thread of the narrative, where the sentiments he has been expressing directly are ridiculed, receives full expression in the line: "Thise been the cokkes wordes, and nat myne" (B 4455). Artful participation in the game of storytelling, both for the Nun's Priest and for Chaucer, requires a transcendence of petty self-interest that is the more difficult to maintain because of the reflection of the artist inherent in any art, even the most objective.

The *Shipman's Tale*, originally written for the Wife of Bath, starts off the fragment without any introduction. A fabliau, it takes the form of a contest in betrayal, in which sex and money become wittingly and cynically interchangeable.[4] The merchant's wife in the tale tries to sell herself to the monk, Don John, only to find that he has borrowed the money from her husband and told him that he returned it to her (as indeed he did) while the merchant was off on a trip. The wife learns of the monk's perfidy in a final bed scene with her husband, who criticizes her for not having told him about the repayment of the debt and for causing, as he fears, "a manere straungenesse" between him and his "cosyn" Don John:

> Telle me alwey, er that I fro thee go,
> If any dettour hath in myn absence
> Ypayed thee, lest thurgh thy necligence
> I myghte hym axe a thing that he hath payed.   (B 1589)

She boldly outfaces him, admitting that she has received the gold:

> What! yvel thedam on his monkes snowte!
> For, God it woot, I wende, withouten doute,
> That he hadde yeve it me bycause of yow,
> To doon therwith myn honour and my prow,
> For cosynage, and eek for beele cheere
> That he hath had ful ofte tymes heere.
> But sith I se I stonde in this disjoynt,
> I wol answere yow shortly to the poynt.
> Ye han mo slakkere dettours than am I!
> For I wol paye yow wel and redily
> Fro day to day, and if so be I faille,
> I am youre wyf; score it upon my taille,
> And I shal paye as soone as ever I may.
> For by my trouthe, I have on myn array,
> And nat on wast, bistowed every deel;

And for I have bistowed it so weel
For youre honour, for Goddes sake, I seye,
As be nat wrooth, but lat us laughe and pleye.
Ye shal my joly body have to wedde;
By God, I wol nat paye yow but abedde!"   (B 1614)

The puns on "taillynge" and "wedde" point up the cynical atmosphere, which the wife is not entirely responsible for creating. She lives
in a household where money is the paramount value, where she receives
admonishment for disturbing her husband in his "countourhous" to call
him to meals, where her husband's activities in bed reflect the state of
his finances. But she has learned her lesson well. She has learned the
importance of appearances from the conjugal lectures showing the
essential contribution that "chiere and good visage" make to a good
credit rating, and has proceeded to spend more than she can wring
from her husband on her appearance, on clothes. She has experienced in
his lovemaking the interdependence of sex and money, and in her affair
with the monk she tries to borrow money and pay it back in bed. "Lene
me thise hundred frankes," she says, and

. . . at a certeyn day I wol yow paye,
And doon to yow what plesance and service
That I may doon, right as yow list devise.   (B 1382)

The technique, she discovers, will work with her husband, but not with
her lover.

The great distinction of the *Shipman's Tale* is the way the respectable
surfaces are maintained. Most fabliaux conclude with some violent or
decisive exposure. This tale carries on its multiple deceptions and
betrayals without once disturbing the amenities and orthodoxies of life
in St. Denis. The monk, who hails from the same town as the merchant,
first establishes himself as favorite house guest of the whole menage,
master and servants alike, before he approaches the wife. "The monk
hym claymeth as for cosynage" (B 1226). The line expresses the two
men's relationship perfectly with what is perhaps a prophetic use of the
word cosynage.[5] The merchant is clearly flattered by the monk's atten-
tions, "as glad therof as fowel of day," and quickly establishes the kind
of relationship that gave the word cozen its meaning of dupe:

> Thus been they knyt with eterne alliaunce,
> And ech of hem gan oother for t'assure
> Of bretherhede, whil that hir lyf may dure.　　(B 1232)

The dialogue between wife and monk in the garden, while the merchant is counting his money, is a model of caution, each of the participants ready to assume a casual demeanor at the least sign of danger. The signals are all green; they quickly get through the necessary preliminaries—the leads that permit retreat, the mutual assurances of secrecy. When they reach the point of closing the deal, they invoke the monk's profession and his "porthors" as guarantors of good faith. The lady's need of money has the noblest of motives:

> But by that ilke Lord that for us bledde,
> For his honour, myself for to arraye,
> A Sonday next I moste nedes paye
> An hundred frankes, or ellis I am lorn.　　(B 1371)

What has started out to be her despair at being linked to a useless husband, despair so intense that she considers running away or suicide, turns out to be worry over an importunate creditor. Not very flattering to the monk, but then Don John has no intention of investing his own money in his mistress-to-be's appearance. He leaves her with an admonition that means more to her than to him: "Gooth now, and beeth as trewe as I shal be" (B 1397). The monk knows by now just how true he can expect her to be. That she brings with her to her garden colloquy with Don John a "mayde child,"

> Which as hir list she may governe and gye,
> For yet under the yerde was the mayde,　　(B 1287)

speaks volumes for the moral tone of fourteenth-century suburban life.

The wife's need to honor Christ and the narrator's final prayer— "God us sende / Taillynge ynough unto oure lyves ende. Amen" (B 1624)—point up the extent to which the forms of religion permeate their lives without having the slightest influence on them. The monk is saying "his thynges" courteously when the wife comes to him. God and a number of his saints, if the words of the wife and the monk are heeded, assist at their meeting. And before they break their fast, "hastily a messe was ther seyd" (B 1441) for the merchant, torn with reluctance from his fingering of what his wife calls "Goddes sonde" (B 1409), and for his wife and his dear friend, fresh from their exchange of vows in the garden. The more delicate the operation, seemingly, the more in need of religious sanctions. When the monk touches his "cousin" for the "hundred frankes," he first wishes him a good journey, invoking God and St. Austyn to speed him on his way; gives him advice on diet in "this hete," asking that God shield him from care; offers his own services for anything that needs doing in his absence; and finally comes to the point—the money for the beasts for the place "that is oures"—adding the ironic prayer, "God helpe me so, I wolde it were youres!" (B 1464). The casual way in which the wife links in rhyme the "Lord that for us bledde" with husbands "fressh abedde" says it all with honest inadvertence. Religious forms merely punctuate their lives.

The tale's emphasis on a formal and empty orthodoxy would have fitted it to the Wife of Bath in the early stages of her development, when she broke into the storytelling after the *Man of Law's Tale*, pushing the Parson aside as a Lollard—

> "We leven alle in the grete God," quod [s]he;
> "He wolde sowen som difficulte,
> Or springen cokkel in our clene corn"   (B 1183)

—and then worried Scripture into support for her opinions and way of life in the first 162 lines of her prologue.[6] The beginning of the tale, with its enthusiastic endorsement of wifely extravagance, and the end, where the wife so skillfully talks herself out of a tight corner, would also have appealed to Alisoun. For the Shipman, on the other hand, the story has only a very general fitness and the particular point that the merchant, whose wine he has no doubt surreptitiously enjoyed, is its butt. For the man who risks his neck in the commerce of the world, the man who only ventures money is fair game and his whole way of life suspect. The placing of the *Shipman's Tale* before the Prioress's may serve only the purposes of contrast. It could conceivably signal a second critique of ways in which religion can be abused.

A comic note is clearly set by the Host in his reaction to the *Shipman's Tale*—"Draweth no monkes moore unto youre in" (B 1632)—and in the exaggerated deference he pays the Prioress as he calls on her for a tale, conditionally, "by youre leve, / So that I wiste I sholde yow nat greve" (B 1638), and "if so were that ye wolde." Apparently the pains she had taken "to countrefete cheere / Of court" have impressed the Host in exactly the way they were intended to.

But if the portrait throws some ironic light on the story of the little clergeon, the language of the story shows no lapses from taste, no slips that reveal clearly an intention on Chaucer's part to satirize the anti-Semitism.[7] Quite the contrary. The Prioress starts out with a prayer to God and the Virgin as fine of its kind as anything Chaucer ever did. The rhetoric of the third stanza with its apostrophe to Mary contains the virgin birth, the Annunciation, and the Trinity, and brings in as well the prefiguring burning bush and the conceit of Mary's humility ravishing the Holy Ghost,

> Of whos vertu, whan he thyn herte lighte,
> Conceyved was the Fadres sapience.   (B 1662)

The prayer, in anticipation of the story and in honor of the Virgin Mother, turns three times to images of children—the middle one the awesome "Fadres sapience," the final one an image for the Prioress's own humility and inarticulateness:

> My konnyng is so wayk, o blisful Queene,
> For to declare thy grete worthynesse
> That I ne may the weighte nat susteene;
> But as a child of twelf month oold, or lesse,
> That kan unnethes any word expresse,
> Right so fare I, and therfore I yow preye,
> Gydeth my song that I shal of yow seye.   (B 1677)

In the tale itself, we are in the realm of absolute values. All Christians are automatically justified in their confrontation with non-Christians. The little clergeon has every right to sing *Alma Redemptoris Mater* as he crosses the Jewry to and from school every day. If the Jews take measures to stop his singing, the cause is the prompting of Satan, our first foe, the serpent, "That hath in Jues herte his waspes nest" (B 1749). Given the values and their certainty, everything else in the tale follows. The little boy who chooses to spend his time learning the hymn to the Virgin, which even his older schoolmate is unable to understand—"I lerne song, I kan but smal grammeere" (B 1726)— has a special grace. The favor of the Virgin will manifest itself even in his death. After his death, as St. John the Evangelist has written, he will still sing, "folwynge evere in oon / The white Lamb celestial" (B 1771). The opposition of good and evil manifests itself in an especially vivid way as the poor widow searches for her child among the "cursed Jues":

> She frayneth and she preyeth pitously
> To every Jew that dwelte in thilke place,
> To telle hire if hir child wente oght forby.
> They seyde "nay"; but Jhesu, of his grace,
> Yaf in hir thoght, inwith a litel space,
> That in that place after hir sone she cryde,
> Where he was casten in a pit bisyde.
>
>   O grete God, that parfournest thy laude
> By mouth of innocentz, lo, heere thy myght!
> This gemme of chastite, this emeraude,
> And eek of martirdom the ruby bright,
> Ther he with throte ykorven lay upright,
> He *Alma redemptoris* gan to synge
> So loude that al the place gan to rynge.   (B 1803)

If we had witnessed the miracle, we too, with the abbot and the whole "covent," would have fallen "gruf . . . al plat upon the grounde,"

    Wepynge, and herying Cristes mooder deere,   (B 1868)

and recalling, as the Prioress (and Chaucer?) did, "'yonge Hugh of Lyncoln" and all the ritual murders attributed to Jews through time and space, from the "Asye" of the tale to the England of its author. So it comes about that the gentlest of poets devoted his art to the cruelest of legends.

The temptation is strong to remember the many times Chaucer denies his responsibility for what the pilgrims say, and to attribute to the Prioress sentiments which we would like to think the poet did not share. No one can fail to see the ways the tale reflects the Prioress's personality.[8] The woman whose tears flow for mice and little dogs has here found the ideal creature to lavish her affection on. The sentimentalized little boy must never attain maturity and independence. He must remain forever defenseless against the world of traps and cruel men, forever dependent, a small living thing for her to fondle and spoil and protect. Martyrdom will conveniently add the *frisson* of horror, the tears of grief, and the satisfaction of vengeance—abundance indeed for the sentimentalist's self-indulgence. The nun who wears on her beads the gold bangle, and who takes such care with her table manners, would hardly express the highest religious ideals. Following as it does the mock religion of the characters in the *Shipman's Tale*, the *Prioress's Tale* presents the distortions of sentimentality, more serious because they have positive rather than negative consequences.

The two views are not entirely incompatible. The tale can reflect the Prioress's personality and at the same time express Chaucer's Christianity. The miracle of the little boy singing after death the hymn to the Virgin recurs in the Prioress's telling of the story, her prayers answered, herself the inadequate instrument of the Virgin's praise. Does Chaucer believe the implicit libel against the Jews, the justification for so many pogroms over the years? The balance on this question is perhaps tipped by what happens when the Prioress stops speaking:

> Whan seyd was al this miracle, every man
> As sobre was that wonder was to se.   (B 1882)

To the sobriety, Chaucer adds the accolade of continued rhyme royal—as if still under the spell of the Prioress, despite the jarring note of Harrie Baillie's crude banter.

The Host displays two principles as major-domo of the entertainment. When he calls on the Monk to match the *Knight's Tale*, he is playing it safe and hoping for a repetition of his success. After the *Prioress's Tale*, as later after the Physician's, he is clearly seeking "comic relief." In this case, he prides himself on seeing beneath the surface: he comments first on the way Chaucer rides along, his eyes ever on the ground; then on his shape, as big as Harrie's own, with evident appeal for the women; finally on his "elvyssh" look. This last point of observation alone warrants the expectation of a "tale of myrthe" and, after Chaucer has mentioned a rhyme he learned long ago, of "som deyntee thyng."

Chaucer richly meets both these expectations and yet fails to satisfy the Host. It must have taken some time for even the most literate pilgrims to know what was happening to them. They would notice first the jog-trot meter:

> Listeth, lordes, in good entent,
> And I wol telle verrayment
>   Of myrthe and of solas;
> Al of a knyght was fair and gent
> In bataille and in tourneyment,
>   His name was sire Thopas.   (B 1907)

Then they would begin to see that the sense has a way of either faltering at the end of a stanza, where the rhythm declares for climax,[9] or giving us some inanity like the name of the knight who was "fair and gent." In the second and third stanzas, it is the first alternative, with "As it was Goddes grace" and "He hadde a semely nose." In the fourth, we return to inanity with the unchivalric reference to the money he paid for his robe—"That coste many a jane." In between the climaxes, are a series of other absurdities, all cut precisely to the requirements of the meter—the explosion of "Poperyng, in the place," as the hero's remote birthplace, the bad pun of a "doghty swayn" with face as white as "payndemayn,"[10] the roses of his lips, the long beard, the bourgeois shoes, hose, and robe. The absurdities reach a real climax at the end of the next stanza:

> Therto he was a good archeer;
> Of wrastlyng was ther noon his peer,
>   Ther any ram shal stonde.   (B 1931)

The idea of a knight winning the ram at wrestling must strike even the most obtuse fan of the romances as peculiar.

The parody extends beyond details to the activities of the hero and the structure of the whole poem. Sir Thopas rides aimlessly about, risking his life in forests infested by wild beasts, "Ye, bothe bukke and hare" (B 1946), falls in "love-longynge" when he hears birds singing, dreams up an elf queen to be his leman, and sets off to find one in the land of Fairye. Opposed by a giant, Sir Olifaunt, he discovers that he has forgotten to arm himself, and takes to his heels under a hail of stones, slung at him David-like by the giant. The first fit comes to a climax with the ceremonial arming of the hero, which one might reasonably expect to happen before he leaves, instead of on his return home.

The jog-trot meter continues without variation for thirteen stanzas, absorbing the absurdities, anticlimaxes, and non sequiturs, the poet either cutting or filling to make each line end-stopped. Then, in the fourteenth stanza, the first variation comes in the form of a two-syllable bob on the first of the three-syllable lines. The weight of more than eighty absolutely regular lines throws its emphasis on what seems at first to be a run-on. The two syllables turn out to be a baffling addition of non-information to what is complete already; a return to regularity of rhythm makes them extrametrical; but the rhyme for lines 4 and 5 shifts to the short third line, and the climactic final line chimes with the bob. The bob, "In towne," and the last line, "By dale and eek by downe," turn out to be rhyme rather than reason. This first irregularity sets off a series of others, but the new irregularities are extensions of the regular pattern, so that we never know whether the wheel-and-bob is coming until it is there. The new pattern establishes itself by repetition, as the good knight invades the land of Fairye, meets Sir Olifaunt, and threatens him with dire consequences when he returns with his armor. The combat itself fails to fill out even a stanza, which returns to the original form; we wait for the wheel-and-bob like the proverbial other shoe; no previous lack of matter has had any formal effect. Instead, we are told, "Yet listeth, lordes . . ."—as if we weren't:

> Yet listeth, lordes, to my tale
> Murier than the nightyngale,
>   For now I wol yow rowne
> How sir Thopas, with sydes smale,
> Prikyng over hill and dale,
>   Is comen agayn to towne.   (B 2028)

The timing so essential to comic effect makes itself felt in the meter.

The gem of a knight appears in a gem of a tale. The number of parallels with extant English chivalric romances shows that Chaucer

in his parody is concentrating rather than exaggerating his effects.[11]
From its chief elements to its smallest detail, the *Thopas* is all of a
piece. Even the spelling and the pronunciation are brought into play—a
really surprising phenomenon where each was as uncertain as it was in
fourteenth-century English. *Forest* not only throws its stress to the
second syllable but lengthens its vowel to rhyme with *best*, *est* (the
direction), and a surprising *almest*. The rhymes in one stanza start
off *was*, *gras* (the green stuff); then *place* becomes *plas*, as *grace* later
becomes *gras* to rhyme with *Thopas*. Distortions of language, non
sequiturs in plot, and absurdities of action pile up as the poem goes into
a second fit with the admonition,

> Now holde youre mouth, *par charitee*,
> Bothe knyght and lady free,   (B 2082)

and with apparently no recollection of what has gone before—the
elf queen, Sir Olifaunt, the land of Fairye. Sir Thopas sleeps in the
open, drinking only water.

But it is too much for the Host, to whom the subtleties of parody
seem the real thing, and who finds nothing amusing in a foolish story
that could go on indefinitely. His interruption saves Chaucer from the
difficulty of bringing to a satisfactory end a parody of the interminable.
It also exposes this judge and reporter of our storytelling contest.
His self-assurance is as absolute as his insensitivity to what has been
happening:

> "Namoore of this, for Goddes dignitee,"
> Quod oure Hooste, "for thou makest me
> So wery of thy verray lewednesse . . ."   (B 2111)

Chaucer's mild reply, affecting a desire to go on with what he must
have been delighted to have interrupted, apparently mollifies the Host,
who offers the poet a second opportunity:

> Sire, at o word, thou shalt no lenger ryme.
> Lat se wher thou kanst tellen aught in geeste,
> Or telle in prose somwhat, at the leeste,
> In which ther be som murthe or som doctryne.   (B 2125)

Chaucer agrees to tell a "litel thyng in prose," a "moral tale vertuous," and apologizes for any differences in wording from the "tretys lyte" which is the source of his story, mentioning particularly an increased number of proverbs. The "sentence," he assures the pilgrims, is unchanged. His statement has been seized on by one school of critics as indicating the meaning behind the whole *Canterbury Tales*, which they assume he refers to as "this tretys lyte."[12] It is true that the statement does not describe his use of his source for the *Melibeus*; but after the references to source material in *Troilus and Criseyde*, many of which acknowledge indebtedness for precisely the passages that Chaucer is inventing, we need not be surprised at his misleading us again. There are plenty of proverbs in the *Melibeus*, even though they are all translations from the *Livre de Melibée et de Dame Prudence*. The curious notion that Chaucer is telling us that his *Canterbury Tales* have all "o sentence," like the Four Gospels, wrenches the meaning of his language in this passage and misrepresents both the Gospels, which are after all four versions of the same life, and the *Canterbury Tales*, which reflect the varied interests and personalities of a motley set of narrators.

The forbidding surface of the *Melibeus* has prevented readers in every age from appreciating the merits it has. Chaucer thought highly of it or he would not have planned to use it as the *Man of Law's Tale* at the beginning of the storytelling, and then later have shifted it to the only slightly less important function of serving as his own second tale.

Two things are especially worthy of recognition about it. One is the extent to which the argument against war has retained its validity. Three-quarters of the rather long story is devoted to the discussion that cancels Melibeus' commitment to war. In the course of the talk, many of the justifications for warfare that we still encounter are taken up. These include dissuasion of the wicked, the prevention of further attack, the having both a just cause and the means to make one's enemies pay for their evil-doing, and finally the defense of one's honor. The first part of the discussion (B 2241–2304) deals with the issue of the prior commitment Melibeus has made to his friends and allies at the end of the council meeting. Prudence's reasons for urging her husband to change are worth quoting:

> For I seye that it is no folie to chaunge conseil whan the thyng is chaunged, or elles whan the thyng semeth ootherweyes than

it was biforn. And mooreover, I seye that though ye han sworn and bihight to perfourne youre emprise, and nathelees ye weyve to perfourne thilke same emprise *by juste cause,* men sholde nat seyn thefore that ye were a liere ne forsworn. For the book seith that "the wise man maketh no lesyng whan he turneth his corage to the bettre." (B 2257; italics mine)

What she says about the preparation for war has also a continuing relevance:

"Warnestooryng," quod she, "of heighe toures and of grete edifices apperteyneth somtyme to pryde. And eek men make heighe toures, and grete edifices with grete costages and with greet travaille; and whan that they been accompliced, yet be they nat worth a stree, but if they be defended by trewe freendes that been olde and wise. And understoond wel that the gretteste and strongeste garnysoun that a riche man may have, as wel to kepen his persone as his goodes, is that he be biloved with hys subgetz and with his neighebores." (B 2528)

Prudence offers her husband two alternatives to war—resort to law or reconciliation with his enemies. It is the latter that she persuades him to accept.

Reconciliation with his enemies has made the allegorical meaning of the story difficult for some critics to follow. For if the three enemies (who enter Melibeus' house through the windows while he is off playing in the fields and wound his daughter in the hands, feet, nose, ears, and mouth) are to be seen as the world, the flesh, and the devil, reconciliation would mean coming to terms with the three enemies of mankind. One critic has simply shrugged his shoulders over the impasse, with the comment that "the mediaeval man was not censorious; he took allegory as he found it." Another has found the answer in the dependence of man on the grace of God for his delivery from evil. For him, the story is showing in the end "that trust in self-defense is the most dangerous vanity of the Christian on his road to God."[13] The difficulty disappears if we remember that in medieval allegory the literal has the determinant role. The other meanings—allegorical, moral, and anagogical—do not represent a reality of which the literal is a mere shadow. Rather all four levels have validity.[14]

As Dame Prudence points out, when she is exploring the causes for the initial violence, Christ "hath suffred that thou hast been punysshed in the manere that thow hast ytrespassed." She goes on to explain:

> Thou hast doon synne agayn oure Lord Crist; for certes, the three enemys of mankynde, that is to seyn, the flessh, the feend, and the world, thou hast suffred hem entre in to thyn herte wilfully by the wyndowes of thy body, and hast nat defended thyself suffisantly agayns hire assautes and hire temptaciouns, so that they han wounded thy soule in fyve places; this is to seyn, the deedly synnes that been entred into thyn herte by thy fyve wittes. And *in the same manere* oure Lord Crist hath woold and suffred that thy three enemys been entred into thyn house by the wyndowes, and han ywounded thy doghter in the forseyde manere. (B 2616; italics mine)

Prudence never makes the mistake of identifying the three enemies as the world, the flesh, and the devil, nor the house with his body, nor the daughter with his soul. Nor does she claim any certainty for her interpretation, recognizing that the "juggementz of oure Lord God almyghty been ful depe," frequently beyond man's understanding, but holding to the belief that "God, which that is ful of justice and of right-wisnesse, hath suffred this bityde by juste cause resonable" (B 2599). In other words, Melibeus has deserved his suffering (as have perhaps most men throughout history), and in this instance the suffering has taken a form especially appropriate. Here perhaps lies the meaning of the wounds in the hands and feet, with the eyes conspicuously not included. The five wounds are almost but not quite equivalent to the five senses. We must not expect one-to-one relationships with allegorical meaning throughout, the sort that one gets in classical or personification allegory.

The other meanings are unusually distinct in the *Melibeus*. The literal level records the vicissitudes of a private citizen in the urban world of thirteenth-century Italy, where the decision on war and peace was often made on a family basis. It is the relevance to the state level of the arguments for and against the resort to force that gives the allegory. Which particular quarrel of the Italian city-states represents the figura, the specific referent of the allegory? This level of meaning in the *Melibeus* has such a generalized value that it can apply to practically any. Its appeal to Chaucer may well have been its relevance to the affairs of his patron John of Gaunt, fighting for a will-o'-the-wisp kingdom in Spain during the late eighties of the fourteenth century.[15]

The moral level is perhaps only too apparent. Proverbs, authorities, and didactic analysis abound in the story. But they come from the characters in the tale. The contrast between the council at the beginning and the one at the end gives an implicit moral meaning. The moral lessons result from the comments of the characters as they try to learn from their own experience. On other occasions, the moral emerges from dramatic interchange, as when Dame Prudence asks her husband what he thinks his wise councillors meant when they advised him to "warnestoore" his house "with gret diligence" (B 2521–22). Thus though the narrative is didactic throughout, it never ceases to be narrative.

The anagoge presents Melibeus as a kind of Everyman, seeking to correct what is wrong in his life by violence against those who have wronged him. Dame Prudence has the insight to recognize that most suffering in this life is deserved, and that the only way to combat evil is, not by violence against others, but by improving one's own conduct. The three enemies have indeed wronged Melibeus. They provide now a test of Melibeus' quality. Resort to violence on his part will simply compound the evil. The enemies of mankind—the flesh, the world, and the devil—are still at work, suggesting actions that will make reconciliation difficult or impossible. Melibeus will succeed against them in the end by reconciling himself to the three who attacked him, forgiving them, and making possible through a right relationship with his fellow man a right relationship with God.

The interaction between the different levels suggests the universality of the "sentence." In his personal and political involvements, man constantly seeks a source of evil outside that he can attack and eliminate. *Melibeus* suggests that the major source of evil, personal or political, is internal; it suggests that the temptation to go after the enemies outside comes from the real enemy and, if acceded to, increases rather than diminishes the tangle of evil.

The *Melibeus* delights the Host, not because of any subtle or profound meaning, but because Dame Prudence reminds him, by contrast, of the external source of evil in his own life—his wife. His response to each of Chaucer's tales is equally insensitive. In the first case, it is ignorantly *against*. In the second case, it is perversely *for*. He has derived from the *Melibeus* the one moral it was designed to combat.

He describes his wife in terms that throw ironic lights on his own life. Most obvious, of course, is the anomaly of a man so blustery and domineering expressing fear of his wife's violence. "I dar nat hire withstonde," he tells us,

> For she is byg in armes, by my feith:
> That shal he fynde that hire mysdooth or seith.   (B 3112)

In two of the three examples he gives of her incitement to violence, he reveals his own violent nature. In the first, for instance, she is simply egging him on as he beats his "knaves" by bringing him the "grete clobbed staves" that he must keep for such occasions, and by shouting encouragement to him. In the third, he is afraid of slaying some neighbor whom she has forced him to fight—"For I am perilous with knyf in honde" (B 3109). The middle instance (shades of the Wife of Bath's portrait) shows churchgoing as the source of quarreling, the wife watching for fellow parishioners who don't do her proper reverence or are "so hardy to hire to trespace."

His wife would appear to be the one person who daunts the Host. Rapidly turning from the defensive to the offensive, he calls on the Monk for a story, points to Rochester as "faste by," and tells him to "brek nat oure game." Though after the Monk has narrated his tragedies, the Host calls him "daun Piers," here he affects not to know his name and innocently inquires whether it is daun John, daun Thomas, or daun Albon.

As he continues to address the Monk, the insulting implication he intended becomes clear. From fine appearance ("ful fair skyn"), to ample diet, to exalted position, to his build, the Host comments on the Monk's qualities. Finally comes the attack direct:

> I pray to God, yeve hym confusioun

That first thee broghte unto religioun!
Thou woldest han been a tredefowel aright.   (B 3135)

The rest of his comments center on the wasted sexual prowess, on the eugenic need for the Pope to grant such men permission to marry, on the way "oure wyves" are attracted by their obvious superiority to "assaye / Religious folk." The Host is extrapolating the final sexual innuendo from all the other resemblances of the Monk to Don John, the wily hero of the *Shipman's Tale*. Having used even the equivalence of sex and money so wittily developed in that tale, he half apologizes and renews the insult in the same breath. You monks, he says,

> mowe bettre paye
> Of Venus paiementz than mowe we;
> God woot, no lussheburghes payen ye!
> But be nat wrooth, my lord, though that I pleye.
> Ful ofte in game a sooth I have herd seye!   (B 3154)

The Monk knows better than to take notice of the Host's insolence. He turns to the problem of what story to tell, making clear that he will join no churl's game but will do his best,

> As fer as sowneth into honestee,
> To telle yow a tale, or two, or three.   (B 3158)

After considering a life of St. Edward, he decides first to tell tragedies, a hundred of which he has in his cell. He then gives the simplest possible definition of tragedy, comments on the hexameters and the prose they are commonly written in, and apologizes in advance for not getting them all in chronological order. The threat of a hundred, plus a life of St. Edward and two or three other stories into the bargain, justifies the interruption at the end of only seventeen tragedies. Without the threat, there would have been no need for the Knight and the Host to intervene, for the tragedies come to an acceptable conclusion at the end of "Cresus," with a general comment on the role that Fortune plays in bringing down "regnes that been proude."

Chaucer apparently went so far as to rewrite the interruption, originally assigned to the Host, to avoid too close a resemblance to the Host's interruption of his own tale.[16] Why was he so intent on a second interruption? Was he using his own early effort, the collection of tragedies, to point up the folly of definitions and strict genres? His own tendency to free his art of formal preconditions shows itself in lyrics that he wrote at about the time he was linking the tales in this fragment. The influence of the French poets of the day, Machaut, Froissart, Deschamps, was all in the direction of strict definition and difficulty of metrical form. Chaucer, on the other hand, took over the envoy, the conventional conclusion for the ballade, and expanded it as an independent, comparatively free, and witty poem. This same tendency may be operating as one of the critical principles in the dramatic arrangements of Fragment B^2. The Monk, the most self-consciously literary of the narrators, prefaces his tragedies with a definition, and has to be stopped by the Knight. His performance serves as prologue to the triumphant conclusion of the long series in a tale that combines genres and inserts digressions, parodies the rules of rhetoric, and revels in its own unique combination of elements.

The series of tragedies, which Chaucer wrote in the 1370's, and which he assigned to the Monk twenty years later, might be termed perfunctory exercises in narrative art. They start off as one-stanza stories in a rather difficult eight-line form which has as its point of focus or emphasis the couplet in the middle. Chaucer discovered almost at once that the verse form would accommodate a two-sentence organization, with one sentence developing a thesis and the other moving away and down, from thesis to antithesis. The first stanza on Samson practically repeats the one on Adam:

> Loo Sampsoun, which that was annunciat
> By th' angel, longe er his nativitee,
> And was to God Almyghty consecrat,
> And stood in noblesse whil he myghte see.
> Was nevere swich another as was hee.
> To speke of strengthe, and therwith hardynesse;
> But to his wyves toolde he his secree,
> Thurgh which he slow hymself for wrecchednesse. (B 3212)

Chaucer apparently saw that he had devised too confining a format in the straitjacket of a single stanza for each tragic victim of Fortune; he retold Samson's story in more detail in nine additional stanzas. This collection is probably Chaucer's first experience with direct narrative (as opposed to the translation of the allegorical *Roman de la Rose* and the love-vision *Book of the Duchess*). It is interesting to watch him as he experiments, and moves from a certain awkwardness through the greater commitment and developing skill of "Cenobia" and "Nero" to the dwindling interest of the final "Cresus." He learned to play the stanza (which he was never to use for narrative again) for more varied and subtle effects, as witness the following on Nero's efforts to escape:

> The peple roos upon hym on a nyght
> For his defaute, and whan he it espied,
> Out of his dores anon he hath hym dight
> Allone, and ther he wende han been allied,
> He knokked faste, and ay the moore he cried,
> The fastere shette they the dores alle.
> Tho wiste he wel, he hadde himself mysgyed,
> And wente his wey; no lenger dorste he calle.   (B 3274)

The syntactical cadences here create an effective counterpoint with line length; the run-on to the single word *Allone*, as the stanza approaches its central climax, and the heavy caesura in the middle of the next line imitate rhythmically the frenetic flight of Nero. The last two lines, with their more nearly regular movement (the sense runs across the semicolon in the final line), bring the agitation almost to rest in Nero's recognition that flight is futile, escape impossible.

Efforts have been made to see in the tragedies a reflection of the Monk's personality. Critics have seized on the antifeminism of the "Sampson" as indicating a bias against women on the Monk's part.[17] But a narrator who does not mention Eve in describing Adam's "mysgovernaunce," who refuses to "accuse" Dianira for sending Hercules the fatally poisoned shirt, and who devotes the longest of his stories to the heroic Cenobia can hardly be accused of antifeminism. Actually, the negative predominates in the Monk's performance. His tragedies reflect the bias of his sources rather than his own. Thus the pity for Hugelino and his sons, starving in the tower, derives from Dante's stark, spare narrative; the great admiration for Alexander reflects his status as the central figure in a medieval narrative cycle; and the dismissal of Cresus as something of a fool follows the treatment of him in

132

the *Roman de la Rose* and Boethius' *De Consolatione.* The Monk expresses in this solemn collection his rejection of the Host's implications and aspersions, and a somewhat limited interest in such a frivolous and unprofitable venture as a round of storytelling.

The Knight's reasons for interrupting come as a surprise from the man whose own tale has a happy ending only after Arcite's "sodeyn fal" from high estate. His preference for success stories in which the hero starts poor and ends rich and happy, stems perhaps from his own position as defender of the status quo. He is, like the Monk, without any real interest in art, though from different motives. Stories featuring repeated falls from high estate make him uneasy for the stability of the society that he has spent his life defending. The dignity of his comments provides a contrasting background for the Host's befuddled and vigorous criticism.

Harrie Baillie has only the vaguest notion of what the Monk has been saying. He manages to dredge up some terms from the "Cresus"— fortune, cloud, tragedy, and biwaille—and to echo the Knight's dismay at the gloom of successive tragedies. Surprisingly, he offers the Monk, as he has done to Chaucer, another chance, and points out that the bells on his bridle, rather than any interest in the story, have kept him from going to sleep and falling from his horse into the mud. He boasts:

> Thanne hadde your tale al be toold in veyn.
> For certeinly, as that thise clerkes seyn,
> Whereas a man may have noon audience,
> Noght helpeth it to tellen his sentence.
>   And wel I woot the substance is in me,
> If any thyng shal wel reported be.   (B 3994)

Guide and boss the agreement has made him—reporter too. But not sole reporter, certainly, or we should be left with only his version. The auditors of the pilgrims have been legion, thanks to the "elvyssh" man the Host first patronises, then forbids to rhyme any further, and treats throughout as an inferior. *Sic transit*, etc. The Host has not fallen off his horse into the mud. But his repeated fall from the high estate that he assumes for himself has been manifest to the many readers of his inconspicuous rival's work.

133

When the Monk curtly refuses the Host's request for a tale about hunting, Harrie takes on another pilgrim whom he somewhat misjudges. His request for a tale from the Nun's Priest is couched in language the more uncomplimentary, since the memory is still fresh of his deference to the Lady Prioress, whom the Priest accompanies, protects, and perhaps even confesses. The Host's comments on the jade touch a sore spot; the horse he rides has no doubt been furnished the Priest by the Prioress. The mildness of his reply and his promise to be "myrie" convey no foreshadowing of what is to follow.

The subtle sophistication of the Nun's Priest's mind, a sophistication that miraculously escapes any touch of cynicism, corruption, or frivolity, shows itself in the brief description of the frugal life led by the widow and her two daughters.[18] The account starts simply, with emphasis on patience and husbandry, as it establishes the setting and the dramatis personae. The word "foond" expresses not just the provision of shelter, food, and clothing but the firm foundation on which their way of life stands. The three sows, the three cows, and the sheep confirm by detail the bare sufficiency of their possessions. But the single sheep "a sheep that highte Malle" (B 4021)— does more. By having a name, the sheep lightens the picture of their life together. Close to the soil and their animals, yes. But filled with love, and imagination, and gaiety, as well. The animals are fellow creatures, not just a source of food and clothing.

As if released by the name, the Nun's Priest carries on his description in a series of witty contrasts: the (sooty) bower and hall, the poignant sauce, the dainty morsels of food, "repleccioun"—no, rather "attempree diete"—"And exercise, and hertes suffisaunce" (B 4029). The "hertes suffisaunce" is subtly present, partly because of the rhyme, in the next line: "The goute lette hire nothyng for to daunce." The ridiculous image of the widow leading the *estampie* in her sooty hall, because not lamed by gout, yields rapidly to a recognition that, yes, in a sense she does dance—that the white and black that she consumes do better than white and red wines could do in helping her escape care and in confirming her sense of security and satisfaction, "For she was, as it were, a maner deye" (B 4036).

Does the extended comparison with court life reveal a hidden motive in the Priest's lively espousal of the widow's simple "suffisaunce"?

134

Without further evidence, it would be pressing the point to stress the Priest's relations with the Prioress. The account of her table manners in the Prologue makes clear that her board favors the white and red, the meats and sauces, specifically excluded from the widow's diet—that in fact the bread served her dogs is of finer quality than the "broun breed" the widow's daughters eat. The Priest, in any event, is not satirizing the "cheere of court" that the Prioress affects, but rather giving a gentle lesson, to the Host perhaps, to the Prioress and the other pilgrims as well, on the true sources of satisfaction in this our life.[19]

The subtlety and wit, the resonance and indirection, the verve and good humor, present in the opening twenty-six lines, continue, with one exception, throughout the *Nun's Priest's Tale*. They are present in the description of that stunning apparition, Chauntecleer, who brings to the widow's hen yard, "enclosed al aboute / With stikkes, and a drye dych withoute" (B 4038), a regal pride, a precision in crowing based on instinct rather than learning, a dazzling and barbered appearance, harem arrangements that a Ptolemy might envy, combined with courtly devotion to the favorite of his seven sister-paramours—and, with it all, a level of imagery and language which rises from the finest in the widow's world, the church organ and the abbey clock, to the level of the most cultured court in Europe.[20] Chauntecleer's lady is "faire damoysele Pertelote."

> Curteys she was, discreet, and debonaire,
> And compaignable, and bar hyrself so faire,
> Syn thilke day that she was seven nyght oold,
> That trewely she hath the herte in hoold
> Of Chauntecleer, loken in every lith.   (B 4065)

Only the "seven nyght oold" reminds us that these are chickens, for all their pretentiousness. When they sing together in the morning it is,

> In sweete accord, "My lief is faren in londe!"
> For thilke tyme, as I have understonde,
> Beestes and briddes koude speke and synge.   (B 4071)

The sudden detail that means "chicken" has only a slightly deflating impact. It seems to result from the narrator's absorption in Chauntecleer's point of view. He does not insist; he merely accepts. Furthermore, he does not condescend as a human being. The chickens deserve our attention as much as people do. As in our own lives, only an occasional detail reminds them of the limitations of their nature.

The thing that disturbs the equanimity of Chauntecleer's world, and that heralds an uproar in the widow's as well, is a dream. We watch the development from its inception, as drama. First, the groans of Chauntecleer on his perch "in the halle," then the wifely concern of Pertelote; the cock's account of his dream, which reveals a failure to identify his natural enemy, for all his accurate knowledge of equinoctials; the hen's shock at her lover's cowardice—"Have ye no mannes herte, and han a berd?" (B 4110)—her refusal to see in a dream anything but evidence of physical disorder, of "repleccciouns" or of "compleccciouns," "Whan humours been to habundant in a wight" (B 4115); and her prescription, wide of the mark like Chauntecleer in failing to identify the fox, based on a thoroughly displayed knowledge of humors, and consisting of a disagreeable and, according to recent criticism, a fatal collection of "digestyves" and "laxatyves" from a medicinal herb garden.[21] Her dismay at her husband's uncockly behavior disappears in her enthusiasm for lecturing and prescribing:

"Pekke hem up right as they growe and ete hem yn.
Be myrie, housbonde, for youre fader kyn!
Dredeth no dreem, I kan sey yow namoore."
 "Madame," quod he, "graunt mercy of youre loore."
(B 4160)

His wife's speech has a number of irritations for Chauntecleer—the disparaging of his cockhood, her assurance that she understands his dreams, his "humors," and himself, her trying to make him eat nasty and disturbing remedies, not least her quotation of an authority in support of her position on dreams. In putting down such an insolent attempt to lecture him, Chauntecleer shows no anger, only dignity, as he stretches his talents to their utmost and for the longest speech within a Canterbury tale (always excepting Dame Prudence) transcends his chicken nature. He takes Pertelote at her weakest point, authorities, and overwhelms her with exempla and citations showing that dreams come true. So engrossed in his subject does he become, that he begins to see the whole matter in intellectual terms. In the three exempla that he tells at length, only one man is the better off for dreaming. The others either fail to heed the warning or cannot effectively evade the fate foreseen in the dream. By the end of the speech, he has persuaded himself that he will be simply another victim:

> Shortly I seye, as for conclusioun,
> That I shal han of this avisioun
> Adversitee. . . . (B 4343)

A victim of dreams, but definitely not of his wife's laxatives: "I hem diffye, I love hem never a deel!" (B 4346).

Having risen above his feathered frailties, and silenced his wife, he indulges himself for some unbuttoned moments in admiration of Pertelote's charms:

> Now let us speke of myrthe, and stynte al this.
> Madame Pertelote, so have I blis,
> Of o thyng God hath sent me large grace;
> For whan I se the beautee of youre face,
> Ye been so scarlet reed aboute youre yen,
> It maketh al my drede for to dyen;
> For al so siker as *In principio*,
> *Mulier est hominis confusio,*—
> Madame, the sentence of this Latyn is,
> "Womman is mannes joye and al his blis."
> For whan I feele a-nyght your softe syde,
> Al be it that I may nat on yow ryde,
> For that oure perche is maad so narwe, allas!
> I am so ful of joye and of solas,
> That I diffye bothe sweven and dreem. (B 4361)

The long speech has finally come to an end. The cock has clearly a weakness for the sound of his own voice, which only his passion for Pertelote can moderate. He cannot resist, at the same time, putting her again in her place. The flattering praise contains the Latin barb which he savors, oblivious of the extent to which it epitomizes his character and foreshadows his fate. In fact, his translation of the Latin is in a sense correct. Because in the beginning woman was man's joy and bliss, she was also his confusion. And will be almost at once again, when the chickens fly from the beams of their house, too confined for lovemaking, and Chauntecleer, forgetting all about his dream and its warning, feathers his love twenty times, "And trad hire eke as ofte, er it was pryme" (B 4368). He has meanwhile displayed the weaknesses the fox will exploit and used the same flattering technique on his wife that daun Russell will use on him. The concupiscence of this new Adam makes him do more than forget his dream; it makes him assume for the benefit of the hens a courage his chicken nature cannot sustain. The strutting like a lion gives way to clucking "whan he hath a corn yfounde." The betrayal of his posturing by his nature suggests what constantly befalls another species of posturing biped.

Having the chickens talk like learned courtly lovers has given the story up to this point a mock-heroic aura. Now the Nun's Priest both employs high style and occasionally makes overt fun of it:

> Whan that the month in which the world bigan,
> That highte March, whan God first maked man,
> Was compleet, and passed were also,
> Syn March bigan, thritty dayes and two ...   (B 4380)

This solemn method of naming a date, with its renewed reference to Adam and the beginning, produces for those who take the trouble to calculate, the irrelevance of May 3; it introduces some pedantically precise astronomical intuitions on Chauntecleer's part, which prove equally irrelevant, as he turns from his crowing to happy observation, with Pertelote, of birds and flowers; and it leads, after the information that a sorrowful event befell him suddenly, to a mocking of rhetorical embellishment:

> For evere the latter ende of joye is wo.
> God woot that worldly joye is soone ago;
> And if a rethor koude faire endite,
> He in a cronycle saufly myghte it write
> As for a sovereyn notabilitee.
> Now every wys man, lat him herkne me;
> This storie is also trewe, I undertake,
> As is the book of Launcelot de Lake,
> That wommen holde in ful greet reverence.
> Now wol I torne agayn to my sentence.   (B 4404)

This is "game" of a high order. The solemn wheeling-out of old saws (shades of the Monk?) gets punctured in the word "saufly" and and the half-line-long flatness, metrical and semantic, of "notabilitee." The further spoofing of the stock true-story claim brings in the first overt antifeminist note (inadvertent?) on the narrator's part. The blow is a glancing one and the recovery is immediate, but it prepares us for what follows.

Enter colfox, villain. Now the Nun's Priest brings in the heavy rhetorical artillery:

> O false mordrour, lurkynge in thy den!
> O newe Scariot, newe Genylon,
> False dissymulour, O Greek Synon ...   (B 4418)

The cursed-murder theme, represented by an impressive but not entirely appropriate set of exemplars, modulates into the conundrum of God's foreknowledge and man's free will. Here for a moment the Nun's Priest's own interest seems to trap him. The argument runs from "symple necessitee" to "free choys" to "necessitee condicioneel," succinctly setting up the basic positions. It could no doubt continue indefinitely, if, as his references imply, the Nun's Priest is well read in Augustine, Boethius, and Bradwardine. He senses that he has gone astray and attempts a quick recovery, only to fall from a digression due to intellectual interest to one expressing the prejudice that has already once appeared, antifeminism:

> I wol nat han to do of swich mateere;
> My tale is of a cok, as ye may heere,
> That tok his conseil of his wyf, with sorwe,
> To walken in the yerd upon that morwe
> That he hadde met that dreem that I yow tolde.
> Wommennes conseils been ful ofte colde;
> Wommannes conseil broghte us first to wo,
> And made Adam fro Paradys to go,
> Ther as he was ful myrie and wel at ese.
> But for I noot to whom it myght displese,
> If I conseil of wommen wolde blame,
> Passe over, for I seyde it in my game.
> Rede auctours, where they trete of swich mateere,

And what they seyn of wommen ye may heere.
Thise been the cokkes wordes, and nat myne;
I kan noon harm of no womman divyne. (B 4456)

This fascinating struggle to transcend self and regain the disguise
of fiction takes place before our eyes. The first effort fails because it
misrepresents the fiction, distorts it to conform with the Nun's Priest's
prejudice. Chauntecleer does not take his wife's advice. His flight into
the yard is not for the purpose of starting her regimen of medicinal
herbs. Rather it has its motivation in his own desires. Far from recover-
ing the fiction, the Nun's Priest finds himself floundering in the kind of
antifeminist cliché he knows to be unworthy. The real significance of
Adam and Eve is not antifeminism, but original sin, man's freedom and
responsibility. The presence of the Prioress has an inhibiting effect, but
the reference to the "auctors" carries on the subject with only the
flimsiest of veils. The return to the mateere-heere rhyme, with which
the passage starts suggests the extent to which he is going around in
circles. Finally, the thought of Chauntecleer frees him. In a sense, these
are the cock's words, and the words of every vain and foolish male
between Adam and Chauntecleer. The Nun's Priest has recovered the
disguise, the distance, the godlike transcendence of human limitation
that fiction at its best can confer.

This struggle of the Nun's Priest marks the climax of the fragment's
interest in the different kinds of commitment, expression, and disguise
that fiction makes possible. His fiction stretches his powers and enables
him to correct the misconceptions of value held by the Host, the Monk,
and the Prioress. At his best he not only sees through the pretensions
of the court that the Prioress simulates and the Host admires, but he
can take delight in observing the absurdities that such a life entails, and
recognize with amusement his own vulnerability to the same entice-
ments. Hence his picture of the regal and pedantic cock with his seven
hens, drawn with an affectionate mockery. Hence the imaginative detail
and the insight into feathered and unfeathered frailty that bring the
picture to life. Chauntecleer has the aspirations of the Prioress to "cheere
of court," and the Monk's irritation at insolence; he has also some of
the weaknesses that the Nun's Priest can see in himself. Only when he
loses his grip on the narrative do we glimpse these vulnerabilities. Does

his understanding of Chauntecleer reflect more of himself than the pedantry and the antifeminism that are overtly revealed? Does the mockery of feminine beauty—"Ye been so scarlet reed aboute youre yen" (B 4351)—point to some susceptibility on his part? If so, the Host's response to his tale has an even more ironical import.

The Nun's Priest, having regained his fictional stance, never again falters. A brief return to farmyard serenity, with the seven hens sunbathing in the sand and Chauntecleer singing more merrily than any mermaid, precedes the crisis of confrontation between cock and fox. Looking at a butterfly and seeing the fox,

> Nothyng ne liste hym thanne for to crowe,
> But cride anon, "Cok! cok!" and up he sterte.   (B 4467)

The fox soothes his ruffled feathers by declaring his friendship and explaining that his purpose is "oonly for to herkne how that ye synge" (B 4480). The fox presents himself as a connoisseur of cock-song, with his interest extending back to the previous generation of Chauntecleer's own family. As he flatters the cock and describes his father's ecstatic singing, he is suggesting behavior to the cock that will make him an easy victim—eyes closed, on tip-toe, neck stretched out. And the cock starts following the directions.

But an occasion of this importance demands some rhetorical flourish —in this case, some lines on the vile role that flattery plays in court— before the cock can start crowing and the fox seize him "by the gargat." Afterwards, come aspostrophes to destiny in which we learn that it all happened on a Friday, to Venus because Friday is her day and Chauntecleer her votary, and to "Gaufred" because the narrator envies him the "sentence" and "loore" he used complaining his master King Richard's death and chiding the Friday on which it occurred. The apostrophes give way to epic similes for the hens' lamentation, and the similes modulate to the uproar and the chase, as the widow and her daughters cry out after the fox and his prey. The rhetorical flourishes and the convulsive responses of men, beasts, birds, and insects prove equally ridiculous and equally futile. The cock's rescue depends on the cock. In his turn, he suggests behavior to the fox (defiance of the pursuers), flies out of mouth and reach when the fox says, "It shal be don," and shows in his response to the fox's efforts to lure him back that even cocks can learn from experience (if it is recent enough).

The cock, the fox, and finally the Nun's Priest feel compelled to sum up their experience in moral terms. The first feels he should keep his eyes open; the second, his mouth shut; the third finds lessons against carelessness, negligence, and trust in flattery. The narrator ends the tale with an admonition and a prayer:

> But ye that holden this tale a folye,
> As of a fox, or of a cok and hen,
> Taketh the moralite, goode men.
> For seint Paul seith that al that writen is,
> To oure doctrine it is ywrite, ywis;
> Taketh the fruyt, and lat the chaf be stille.
> Now, goode God, if that it be thy wille,
> As seith my lord, so make us alle goode men,
> And brynge us to his heighe blisse! Amen.　　(B 4636)

It is worth noting that the repetition of "goode men" occurs in a different context and with the implications of context strengthened by rhyme. The "amen" that ends the prayer underlines the difference of tone in the preceding admonition. The Nun's Priest is expressing the "sentence" of the narrative in his acknowledgment that all men need God's help to be good. The echoes of the Lord's Prayer bespeak his sincerity.[22] In his admonition to the "goode men" who hold the tale a "folye," the rhyme with "hen" suggests a different attitude. For those who cannot see relevance in a Chauntecleer's adventure—who find in the pride, the pedantry, the vanity, and the stupidity of chickens, experiences beneath their notice—who fail to appreciate the wit and urbanity, the good humor, the delight in living things, the balance and the taste and the gusto that the Nun's Priest brings to the tale—who must discard what is not doctrine as chaff through a misinterpretation of what St. Paul says[23]—for those "goode men" there is the fruit of three separate morals. They can keep their eyes open, their mouths shut, and be on the alert for flattery.

If the good men err on one side, the Host errs on the other. The enthusiasm of his response indicates that he has listened more closely to the Nun's Priest than to the Monk. What he has heard and understood is another matter. The sexual insinuations that begin in his request to Chaucer for a tale, and that have insulting dimensions when he calls on the Monk, have apparently found stimulus in the "murie tale of Chauntecleer." For they come out in even stronger terms as he praises the Nun's Priest for his tale and for his potential as a treader of hens. The only portrait Chaucer gives us of Sir John is the Host's admiration for his "braunes," his great neck, his "large breest," his sparhawk's eyes, and his dark manly color. The figure he ascribes to the Priest confirms his role as sole companion and protector of the two nuns on their journey.[24] But Harrie's appreciation shows little grasp of the complexity of the Priest's character. The frailties of Chauntecleer may indeed reflect the narrator's own. But they are ones he has under control, as the mockery of his fiction testifies. Of the ones he overtly reveals in the moments of direct expression, the antifeminism reflects the excess in a battle long since won. He is more likely to err in a blanket condemnation of women than in the kind of *Frauendienst* the Host refers to.

Chaucer calls him, in the introduction to his tale, "This sweete preest, this goodly man sir John" (B 4010). Their association, Chaucer's and the Nun's Priest's, extends beyond their presence as narrators in the same fragment and beyond the enthusiasm with which Harrie Baillie has misinterpreted their stories. They share also a delight in the variety of living things, a preference for implicit morality, a slightly pedantic concern with the paradox of God's foreknowledge and man's free will, a penchant for the opportunities the spirit of play can provide, and an interest in the literary effect new combinations of genre and style can make. The *Nun's Priest's Tale* and this fragment of the *Canterbury Tales*, indeed the *Canterbury Tales* as a whole, exemplify these qualities.

the wife of Bath's influence

"It dooth myn herte boote"

1. Fragment D—"Barly-breed"

THE Wife of Bath occupied Chaucer's creative energies intermittently over a considerable period of time. For no other of the pilgrims do we have the kind of evidence for development that we have for her.[1] The original narrator of the *Shipman's Tale*, she became the instigator for the series of stories called the marriage group at approximately the same time the fabliau about Don John and the merchant's wife was being used to lead off the B² fragment. Most critics have assumed that her new position would follow closely the B² fragment, and one has even suggested that she was intended to break in unannounced at the end of the *Nun's Priest's Tale*.[2] If Chaucer had intended this sequence, he could easily have made his intentions clear; he would certainly not have created in his references to place and time the kind of difficulties we encounter in trying to make the tales influenced by the Wife fit the road between Rochester and Canterbury. These references and, in addition, the Host's response to the *Merchant's Tale* suggest that Chaucer had a more important function in mind for her.[3]

The conception of the *Canterbury Tales* involved an inherent conflict, the conflict between the pilgrimage, with its goal the martyr's shrine in the Cathedral at Canterbury, and the game of storytelling, with its purpose the entertainment of the pilgrims throughout their journey. A critical moment would occur when the pilgrims started on the return journey. Could the interest in the work not just survive the retracing of the pilgrims' steps, the letdown inherent in facing back; could it develop in new ways related to a growing intimacy of association;

could it transmute the patterns associated with the pilgrimage and those
associated with the storytelling into comedy of an order only hinted at in
the earlier fragments? In seeking to provide a positive answer to these
questions, Chaucer detached the Wife's developing confession from the
Man of Law's Epilogue and moved it to a position on the homeward
journey.[4]

The Wife of Bath's Prologue has three clearly defined parts: her
discourse on the permissibility of more than one marriage, her account
of life with her first three husbands, and the more detailed description of
her experiences with the last two. The distinction between the parts,
the digressions within the parts, and the voice that gives an unmistakable
unity to digressions and parts reflect the paradoxes inherent in the Wife
of Bath's personality.[5] She lights on two of these paradoxes at the very
beginning of her monologue:

> Experience, though noon auctoritee
> Were in this world, is right ynogh for me
> To speke of wo that is in mariage.   (D 3)

Experience is enough for her, she says, and later she will indicate her
enthusiasm for this kind of evidence: "Of fyve husbondes scoleiyng
am I" (D 44f). But her enthusiasm for authority is no less evident as
she argues her way out of the tight corner a misinterpretation of scripture has put her in:

> But me was toold, certeyn, nat longe agoon is,
> That sith that Crist ne wente nevere but onis
> To weddyng, in the Cane of Galilee,
> That by the same ensample taughte he me
> That I ne sholde wedded be but ones.
> Herkne eek, lo, which a sharp word for the nones,
> Biside a welle, Jhesus, God and man,
> Spak in repreeve of the Samaritan:
> "Thou hast yhad fyve housbondes," quod he,
> "And that ilke man that now hath thee
> Is noght thyn housbonde," thus seyde he certeyn.
> What that he mente therby, I kan nat seyn;
> But that I axe, why that the fifthe man
> Was noon housbonde to the Samaritan?   (D 22)

Later we learn why this text has such impact on her, why the mention of a fifth husband triggers her anxiety and leads her to read the passage as denying the validity of fifth marriages. Meanwhile she marshals evidence from the Old and New Testaments in an effort not only to justify successive marriages but also to defend marriage against virginity.

The vehemence of her defense throws into sharp relief the "wo" she speaks of experiencing in marriage. Which brings us to the second paradox: strange woe indeed that moves her to thank God repeatedly for five marriages, welcome the thought of a sixth,[6] and envy the pleasures of a Solomon—woe that expresses itself in such doleful accents as,

> I wol bistowe the flour of al myn age
> In the actes and in fruyt of mariage. (D 114)

Later she speaks of a husband as debtor and thrall, who will have his "tribulacion / Upon his flessh" in the insatiable sexual demands she makes of him. But the picture is hardly borne out in any of her marriages —not in the first three, where her husbands gave her little satisfaction: "And yet in bacon hadde I nevere delit" (D 418)—not in her fourth, where her reveling husband was seldom if ever at her disposal—not in her fifth, where she at first burned in frustrated desire for her husband and later found fulfillment in a mutual affection. When the Pardoner interrupts, she speaks again

> Of tribulacion in mariage,
> Of which I am expert in al myn age,
> This is to seyn, myself have been the whippe. (D 175)

The anomalies and contradictions in her attitude toward marriage provide a clue to the impression the Wife makes on us. She is both an imposing and a comic figure. She reflects in her character two of the drives that psychoanalysts have found central in their study of human personality, the drives for sex and for power. She has at the same time a voracious appetite for experience of every kind, an indomitable spirit that outlives and transforms adversity, and a vehemence in expressing herself that combines opposites and overrides contradictions.

Her impression of herself as being the "whippe" comes from her memories of her first three husbands, whom she introduces as the "goode" ones because the problems they presented were relatively simple. She hardly expected emotional fulfillment from them:

> Unnethe myghte they the statut holde
> In which that they were bounden unto me.
> Ye woot wel what I meene of this, pardee!
> As help me God, I laughe whan I thynke
> How pitously a-nyght I made hem swynke!
> And, by my fey, I tolde of it no stoor.　　　(D 203)

The word "stoor" reminds her of her reasons for marrying such unlikely old codgers—the treasure which she took care to have under her control before the ceremony. Not even their wealth makes them distinct from one another in her mind. She continues to treat the three as one, giving us a vividly dramatic account of how she kept them under control. She sees her rule as both tyrannical and benevolent:

> I governed hem so wel, after my lawe,
> That ech of hem ful blisful was and fawe
> To brynge me gaye thynges fro the fayre.
> They were ful glad whan I spak to hem faire;
> For, God it woot, I chidde hem spitously.　　　(D 223)

The chiding consists of a mixture of complaint over the husbands' niggardliness—"I sitte at hoom, I have no thrifty clooth" (D 238)—over their interest in other women—and, above all, over their drunken chiding and preaching to her. She complains of their complaints before they have a chance to complain. She even goes so far as to complain of their complaints at her complaints:

> Thou seist also that it displeseth me
> But if that thou wolt preyse my beautee,
> And but thou poure alwey upon my face,
> And clepe me "faire dame" in every place.　　　(D 296)

She admits that it was all invented:

> Lordynges, right thus, as ye have understonde,
> Baar I stifly myne olde housbondes on honde

> That thus they seyden in hir dronkenesse;
> And al was fals. . . . (D 382)

Her complaints shifted without warning to admonitions and expressions of endearment—to admonitions that they should trust her (D 318 ff.), that they should be satisfied with the love she gave them and not worry what others were getting if they had enough (D 326 ff.), and that, since men are more reasonable than women, they should give way to her in the interests of peace (D 434 ff.)—to expressions of endearment that must have seemed to the poor old men more threatening than the sharpest tongue-lashing—"Com neer, my spouse, lat me ba thy cheke!" (D 433); and again:

> What eyleth yow to grucche thus and grone?
> Is it for ye wolde have my queynte allone?
> Wy, taak it al! lo, have it every deel!
> Peter! I shrewe yow, but ye love it weel. (D 446)

The theory is quite simple. As the Wife puts it:

> Whoso that first to mille comth, first grynt;
> I pleyned first, so was oure werre ystynt. (D 390)

She has always, as further insurance, her certainty that "half so boldely kan ther no man / Swere and lyen, as a womman kan" (D 228). Throughout sounds her delight in remembering a drama in which the only speaking part was hers, the listening being shared by three nameless old men who lost all further identity when they became her husbands.

The fourth husband is nameless too, and one gathers from what the Wife avoids saying, as well as what she says, that the marriage was disastrous. She calls him first a reveler. No doubt she expected a reward after her three dutiful ventures into matrimony for profit, the reward of a gay young lover-husband. She quickly disabuses us:

> My fourthe housbonde was a revelour;
> This is to seyn, he hadde a paramour. (D 454)

Her thoughts have a way of blanking out her fourth husband. They skip first to the gay youth she led, dancing and singing and drinking; then to the connection between liquor and sex; and finally to the joy of remembering it all:

> But, Lord Crist! whan that it remembreth me
> Upon my yowthe, and on my jolitee,
> It tikleth me aboute myn herte roote.
> Unto this day it dooth myn herte boote
> That I have had my world as in my tyme.   (D 473)

Here the line of ten words comes to justify, with its weight on world and time, the suspension of the two preceding lines with their complementary effort to find the right words for the feeling of deep pleasure and with the remarkable rhyme sequence herte roote—herte boote, authenticating the physical sensation suggested by "tikleth." The great digression continues with her recognition of the reduced potential that comes with age, and her determination, in spite of it, "to be right myrie." She has to drag herself back to the humiliating disappointment of her fourth marriage, and begins again: "Now wol I tellen of my fourthe housbonde" (D 480).

She tells us the "greet despit" she had in her heart over his love for another, and how she got even with him by making him "of the same wode a croce":

> Nat of my body, in no foul manere,
> But certeinly, I made folk swich cheere
> That in his owne grece I made hym frye
> For angre, and for verray jalousye.
> By God! in erthe I was his purgatorie.   (D 489)

She goes on to describe the circumstances surrounding her fondest memory of him—dead—which in turn, by a process we understand only when she comes back to the subject of his death, reminds her— "Now of my fifthe housbonde wol I telle" (D 503).

The Wife of Bath's assurance of manner has so carried all before her that no one questions the myths she has invented to cover the long years of her fourth marriage.[7] She tells us she made her fourth husband jealous, "Nat of my body, in no foul manere." But the earlier effort to describe the marriage proceeds from dancing, singing, and drinking to sex, and later she admits to the overwhelming Venerian influence in her life,

> That made me I koude noght withdrawe

149

> My chambre of Venus from a good felawe. (D 618)

And lest we misunderstand her, she makes her meaning even more explicit:

> I ne loved nevere by no discrecioun,
> But evere folwede myn appetit,
> Al were he short, or long, or blak, or whit;
> I took no kep, so that he liked me,
> How poore he was, ne eek of what degree. (D 626)

"Nat of my body" cannot be true of her relations with other men during this marriage that lasted until she was forty. The jealousy of the reveler-husband turns out to be equally mythical, as she inadvertently dwells on the revealing times of happiness, when he was away in London or she was off on visitation to vigils, processions, preaching, pilgrimages, miracle plays, marriages—

> And wered upon my gaye scarlet gytes.
> Thise wormes, ne thise motthes, ne thise mytes,
> Upon my peril, frete hem never a deel;
> And wostow why? for they were used weel. (D 562)

The jealous husband?—who spent his Lent in London and permitted her three journeys to Jerusalem, not to mention the minor liberties nearer home?

Which brings this enthusiast for marriage into her forties with a strange set of husbands to recall. The first three have at least fed her passion for power and have had the grace to die early and set her free for new ventures. The fourth has only had the grace to die. The death she had no doubt longed for over the years has an even more vivid place in her memory because of the role her fifth husband played at the funeral—and was already playing in her heart. For she had dallied with him in the fields one Lent and arranged that he should marry her if her husband should die. And she had borne him "on honde" he had enchanted her—a "soutiltee" taught her by her mother—telling him she had dreamt of him all night, that he was trying to kill her, and her bed was all full of blood, meaning gold "as me was taught"—

> And al was fals; I dremed of it right naught,

> But as I folwed ay my dames loore,
> As wel of this as of othere thynges moore. (D 584)

At this point she loses the thread of what she is saying. For one so voluble, with so much of consuming interest to talk about, how could this happen? The answer is Jankyn, the named fifth husband. The man she cannot mention without blessing, whose blows she still feels "on my ribbes al by rewe," who was so fresh and gay in bed and at the same time "of his love daungerous to me"—Jankyn has driven from her mind for the moment the minor obstacle of a living husband:

> A ha! by God, I have my tale ageyn.
> Whan that my fourthe housbonde was on beere . . . (D 587)

The memory of Jankyn following the corpse—

> . . . me thoughte he hadde a paire
> Of legges and of feet so clene and faire
> That al myn herte I yaf unto his hoold (D 599)

—this image, for her so rich in anticipated fulfillment that she leaps ahead from the legs she saw to the feet she was later to know, releases a set of remarkable reminiscences, linked and disparate and unique, that express what it means to be *the* Wife of Bath—Jankyn's twenty years, her forty; her "colt's tooth" and the attractive gap in her teeth; the print on her of "saint" Venus' seal; herself lusty, fair, rich, young (!), attractive; with, on her husbands' say-so, the best possible *quoniam* (note the use of a third language to find names good enough for it); her Venerian feeling; her Martian heart . . . And suddenly—"Allas! allas! that evere love was synne!" (D 614). That too—the regret, the recognition of standards by which she might be judged, and the failure to see that love was never sin—but it lasts only for a line, overwhelmed at once by the compulsions of her nature.

What we are witnessing in the Wife's long monologue is a new kind of comic drama, led up to by the Host's soliloquy on his wife and, even more significantly, by the Canon's Yeoman's account of his seven years' apprenticeship to alchemy.[8] The Wife is drawing on the illusions of a lifetime with roots in racial archetypes. Her conscious search for power and sexual fulfillment had taken her, up to this point in her

151

narrative, through a series of disastrous experiences, four grim marriages
and innumerable casual couplings, all consumed voraciously and transformed by the tough resilience of her nature into a triumphant set of
reminiscences and a confident set of opinions. What she was subcon-
sciously seeking in her frenetic journeys, geographical and matrimonial,
gives validity, conviction, and a kind of integrity to the distortions of
experience that her mind emits. This thing she was seeking emerged in
identifiable form, though still unrecognized by her, at the moment of
crisis in her fifth marriage.

Her marriage to Jankyn had started as inauspiciously as the others.
Despite the agreement and her efforts to follow her mother's prescrip-
tions, she found she had to sign over her wealth to bring him to the
altar. She endured this humiliating reversal of her first three marriages.
She endured the long nights, listening to him read aloud from his book
of wicked wives. She continued to walk as before "from hous to hous,"
to speak her mind—"Ne I wolde nat of hym corrected be" (D 661)—
and to endure the reprisals she still feels on her ribs. One night, as he
read on and on to her, she could stand it no longer. She ripped three
leaves from the accursed book and struck him so that he fell over
backward into the fire. Furious, he leapt up and dealt her a blow on
the head hard enough to knock her out and to make her for the rest of
her life "somdel deef."

> And whan he saugh how stille that I lay,
> He was agast, and wolde han fled his way,
> Til atte laste out of my swogh I breyde.
> "O! hastow slayn me, false theef?" I seyde,
> "And for my land thus hastow mordred me?
> Er I be deed, yet wol I kisse thee."
>   And neer he cam and kneled faire adoun,
> And seyde, "Deere suster Alisoun,
> As help me God! I shal thee nevere smyte.
> That I have doon, it is thyself to wyte.
> Foryeve it me, and that I thee biseke!"
> And yet eftsoones I hitte hym on the cheke,
> And seyde, "Theef, thus muchel am I wreke;
> Now wol I dye, I may no lenger speke."   (D 810)

The violence she provoked for love almost ended her life. Then against all her theory and habit, along with the characteristic accusation, she made of what she thought were her last words an expression of her love that got through to him. The miracle occurred that no amount of stubborn struggle with weapons of the war between the sexes could have effected.[9]

The Wife of Bath can describe what happened, but still does not understand. She does not understand that what she had been seeking she finally attained. At least she cannot name it. She thinks of it as power, sovereignty in marriage. Its proper name is love. The significant result of the outbreak of violence is not the burning of the book or the transfer of the property back to the Wife of Bath. It is Jankyn's change of heart, to which these events testify. It is the pattern of their life together:

> God helpe me so, I was to hym as kynde
> As any wyf from Denmark unto Ynde,
> And also trewe, and so was he to me.   (D 825)

The Wife's unusual frankness, her willingness to speak of herself without shame and without reservation, her volubility and her spontaneity make what she says plausible. She believes what she tells us. Yet between the details of her life and the conclusions she comes to, the judgments she makes, there are patent disparities, distortions, and falsifications. In this gap between experience and the theoretical structure that the Wife forces her experience into, lie the implicitly expressed but unspoken, because largely unrecognized, aspects of her nature— her contradictions, her aggressions, her self-deceptions, her illusions, as well as her thorough humanity, her courage and resilience, her perseverance. The meanings of her monologue thus go far beyond what she intends, and sometimes in quite another direction.

On the details of her own experience, we can usually trust her. But not always on generalizations, and seldom on what she tells us of other people's feelings. For instance, her claim that she was her fourth husband's "purgatorie," that she made him jealous but "nat of my body," has to be weighed against other evidence: the implications of her statements about the connections between liquor and sex, about her inability to refuse men, about the journeys she made and the motivation for them, and, in the case of her husband's jealousy, his willingness to be separated from her over extended periods of time. The claim must also be somewhat discounted because of the support it lends to her image of herself as a successful practitioner and hence an authority on marriage. When she tells us that her old husbands were "ful blisful," that she won Jankyn's love by following the shrewd counsel her mother had given her, and that in her fifth marriage she was, among other things, still young, the context itself gives her the lie.

The image of herself as the victim of Martian and Venerian influences is closer to reality. She is indeed cruel and lustful. But the cruelty stems from policy rather than malice, and the lust does not quite destroy her capacity for love. The very energy she brings to all aspects of life, to experience and theory, prevents her from adjusting the latter to the former and leads her to force onto the procrustean bed of sovereignty over husbands the only real happiness she ever had in marriage. It prevents her from seeing what really happened at the crisis of her life—from understanding the part that weakness and tenderness played in her request for a kiss, and the response in kind that her tenderness inspired in Jankyn. Is her failure to remarry evidence of another unwitting lesson learned at Jankyn's charming feet—a lesson she is so little conscious of that she can still glibly say, "Welcome the sixte"?

That she draws responses from pilgrims, even while she speaks, foreshadows the influence she is to have on a whole series of the stories. The two who interject themselves, the Pardoner and the Friar, have in common the hypocritical misuse of the Church's power to absolve, and the Summoner, who attacks the Friar for his interruption, shares with the other two the ignorant and superstitious victims on whom they prey. Do they see in the Wife of Bath a possible source of profit, or are they merely fascinated by the blatant success of a fellow operator? In any event, she shows herself capable of handling these scoundrels who make a thriving business of the corruption of others. The Pardoner's pretense of wanting to marry, she sees through at once. She reduces him by an assertiveness that only thinly disguises her contempt for his lack of virility. He quickly subsides from crass mockery of the Wife's position to an acquiescence qualified only by his reference to "us yonge men." The Summoner, whose eagerness to put down the Friar suggests the pathological, she does not deign to notice.

154

But she apparently sees the Friar as an antagonist who deserves her best effort. As if sensing an opportunity to avenge her sex's wrongs at his hands, she mimics his own suavity of manner, affecting to ask his permission to "telle forth" her tale. She even makes use of the prayeres-freres rhyme, which Chaucer picked off the Friar's tongue to serve as characteristic of his tone of voice in the General Prologue, and which the Summoner will later mimic with devastating effect. As she uses the rhyme, she seems to be praising the industry of friars for blessing into oblivion the fairies that many hundreds of years ago infested England:

> For now the grete charitee and prayeres
> Of lymytours and othere hooly freres,   (D 866)
>
> .   .   .   .
>
> This maketh that ther ben no fayeryes   (D 872)

—to the great benefit of women, she hastens to add, who now find under bushes and trees only the friar, "And he ne wol doon hem but dishonour" (D 881). Clearly gratuitous, since friars will play no part in her tale, her comments show her taking Huberd's measure, as she has earlier the Pardoner's, and thoroughly enjoying the elaboration of her comment which puts off the coup de grace for some twenty lines.[10]

Her fiction turns out to repeat some of the inadvertent meanings of her monologue. She has distorted to her own purposes Arthurian romance, sending her knight on a worldwide quest for an answer to the question, "What do women want most in the world?" The answer comes both in a public proclamation—"sovereignty over husband and lover"—and in a marriage-bed demonstration which makes clear the advantages of the proclaimed solution. It is worth noting that after the initial rape by the knight all the important decisions are made by women. The Wife presents a world in which, on the surface at least, women save men from the consequences of their folly and guide them to a happiness they would never find on their own. At the same time, the heroine, an old hag, transforms herself into everything the hero could want in a wife, a miracle in which Alisoun finds vicarious fulfillment, living as she does on her belief in being able to carry it off herself.[11] She finds, too, in her fiction the further gratification of being able to discuss at some length subjects close to her heart, like the things women most desire and the nature of true gentilesse. In her confidence that she has shown, in fictional form, the validity of her theory on marriage, she can end her story in a prayer for

> Housbondes meeke, yonge, and fressh abedde,
> And grace t'overbyde hem that we wedde;
> And eek I praye Jhesu shorte hir lyves
> That wol nat be governed by hir wyves;
> And olde and angry nygardes of dispence,
> God sende hem soone verray pestilence! (D 1264)

Despite the control she can exercise as creator in her fictional world, despite the supernatural powers she confers on her heroine, elements in her tale resist her didactic purpose and present an underlying pattern in accord with the implications of her monologue. We find, for instance, the same disparity between theory and experience. Each crisis of her story presents this disparity with increasing significance. Theoretically, the knight has earned by his rape the death penalty, from which the queen and her ladies provisionally reprieve him. When the knight, instructed by the old hag, gives his answer to the assembled ladies and all agree that he has passed his ordeal, the theory as to what women most desire is proclaimed. But almost at once the old hag has an opportunity to practice what she has preached, and her desires do not accord with the theory. She turns down the knight's offers of money, of anything but his "body."

> "Nay, thanne," quod she, "I shrewe us bothe two!
> For thogh that I be foul, and oold, and poore,
> I nolde for al the metal, ne for oore,
> That under erthe is grave, or lith above,
> But if thy wyf I were, and eek thy love." (D 1066)

The first of her two desires she can compel. She soon finds herself in bed with a reluctant husband who tosses and turns in an agony of shame. The knight's love is another matter. Her reply to his criticism of her birth, poverty, and old age merely puts off the decision. She will need more than a good argument to win his love. Her offer of alternatives continues the wifely instruction and answers his criticism of her ugliness. The knight finds the alternatives equally distasteful and in his indifference tells his wife to choose the one she would like:[12]

"Thanne have I gete of yow maistrie," quod she,
"Syn I may chese and governe as me lest?"
"Ye, certes, wyf," quod he, "I holde it best." (D 1238)

Having paid lip-service to the theory, the wife then gives him what she knows he wants—beauty, youth, her faithful love, and even her obedience (D 1255). Then and only then does she get the second and more important of her desires, his love. The dilemma of the alternatives is thus mere pretense. It takes a miraculous transformation to win a man's love, a transformation that matches the one the Wife actually effected when *in extremis* she begged Jankyn for a kiss.

The Arthurian setting of the Wife's tale seems at first a discordant note. What has this practical and domineering woman to do with questing knights, with the romance of fair damsels in distress, with the hunger for the marvelous that so frequently kept King Arthur from his feast at the round table? The matter of Britain, like the authorities quoted with such enthusiasm in her monologue, she absorbs and compels to serve her purposes, from the need to check a friar's impertinence to the promulgation of her theory on happiness in marriage. The incongruity remains to reflect the incongruities in her life, the elements that resist her will, the others that divulge her own quest. Her voice is at times somewhat muted by the requirements of narrative. But it sounds in the beginning in the list of buildings that friars busy themselves in blessing; at the end, in her prayers for the reward and punishment of husbands; and in the middle, with her digression on the things women desire:

And somme seyen that we loven best
For to be free, and do right as us lest,
And that no man repreve us of oure vice,
But seye that we be wise, and no thyng nyce.
For trewely ther is noon of us alle,
If any wight wol clawe us on the galle,
That we nel kike, for he seith us sooth.
Assay, and he shal fynde it that so dooth;
For, be we never so vicious withinne,
We wol been holden wise and clene of synne. (D 944)

The Friar takes the initiative in commenting on the Wife's tale and in renewing the quarrel with the Summoner. His mind is primarily on the latter, as is testified by the "maner louryng chiere" he has made on his enemy. He comments on the Wife's didacticism out of recognition that he cannot take up his battle with the Summoner without first alluding to the story just finished, rather than out of any desire to repay the Wife in kind for her linking of elf and friar. The Summoner, feeling that he has come out ahead in their early exchange and can continue to give as good as he gets, will have none of the Host's efforts on his behalf. In fact, he may even now have in mind what he hopes will prove the knockout blow at the end of his tale, for he ends his remarks with the otherwise puzzling threat: "And his office I shal hym telle, ywis" (D 1297).

Although he is taking the initiative in renewing their quarrel, the Friar keeps his animosity under reasonable control. Only at the beginning, where he attacks the Summoner's vicious conduct directly, does he leave himself open to a counterblow:

> For thogh this Somonour wood were as an hare,
> To telle his harlotrye I wol nat spare;
> For we been out of his correccioun.
> They han of us no jurisdiccioun,
> Ne nevere shullen, terme of alle hir lyves.—
>   "Peter! so been the wommen of the styves,"
> Quod the Somonour, "yput out of oure cure!"   (D 1333)

The connivance of the summoner with the malefactors he is supposed to punish, with the bawds and the prostitutes, his acceptance of bribes from the wealthy, and his dishonesty vis-à-vis his master the archdeacon make up the bulk of the attack. Actually this description of the archdeacon-summoner team has no real connection with the story itself. It serves the Friar's vindictive rather than his aesthetic ends.[13]

The narrative is almost all dialogue. The summoner is off to squeeze a bribe from an innocent widow. From the moment of encounter with the yeoman, whose hat has ominous "frenges blake," we watch the summoner dig himself more and more deeply into the pit. His carelessness of the increasingly explicit warnings he receives not only indicates his insolent and cynical depravity but is intended to satirize the similar fecklessness in the character of the pilgrim. The fiend identifies himself and tells his companion that he would ride to the ends of the earth for a prey, that he and his fellows take whatever shape will facilitate their purposes, that the summoner will be able without further instruction from him to hold a university chair in fiendly studies and outdo Virgil and Dante in firsthand knowledge of hell. Meanwhile he has addressed his newly sworn brother as "leeve sire somonour" (D 1474), cutting through the pretense of his being a bailiff out to collect rents. This ominous dialogue merely whets the summoner's curiosity. His insistence on tying himself ever more closely to a devil has a dramatic justification in his hope to pick up tips for his business of extortion, as well as in the natural affinity of two such beings. The introduction of the supernatural element suggests as further meaning the way a commitment to evil escalates, blinding the victim to his loss of freedom. The damned soul wills his damnation as the summoner his association with the devil. Both are oblivious to the danger they are incurring.

Two lively episodes close the narrative and contribute to this anatomy of damnation. The farmer cursing his horses, his cart, and his hay deceives the summoner into a superficial assumption: that he has consigned them all to the devil. The devil disabuses him. The world is not run on trivial principles. In introducing himself, he has explained:

> My wages been ful streite and ful smale.
> My lord is hard to me and daungerous,
> And myn office is ful laborous,
> And therfore by extorcions I lyve.
> For sothe, I take al that men wol me yive.
> Algate, by sleyghte or by violence,
> Fro yeer to yeer I wynne al my dispence. (D 1432)

The fiend, not yet identified, shows here the "sleyghte" he lives by. The statement is both deceptive and true. He does indeed live by extortions, make his expenses by deception and violence. The extortions, the deceptions, and the violence are not his own; rather they are the means by which men will him what he takes. Later he explains his subjection to God's purposes, and in the details he gives of his duties we can see why his wages are "ful streite and ful smale." Finally, with the carter and his bemired team, we get further instruction. Men must really mean what they say. It must not be a momentary whim, irritation, or even, by implication, a temporary fall from grace.

The summoner proposes to teach the poor fiend, who has earned "nothyng upon cariage," a lesson. He outlines his plan for extortion, emphasizing the widow's innocence, her poverty, and the high proportion the amount of his bribe will bear to her resources. He boasts:

> But for thou kanst nat, as in this contree,
> Wynne thy cost, taak heer ensample of me.   (D 1580)

The fiend is on the point of making, rather than taking, an example. The extortion he lives by is about to occur. The hard terms of his service will manifest themselves. The summoner understands nothing of what he has been so plainly told. He even responds to Mabely's request that he show her his charity:

> "Nay thanne," quod he, "the foule feend me fecche
> If I th'excuse, though thou shul be spilt!"   (D 1611)

He then receives mercy where he has shown none. The widow, asked if she really means it when she consigns him to the devil, qualifies her curse, "but he wol hym repente." The summoner echoes in his reply his fiend-companion's earlier explanation about the carter, "It is nat his entente" (D 1556). He gives it the edifying finality of rhyme: "Nay, olde stot, that is nat myn entente" (D 1630). He thus shuts the door on his final chance and at the same time illustrates the hard terms on which the fiend lives. It is clear from the summoner's early account of himself that he has willed his soul to the devil long since:

> I spare nat to taken, God it woot,
> But if it be to hevy or to hoot.
> What I may gete in conseil prively,
> No maner conscience of that have I.
> Nere myn extorcioun, I myghte nat lyven,
> Ne of swiche japes wol I nat be shryven.
> Stomak ne conscience ne knowe I noon;
> I shrewe thise shrifte-fadres everychoon.   (D 1442)

But repentance would still save him and send the fiend away empty-handed. The summoner gets the special grace of Mabely's reminder. He ignores it; he wills his damnation.[14]

The Friar, after his direct condemnation of the Summoner's practices at the beginning of his tale, climbs to a firmer theological position and fictionally arranges it so that the Summoner condemns himself. Having sent him in the fiend's grip to hell, "Where as that somonours han hir heritage" (D 1641), he proceeds with infuriating unction to pray:

> And God, that maked after his ymage
> Mankynde, save and gyde us, alle and some,
> And leve thise somonours goode men bicome!   (D 1644)

There follows what is clearly an epilogue to the tale:

> "Lordynges, I koude han toold yow," quod this Frere,
> "Hadde I had leyser for this Somnour heere . . ."   (D 1646)

What he so smugly tells us he could have spent his time on are the punishments of hell. A thousand winters would not have sufficed. The rancor against the Summoner does not disturb his theology as he prays that we be kept out of Satan's grasp, admonishes us that we be always on the alert, and reassures us that no man is tempted beyond his strength. But his rancor returns, at the end, to suggest within whose reach he is placing his own soul at that very moment:

> And prayeth that thise somonours hem repente
> Of hir mysdedes, er that the feend hem hente!   (D 1664)

The Host has no opportunity to get in a word. The fury the Summoner feels at being suavely exposed as self-condemned, and then unctuously prayed over, requires a physical release. Stretching himself to his full height in his stirrups does not suffice to contain his passion. He quakes like "an aspen leef" in its grip. The anger he feels, possesses his fiction as well. Three times he must cover the fictional friar with anal discharge before he can feel purged of his emotion. Anger, in fact, becomes an important thematic element in the main story he tells against friars. But the friar's sermon against anger, which prepares us ironically in the fiction for the friar's enraged departure, suffers a distorting influence, as we shall see, from the Summoner's passion. Indeed, in order to bring about his third defilement of the friar, the Summoner violates the limits of his narrative and imposes on his characters a false motivation. In doing so, he fully carries out the threat made in his initial exchange with the Friar, at the end of the Wife of Bath's Prologue. He there catches up the Friar's "er that I go" with his own "er I come to Sidyngborne," and his rival's "swich a tale or two" (D 842) with his own "tales two or three." Even the Friar's anticipated effect—"That alle the folk shal laughen in this place"—he echoes and changes:

> That I shal make thyn herte for to morne,
> For wel I woot thy pacience is gon.   (D 849)

He no doubt considers the episode at the lord's house a third narrative to add to the vision of friars in hell and to the main story, having as it does a new cast of characters with the exception of the friar, and for its central concern an abstract problem of aerodynamics which the friar would not for a moment have sought help in solving. The Summoner, having, in his own mind, successfully raised the ante in every aspect of the relationship with the Friar, and having finally regained the patience that he has accused the Friar of losing, subsides without the usual blessing, but with a reminder of what he undertook at the beginning of the quarrel: "My tale is doon; we been almoost at towne" (D 2294). Actually, the Summoner has done more than he realizes or intended. In addition to thoroughly carrying out his program against the Friar, he has given the *Friar's Tale* an unintended complement. If the protagonist of the *Friar's Tale* is self-condemned, the narrator of the *Summoner's Tale* is self-exposed.

The antagonists in this quarrel have a real instinct for the jugular, despite the contrast between them in manner and station. Each seizes on an aspect of the other's nature that is featured in the General Prologue, the Friar on the suggestion of hell-fire in the Summoner's visage, the Summoner on the suave hypocrisy of the Friar's speech. Each relentlessly exposes the other in a style reflecting his nature, the Friar with a smoothly controlled sophistication, the Summoner with a mocking and passionate vulgarity. The Summoner, coming last, has a slight advantage: he can build to some extent on his rival's performance. In his opening narrative, which he wants no one to mistake for his turn at storytelling, he does a masterful job of using the Friar's concluding remarks against him.[15] The Friar has precisely the position of the character in the Summoner's story before he is enlightened by the angel: he has an exhaustive knowledge of the pains of hell, along with a smug delight in his own immunity. The story quickly dispels his illusion of immunity, suggesting as his destined home, "his heritage of verray kynde," a place especially distasteful to a man so fastidious in his dress and habits. The Summoner makes no mealymouthed pretense of praying for his victim:

> God save yow alle, save this cursed Frere!
> My prologe wol I ende in this manere. (D 1708)

To make sure that the pilgrims recognize the hero of his main tale, the Summoner starts him off preaching on the pains of hell.[16] He does not make the Friar's mistake of a long opening description with only a tenuous connection to the plot. He lets us watch this "lymytour" on a specific day, urging the people to pay his brethren for trentals, and contrasting the efficacy of masses "hastily ysonge" with the single mass a day of the parish priest:

> "Delivereth out," quod he, "anon the soules!
> Ful hard it is with flesshhook or with oules
> To been yclawed, or to brenne or bake.
> Now spede yow hastily, for Cristes sake!" (D 1732)

He draws from the Friar a most revealing interjection, not for the way the limiter he is describing has reduced begging to a system, with a second friar writing the names of the donors on a slate and a "sturdy harlot" carrying the loot in a sack on his back, not for the suggested rapacity of their begging, their willingness to take anything from a bushel of wheat to a halfpenny, but rather for the implication that people do not receive what they pay for, an implication that would certainly hurt business if it were believed:

> And whan that he was out at dore, anon
> He planed awey the names everichon
> That he biforn had writen in his tables;
> He served hem with nyfles and with fables.
> "Nay, ther thou lixt, thou Somonour!" quod the Frere. (D 1761)

163

The Summoner certainly wins the battle of the interjections.

He continues to score with his picture of the friar arriving at Thomas's house and settling down in comfort while his fellows go on to the inn. The condescension, the hypocritical self-effacement, the pretended concern with Thomas and his family, the reiterated claim to a special sanctity for himself and his brethren, the flirtatious advances to the wife before the sick husband's eyes and his acceptance of her version of the husband's angry conduct, and, through it all, the sanctimonious sweetness of tongue come through dramatically in the friar's speech. The satire is devastating and beautifully articulated. In response to the wife's complaint, the friar starts to lecture Thomas on his ire, but is distracted when the wife interrupts to ask what he will have for dinner.

> "Now, dame," quod he, "now *je vous dy sanz doute*,
> Have I nat of a capon but the lyvere,
> And of youre softe breed nat but a shyvere,
> And after that a rosted pigges heed—
> But that I nolde no beest for me were deed—
> Thanne hadde I with yow hoomly suffisaunce.
> I am a man of litel sustenaunce;
> My spirit hath his fostryng in the Bible.
> The body is ay so redy and penyble
> To wake, that my stomak is destroyed.
> I prey yow, dame, ye be nat anoyed,
> Though I so freendly yow my conseil shewe.
> By God! I wolde nat telle it but a fewe."   (D 1850)

The word that her child died soon after his last visit inspires him to claim a revelation of the child borne to bliss within a half hour of his death, not just for himself but for "oure sexteyn and oure fermerer" as well, and to invent the resulting *Te Deum* by the whole convent and a special orison of thanksgiving by him. The mention of prayer sets him off on his favorite subject, the special sanctity of friars and the resulting efficacy of their prayers. The next seventy-eight lines constitute a paean to the clennesse, fastynge, poverte, humblesse, and chastite of friars, with the gluttony and drunkenness of other clergy and all laymen brought in as contrast. Four times the rhyme freres-preyeres recurs,[17] drawing around it the magic words and claiming the special power. The final lines are vivid as they condemn the swimmers in "possessioun," like Jovinyan—

> Fat as a whale, and walkynge as a swan,
> Al vinolent as botel in the spence   (D 1931)

—and envisage the prayers of friars that "humble been, and chaast, and poore" springing "as an hauk up at a sours" to God's two ears, ending with the warning to "Thomas! Thomas!": "Nere thou oure brother, sholdestou nat thryve" (D 1944).

Thomas's complaint that the prayers have not cured him, though in a few years he has spent many pounds on "diverse manere freres" (rhymed here significantly with yeres; only the friar uses the preyeres-freres rhyme in the *Summoner's Tale*), forces the friar to devote another twenty-six lines to Thomas's folly in giving to anyone but him: "Youre inconstance is youre confusioun" (D 1958); "Youre maladye is for we han to lyte" (D 1962); "What is a ferthyng worth parted in twelve?" (D 1967)—with perhaps an unintended suggestion to Thomas, if this friar also lisps.[18] Only then does he find it possible to continue his lecture to Thomas on anger, begun before the good wife took his order for dinner.

Here the Summoner falters. The real Friar would surely have kept his bearings in a sermon on one of the seven deadly sins. The economy of the story also requires from the friar a straightforward condemnation of the passion he will himself fall victim to. But the friar's lecture to Thomas keeps veering off the point. The image of the serpent in the grass, ready subtly to sting, turns out to be, not sin, but woman. The sermon warns against strife with women, against setting "an irous man" in high estate, and against telling their vices to any but the poor and the powerless. It returns occasionally to the straightforward condemnation of anger, and on the first of these occasions displays the envious contempt for the secular clergy which is one of the friar's obsessive themes:

> This every lewed viker or person
> Kan seye, how ire engendreth homycide.   (D 2009)

The speech is thus not a lapse on Chaucer's part from the dramatic situation.

At the end of the Cambises exemplum, a lesson is drawn that reflects the cultivation of the rich and powerful by the Friar:

> Beth war, therfore, with lordes how ye pleye.
> Syngeth *Placebo*, and "I shal, if I kan,"
> But if it be unto a povre man.
> To a povre man men sholde his vices telle,
> But nat to a lord, thogh he sholde go to helle.   (D 2078)

Here the economy of the story is yielding to the Summoner's anger at the Friar. Their vices take the two in opposite directions on the social scale, the Summoner into an alliance with prostitutes and pimps, the Friar to association with the wealthy and powerful. The Summoner, in attacking the Friar's sycophancy, is undercutting a social superiority that is especially galling to him.

The three exempla provide the one point of consistency in the sermon and suggest an origin even more at odds with the structure of the narrative. In all of them the angry man is powerful enough to sweep all before him. The judge condemns to death the three innocent knights; Cambises demonstrates his steadiness in drink by killing the lord's son; and Cirus succeeds in reducing the river Gysen to a brook. The Summoner has accused the Friar of losing his patience in their initial exchange. The irony of the furious Summoner telling a story which uses anger as the mainspring of its plot reaches its epitome in the exempla. The Summoner finds a vicarious fulfillment in the obliterating anger of these men.[19] He cannot resist the opportunity, just as later he cannot resist putting the Friar at the hub of the wheel. The aesthetics of the situation, already compromised by the earlier veerings from the sermon's function in the tale, give way to the satisfying release of that flesh-quaking passion.

At the end of the sermon, the Summoner recovers his narrative balance and finishes out his fiction with the presentation by the angry Thomas of his enraging gift. The carrying on of the story beyond the departure of the friar could be justified only by some attempted revenge on his part. His arrival at the lord's court, speechless in his fury, seems to be preparation for just such an attempt. But with the telling of his story, the "odious meschief" the friar and his order have suffered undergoes a subtle change from the insult of being given a fart instead of something valuable. What the friar complains of to the lady of the house is the charge,

> To parte that wol nat departed be,
> To every man yliche, with meschaunce! (D 2215)

The lord has also changed from offering to help the friar in his revenge. He is now filled with wonder at the churl's shrewdness in presenting the friar such an impossible problem in "ars-metrike." The modulation serves the Summoner's blind purpose, if not the cause of narrative verisimilitude.[20] The clever squire can now show that the problem is not insoluble, and the Summoner can subject the Friar to one more anal indignity. To be unaware of what this repeated defilement of his enemy means in terms of self-exposure is to be furious indeed.

What makes the *Summoner's Tale* effective is the skillful mockery of the Friar's mellifluous accent and of the basic hypocrisy that underlies it. Detail after detail strikes home. In contrast to the *Friar's Tale*, the details add up to no implicit meaning. The simple irony of the preacher against anger arousing anger in his listener, and then becoming enraged himself, provides no special insight into anger. The issues involved are trivial; the resolution results from a vulgar if well deserved trick; only the satire against clerical abuse and hypocrisy raises it above the level of the typical fabliau. In its relationship to the Summoner's passion, the tale has its most significant value. What motivates the story in the first place makes for the effectiveness of the detailed mockery, distorts the sermon and finds expression in it, carries the fiction beyond its limits, and exposes the narrator's anal fixation. The conflict between Friar and Summoner thus provides a contrast between the successful objective correlative and the subjectively distorted artifact. The Friar's advantage in aesthetics is canceled by his involvement in a quarrel with the Summoner. His vows would make natural the humblest and lowliest of associations. The hypocrisy that the Summoner exposes accounts for his status in society. Among the many-faceted ironies of this quarrel, the final one is perhaps that the revelations each character makes of himself and his enemy can damage only the Friar.

The three stories of Fragment D have some interesting interrelationships. The quarrel of the Friar and the Summoner starts while the

Wife is still speaking, and holds the stage as soon as she finishes, effectively postponing any discussion of the issues she raises about marriage. The fragment is the most thoroughly dramatic of all. Each of the tales expresses the personality of the teller, and the first and third have at times a special idiom associated with the teller. None of the three stories would have a chance for the prize, and only the Friar's has any real distinction as narrative art. On the other hand, each reflects strongly the purposes of the teller, and each goes beyond those purposes in unintentional revelation. The aggressiveness that the three narrators share not only contributes to their self-exposure but helps to create that final level of meaning, the sense of a universe where men's appetites are inevitably ordered. Men are nowhere so free as in their games, nor, paradoxically, so responsible. Wife of Bath, Friar, and Summoner participate in the storytelling with abandon. The quarrel between Friar and Summoner reflects the mean and narrow purposes of the men involved. It ends with a tale so dominated by the passion of the teller that he is unaware of a self-exposure almost indecent. The wife's autobiographical monologue sets before us the most startling of the pilgrim personalities. The repercussions will be felt beyond the fragment, in the *Pardoner's Tale* and in the marriage group.

2. Fragment C—"Deeth"

Fragment C is the only part of the *Canterbury Tales* that has no indication of time or place. We depend entirely on its relation to other fragments for evidence of its position in the sequence of tales. Scholars have placed it on the basis of such relationship both near the beginning and near the end.[21] The fact that the Pardoner interrupts the Wife of Bath when she is discussing the debt husbands owe to their wives makes likely a position near Fragment D. Since the interruption would come as an anticlimax after the Pardoner's remarkable performance, most recent critics see the Wife of Bath's Prologue as preceding, and some as even inspiring, the Pardoner.[22] A similar relationship is perhaps to be seen in the Pardoner's supposition, while he is congratulating the pilgrims on the good fortune of having him with them to "assoille" them of guilt they may incur as they travel:

Paraventure ther may fallen oon or two

168

Doun of his hors, and breke his nekke atwo.   (C 936)

In the Manciple's Prologue, which takes place within a mile or two of Canterbury, the drunken Cook does fall off his horse. The episode provides a possible inspiration for the Pardoner's comically exaggerated remarks and gives a very slight confirmation to the position we have assigned both the Wife and the Pardoner, on the first day of the homeward journey.

The *Physician's Tale*, which opens the fragment without introduction, is one of the earlier written of the *Canterbury Tales*.[23] It bears some resemblance in narrative manner to the stories in the *Legend of Good Women*. While it is a reasonable tale for the Physician to tell, it has no special relevance to his character. It functions dramatically and thematically in the *Canterbury Tales* mainly by reason of its effect on the Host. The beheading of the heroine by her father Virginius, in order to preserve her from the wicked judge Apius, moves Harrie more deeply than anything else that happens in the pilgrims' fictional worlds. The part that beauty plays in causing her death disturbs him especially: "Allas, to deere boughte she beautee!" (C 293). Neither condemnation of judges and lawyers nor the generalization that gifts of Fortune as well as those of Nature cause harm and death can ease his spirit. He keeps returning to the tale: "This is a pitous tale for to heere" (C 302).

Another unsuccessful effort to dismiss his feelings brings in a complicating element, a reminder that the Host as literary critic is a comic figure. He begins to trip over his language as in praise of the Physician he picks out a comparison that would have little appeal for the skeptical doctor:

> So moot I theen, thou art a propre man,
> And lyk a prelat, by Seint Ronyan!
> Seyde I nat wel? I kan nat speke in terme.   (C 311)

His reaction to the laughter his mistake arouses compounds the comedy: not his technical terms, but (of all things!) his oaths have been at fault. In reverting to his sorrow over the hapless Virginia's death, he gets his heart pangs, in their Latinate form, confused with the princes of the Church:

> But wel I woot thou doost myn herte to erme,

That I almoost have caught a cardynacle.   (C 313)

Of the three possible remedies, "triacle," "moyste and corny ale," or a "myrie tale," only the third is readily available. Turning to that "beel amy," the Pardoner, he calls for the comic relief which he has himself been providing for others: "Telle us som myrthe or japes right anon" (C 319).

The Pardoner, in assenting, first takes advantage of the rhyme the Host has left him to mimic Harrie's unintentional vulgarity, "by Seint Ronyon," and then for the refreshment the Host hasn't available, resorts to his own private "ale-stake," the Summoner:[24]

A gerland hadde he set upon his heed
As greet as it were for an ale-stake.
A bokeleer hadde he maad hym of a cake.   (A 668)

While he is drinking and eating, the "gentils" object. They want no "ribaudye," which apparently they think the Pardoner well able to provide, but "som moral thyng." The Pardoner again assents:

"I graunte, ywis," quod he, "but I moot thynke
Upon som honest thyng while that I drynke."   (C 328)

This natural give-and-take between the pilgrims, set in motion by the Host's heartache over Virginia, a fictional character in the game he has invented, and by his desire for "myrthe" to ease his pain, has already touched the theme that will provide its climax. The Host's instinct for "sooth pley, quaad pley," which in earlier fragments has numbered among its victims the Cook, Chaucer, the Monk, and the Nun's Priest, has just now lighted on the epithet "beel amy" for the Pardoner. A foreshadowing of his later insult to the Pardoner's virility, it recalls the portrait in the General Prologue and suggests a motive for the remarkable performance that follows.[25]

The Pardoner will give to each what he has requested, "myrthe" and "japes" to the Host, "som moral thyng" to the gentlefolk; but the morality will serve a cynical purpose, and the japing revelers will end like Virginia in death.[26] He will also seek for himself a success that does not involve money—a recognition of his talents by an audience more critical and sophisticated than the one he usually faces and bilks. He will gain a recognition wider than the one he seeks. The startling image of gold as death, which ordinarily serves his cupidity, will for this audience expose it, and will expose also the vanity of the ends his striking talents serve. At the same time, he will gain unexpected satisfaction from doing as game what he habitually does only for profit, from sharing a part of his real life with the pilgrims, from improvising a performance that includes and "places" his habitual one. His effort to prolong the association, to continue sharing with his audience by mocking the relics and pardons he traffics in, has an unintended and, for him, shattering result, the exposure of the part of his real life he has sought to conceal. This eunuchhood that emerges as willful avarice, the talent as speaker and actor that makes worldly success possible, his basic dissatisfaction with the limitations of life—these emerge from the series of illuminating moments in his performance, from the use he makes of a second audience, from the revelation of his self-indulgences and aggressions, from the imagery of his sermon, from the apparition of the old man, from the discovery of gold that is really death, from the blessing of the pilgrims, from the mock hawking of his pardons, and from the quarrel with the Host.

The Pardoner is histrionic to his finger tips. Those critics who assign the revelations of his monologue to a medieval literary convention,[27] who claim that no one would make such a confession in public, are missing much of the complexity of motive that his performance before the pilgrims involves. He starts out at once to create for the pilgrims the typical scene of his preaching. Before we can really take in what is happening, he has a second audience, an imaginary one, that he is addressing directly, showing them his relics, making them feel the need to pay him for the magic powers he convinces them he wields. Then he steps back again and talks to the pilgrims about the peasant audience, about the techniques he uses in duping them, finally about his own way of life. Clearly he enjoys the challenge of his customary work. At the same time, he has nothing but contempt for the ignorance of his victims. To the pilgrims he can openly express his contempt and expect them to share it. By insinuating this common ground, he is trying to make them to some extent his accomplices. Those who resist, who hold themselves off in moral dudgeon, can join the peasants and earn his scorn. In any event, so far from his customary haunts, he has nothing to fear. He can superimpose on his role of the preacher, calling people to repent their sins, the role of the honest cynic, who knows the worst that can be said of himself and says it.

Inspired by this new audience, he improvises a new performance, contrasting in tone with the old even as it describes the old. He takes the pilgrims at once behind the scenes.

> "Lordynges," quod he, "in chirches whan I preche,
> I peyne me to han an hauteyn speche,
> And rynge it out as round as gooth a belle,
> For I kan al by rote that I telle.
> My theme is alwey oon, and evere was—
> *Radix malorum est Cupiditas.*"   (C 334)

The informality and spontaneity and frankness find expression in short descriptive cadences, arranged in a temporal and linear order: "First . . ." (335), "Thanne . . ." (347), "Thanne . . ." (350). The sentences fit themselves without strain to the line length, with every line end-stopped. Inversions occur in two sentences (337 and 342). The first of these leads to a slight elevation of style; the Pardoner's license to preach carries him temporarily into an ordering of language designed to strike awe and put his rights beyond question:

> Oure lige lordes seel on my patente,
> That shewe I first, my body to warente,
> That no man be so boold, ne preest ne clerk,
> Me to destourbe of Cristes hooly werk.   (C 340)

Here the suspension created by "ne preest ne clerk," following the stress-heavy "no man be so boold," prepares for the inversion, syntactic and metrical, and the special idiom "destourbe of" in the last line. The second inversion results from natural emphasis rather than rhetorical ordering:

> Bulles of popes and of cardynales,
> Of patriarkes and bishopes I shewe.   (C 343)

The direct address to the peasants employs a strikingly different rhythm and syntax. It illustrates what he means by "hauteyn speche":

"Goode men," I seye, "taak of my wordes keep;
If that this boon be wasshe in any welle,
If cow, or calf, or sheep, or oxe swelle
That any worm hath ete, or worm ystonge,
Taak water of that welle and wassh his tonge,
And it is hool anon; and forthermoore,
Of pokkes and of scabbe, and every soore
Shal every sheep be hool that of this welle
Drynketh a draughte. Taak kep eek what I telle:
If that the good-man that the beestes oweth
Wol every wyke, er that the cok hym croweth,
Fastynge, drynken of this welle a draughte,
As thilke hooly Jew oure eldres taughte,
His beestes and his stoor shal multiplie." (C 365)

The syntax of the passage is complex, with the meaning repeatedly suspended for subordinations. It is also unified by dependence of the whole passage on the first if-clause (353). The fourteen lines fall into periods of four and a half, three, and five lines, with the remainder devoted to the two minatory injunctions. These two injunctions (note the way "Goode men" and "good-man" point up the virtual repetition) and the repetition of the key phrases—"wasshe in any welle" (353), "that welle and wassh" (356), "of this welle / Drynketh a draughte" (360), and "drynken of this welle a draughte" (363)—bind the three periods together into a single cadence, which is strengthened by the fact that the first two periods end in a medial pause (357 and 360) and the third (and longest) ends in the first line of a couplet (365). The solemnity of tone is reinforced by the way the speech cadence cuts across the metre and rhyme without breaking the rhythm. An especially fine rhythmic imitation of the syntactic suspensions is effected by the reversal of stress after the caesura (362) and the unusually strong headless line with early caesura (363) at the crest of cadence in the third period (note too the alliterations):

Wol every wyke, er that the cok hym croweth,
Fastynge, drynken of this welle a draughte. (C 363)

No sheep's shoulder bone has ever had a nobler incantation.

The Pardoner ends his sample of "hauteyn speche" with the "gaude" by which he cons his victims into being afraid not to give. He then reverts to his informal manner to express pride in his income and the joy he takes in becoming the instrument of his avarice.

> Myne handes and my tonge goon so yerne
> That it is joye to se my bisynesse. (C 399)

He keeps emphasizing the motive for his preaching. The subject is always avarice, in order "to make hem free / To yeven hir pens, and namely unto me" (C 402). The repeated acknowledgment of his own vice of avarice and his denial of any intention to win his listeners from sin, whatever the actual result of his preaching, suggest some ulterior motive—the concealment, in exaggerated self-exposure, of aspects of his life he would not have others see.

Twice he loses the tone of amused objectivity in describing his way of life to the pilgrims. He has no mercy on those who oppose him, and takes advantage of the pulpit to defame them, not by name, but recognizably nonetheless. An unpleasant malice mars the image he projects of himself as he talks of stinging his enemy with his "tonge smerte" and spitting out his "venym under hewe / Of hoolynesse." The second occasion for loss of objectivity is when he asks the question:

> What, trowe ye, that whiles I may preche,
> And wynne gold and silver for I teche,
> That I wol lyve in poverte wilfully? (C 441)

The answer comes pouring out of what he "wol" and "wol nat" do. Manual labor and the apostles' way of life are out.

> I wol have moneie, wolle, chese, and whete,
> Al were it yeven of the povereste page,
> Or of the povereste wydwe in a village,
> Al sholde hir children sterve for famyne.
> Nay, I wol drynke licour of the vyne,
> And have a joly wenche in every toun. (C 453)

The litany of "I wol," coming six times in twelve lines (always at or near the beginning), pauses only for the aggression against others, this time not his "enemies," but unfortunates whose interests might interfere with his profiteering at their expense.[28] The outburst is in response

to a question he has asked himself, and it ends with an assertion of a
sexual appetite that both Chaucer and the Wife of Bath would judge
to be an empty boast. Assertiveness, aggression, and an overinsistence on
self-exposure only partially conceal the insecurity and isolation of the
Pardoner's life. The joy in his hypocritical exercise of skill stems partly
from the escape it affords him. While he is hypnotizing the peasants
with his "hauteyn speche," he is busy, distracted, taken out of himself.
The amount of his annual income has a special value for him. It is a
definite figure that impresses others, and that he cannot doubt as a
symbol of his own success.

Before beginning his tale, he again reassures the pilgrims. Though
vicious himself, he can tell a moral tale, the kind he is used to preaching
for profit. He thus retains his imaginary audience. But he has placed
himself in a slightly different relationship to the pilgrims. They want
the morality that he customarily preaches. They must move closer to
the village listeners. He will no longer be in and out of his role as
preacher. He will be addressing both audiences simultaneously. Those
pilgrims who want can see the performance as exemplary of his skills.
The others can take the morality straight.

The story modulates rapidly into a sermon on the evils of the tavern.
The Pardoner is not only using morality for an immoral purpose but
turning the aesthetics of the situation upside down to do it. The
exemplum has swallowed the sermon of which it is ordinarily a part,
and then the sermon proceeds to spawn new exempla: the tavern, that
"develes temple" haunted by the "yonge folk," dancing, gambling,
swearing, eating and drinking "over hir myght," who do the devil sacrifice "By superfluytee abhomynable" (C 471). The line, filled up by
the two words, suggests its subject; the specific meaning will become
clear with the later repetition of the word "superfluytee."

> And right anon thanne comen tombesteres
> Fetys and smale, and yonge frutesteres,
> Syngeres with harpes, baudes, wafereres,
> Whiche been the verray develes officeres
> To kyndle and blowe the fyr of lecherye.　　　　　(C 481)

The tavern furnishes a model for the sermon's bewildering display
of rhetoric, authority, exemplary narrative, and vividly realized detail:

O glotonye, on thee wel oghte us pleyne!
O, wiste a man how manye maladyes
Folwen of excesse and of glotonyes,
He wolde been the moore mesurable
Of his diete, sittynge at his table.
Allas! the shorte throte, the tendre mouth,
Maketh that est and west and north and south,
In erthe, in eir, in water, men to swynke
To gete a glotoun deyntee mete and drynke!
Of this matiere, o Paul, wel kanstow trete:
"Mete unto wombe, and wombe eek unto mete,
Shal God destroyen bothe," as Paulus seith.
Allas! a foul thyng is it, by my feith,
To seye this word, and fouler is the dede,
Whan man so drynketh of the white and rede
That of his throte he maketh his pryvee,
Thurgh thilke cursed superfluitee.   (C 528)

The "cursed superfluitee" finds a reflection in the rhapsodic style with the vivid scenes interspersed. Yet the Pardoner keeps what he is doing under some control. The passage above, for instance, forms one of the two sections on excessive eating, followed by two sections on drunkenness, followed in turn by two connected sections on gambling and swearing. The sermon topics derive from the revels of the "yonge folk" in the tavern at the beginning, and include the rather slighted subject of lechery induced by drunkenness, as well as gluttony, "hasardrye," and blasphemous oaths. The brief biblical exemplum of Lot and his daughters alone represents lechery; it leads to a second biblical exemplum, Herod under the influence of wine ordering John the Baptist's death, with no mention of Salome. This second exemplum thus becomes part of the bridge passage from Lot's drunken incest to the story of Adam and Eve and the consideration of excessive eating, a bridge passage that also includes a saying of Seneca on drunkenness and several apostrophes to gluttony.

The quoted passage has a kind of form, not clearly articulated as the broad outlines of the sermon are, not repeated in the other short sections,

176

but growing out of the subject matter itself. The maladies; the man sitting at his table, who if he only knew would be "mesurable," but as things are, alas, betrayed by his own appetites; the sudden contrast from short throat and tender mouth (representing appetite) to labor through the four points of the compass and three of the four elements to gather the "deyntee mete and drynke," which then in a quotation from Paul is partly digested, and finally (though it is a foul thing to say) in part vomited up, turning the short throat into a privy, and by a clarifying repetition doing the devil sour sacrifice—the elements, disparate in every respect, fuse under the compelling energy of the Pardoner's imagination. That imagination expresses itself in the sermon in a series of lurid images, the cast-up of his experience of the sins he decries, which vicariously he enjoys again. We watch with him the cooks in their frenetic activity; feel the marrow slipping through the "golet softe and swoote"; taste the sauce, designed with all its spices "by delit, / To make hym yet a newer appetit" (C 546); smell the foul breath and hear the "Sampsoun"-sounding belches of his companions; distinguish the ingredients of diluted or spiked wine with the palate of a connoisseur; find ourselves unexpectedly at the town of Lepe in Spain eructing "Sampsoun"; hang on the roll of the "bitched" bones with Christ-mangling oaths; and calculate the chances for a dagger-thrust to the heart of a probably cheating, certainly winning opponent.

The sermon glosses the final part of the Pardoner's monologue, dramatizing the willful self-indulgence he there asserts. The gloss on one element of his vaunted way of life is almost a blank. The "wenche in every toun' has nothing in the sermon to match the gratification of his other appetites. Yet the opportunity is there in the assortment of female venders frequenting the tavern and the lechery that drunkenness stimulates. His imagination dwells most fondly on food and drink, secondarily on gambling (why gamble for what is so plentifully available without taking a chance?), and not at all on women. He also furnishes us with a hint as to his audience. In mid-sermon, he says, "But herkneth, lordynges," (573), a form of address he would use only to the pilgrims (see C 329). In reverting to his exemplary narrative, he uses the ambiguous "sires" (660), used earlier in addressing the peasants, and later the pilgrims (366 and 915). This evidence confirms what we noted at the beginning of the tale. The Pardoner is directing his tale and the included sermon at both pilgrims and peasants simultaneously.

If the Pardoner lets himself go in the sermon, he reins himself in when he returns to his story. The proportions and the detail of the narrative are under firm control. The tale proceeds in a series of dramatic interchanges, seemingly casual. Yet at almost the exact mathematical center, the three rioters discover Death and think they have stopped looking for him. The ironies of the gold as unrecognized death find a concise expression in the single line, "No lenger thanne after Deeth they soughte" (C 772). Before the line, just two scenes, approximately equal in length, bring the drunken revelers to their discovery. After the line, three sequences record their plotting with and against one another; a fourth and final one of only fifteen lines effects their deaths.

The early scenes are rich in omen. The corpse that the revelers casually inquire after turns out to be a friend and companion. Hearing of the slaughter that the privy thief Death has made this pestilence, one of the rioters asks arrogantly, "Is it swich peril with hym for to meete? / I shal hym seke" (C 694). The three plight their words "To lyve and dyen ech of hem for oother" (C 703). Most ominous of all is the old man they meet.[29] He has a dignity and courtesy that survive the aggressive accusations of the three "riotoures." The confrontation represents more than the age-old conflict between the generations. The young men, in swearing brotherhood and uniting in the altruistic and impossible mission against Death, have adopted the suspicious self-righteousness of the fanatic. They assume that their purpose takes priority over all others, and that men must either support them or be regarded as enemies.

The old man they haven't the patience to listen to gives them an oblique and mysterious answer when one of the revelers asks him why he lives so long in "so greet age":

> This olde man gan looke in his visage,
> And seyde thus: "For I ne kan nat fynde
> A man, though that I walked into Ynde,
> Neither in citee ne in no village,

That wolde chaunge his youthe for myn age;
And therfore moot I han myn age stille,
As longe tyme as it is Goddes wille." (C 726)

The inebriated and unwonted idealism of the rioters' quest receives an implicit rebuke in this answer. The search for Death is appropriate to the old man; no young man really wants the certainty of soon meeting him.[30] The facetiousness of the old man's reply that has this deeper import turns more serious in his recognition of God's will. The fact is that the killing of death, even if it were possible, would not for this old man improve the conditions of human existence: "Allas! whan shul my bones been at reste?" (C 733). After vividly projecting the limited conditions of his life as in effect a quest for death and thus a tacit and inadvert comment on the drunken revelers' quest, the old man reminds his interlocutors that they may well some day be in his state:

Ne dooth unto an oold man noon harm now,
Namoore than that ye wolde men did to yow
In age, if that ye so longe abyde.
And God be with yow, where ye go or ryde!
I moot go thider as I have to go. (C 749)

The revelers hear only what they want to hear. They miss the special meanings that, without anyone's willing them or even being aware of them, this encounter has. The old man has spoken about Death; he must be his spy. And indeed the old man knows where the young can find Death:

... turne up this croked wey,
For in that grove I lafte hym, by my fey,
Under a tree, and there he wole abyde;
Noght for youre boost he wole him no thyng hyde. (C 764)

The natural and the supernatural mingle in the old man's wisdom, his acceptance of his own limits, his willingness to continue his painful way "thider as I have to go." His style, from which experience has burned out all but his general humanity, brings to mind archetypal characters like the wandering Jew, mythical seers like Teiresias, allegorical figures like Death or Old Age. That he retains a certain impenetrability, that he refuses to yield the key to his mystery, certifies the instinctive grasp on artfulness which Chaucer grants to the Pardoner.[31]

The gold does what the old man could not do. It deflates the young men's idealism. It sobers them. It brings them back to ignoble and tavern-bound motives. The desire to keep the gold against any claim from outside their fellowship quickly becomes the desire of each to keep the gold for himself. The Pardoner does not speed the pace of his narrative, however, We watch the three discussing how to secure their treasure. We watch the two plotting the death of the third, and the one buying the poison, the bottles, and the wine.

With the three men dead and the gold intact, the Pardoner gives in for a moment to rhetorical temptation. He apostrophizes the sins of the tavern and the general sins of mankind. Then he turns to the imaginary peasant audience and starts his pitch:

> Now, goode men, God foryeve yow youre trespas,
> And ware yow fro the synne of avarice!
> Myn hooly pardoun may yow alle warice,
> So that ye offre nobles or sterlynges,
> Or elles silver broches, spoones, rynges.   (C 908)

If there is any question whose spoons and rings the Pardoner is soliciting, he clears it up in his request to "ye wyves" for "youre wolle." The moral of his preaching is thus money for the Pardoner:

> I yow assoille, by myn heigh power,
> Yow that wol offre, as clene and eek as cleer
> As ye were born.   (C 915)

The Pardoner pays his fellow pilgrims the compliment of excluding them from the appeal for funds. He now turns to them and gives them a gratuitous blessing:

> And lo, sires, thus I preche.
> And Jhesu Crist, that is oure soules leche,
> So graunte yow his pardoun to receyve,
> For that is best; I wol yow nat deceyve.   (C 918)

What follows is a comedy of misunderstanding and inadvertent insult that unexpectedly exposes the Pardoner's eunuchhood. From the earliest distinction he has made between peasants and pilgrims he can not intend, as some critics have urged,[32] to sell his services to his companions. Hearing the serious claims of the first few lines, some of the pilgrims might indeed be in doubt over his meaning. But as he warms to his parody and suggests taking pardon on the go, "Al new and fressh at every miles ende" (C 928), with the appropriate payment on each occasion, few of his listeners can be deceived. The Pardoner so much enjoys performing, and the unexpected courtesy of his blessing has won so favorable a response that he is trying for an additional success. The blessing carries a recognition of the preceding sales pitch as fraudulent. He now mocks for the pilgrims his own venal histrionics. It is perhaps his freest moment. He has won for himself a temporary release from the avarice that grips his life. He is sharing with others an enjoyment.

Unfortunately for the Pardoner's playful purposes, the Host, as we saw in the case of Chaucer's *Sir Thopas*, has no ear for parody. When the Pardoner singles him out and offers him a bargain in pardons, the Host, with the ronyon mistake still in mind, takes no chances and makes it clear that whatever the game is he is not playing it. The Host has in fact been the one to ask for "japes." The Pardoner has every right to expect that his mockery of his own profession will be continued in a form he can reply to. Even at that, Harrie's denigration of the relics would not cause any particular anger. But "coillons" hits not at the relics but at the man. From the Host's reaction to the Pardoner's anger, he has no intention of deadly insult:

> "Now," quod oure Hoost, "I wol no lenger pleye
> With thee, ne with noon oother angry man."　　(C 959)

At the same time, his philosophy of "pleye" as revealed in earlier encounters with the Cook and the Monk—"A man may seye ful sooth in game and pleye" (A 4355)—would not prevent him from rubbing salt into a wound. The Host's insensitivity has put the fellowship of the pilgrims in some jeopardy.

The Knight, recognizing the crisis, steps in and re-establishes harmony. Chaucer calls him "worthy" again, and the Knight shows no perfunctory understanding of the situation as he first quiets the pilgrims' laughter, then soothes the Pardoner's hurt feelings, and urges the Host to take the initiative in the reconciliation. The kiss of peace that results is a tribute to the Knight's sense of responsibility and delicacy of feeling.

The episode of the Pardoner's anger concludes a remarkable series of incidents that Chaucer must have intended us to notice. The song that the Summoner and the Pardoner sing; the line in the Prologue summing up the general physical impression the man makes, "I trowe he were a geldyng or a mare" (A 691); the Pardoner's interruption of the Wife of Bath; his vaunt of having a wench in every town; his avoidance of lechery in the sermon on tavern sins; and now his anger at the Host's remarks on his testicles must indicate a lack of virility in the Pardoner, an effort on his part to conceal this lack, and a resulting sensitivity to anything that could be construed as a reference to it. This aspect of his life accounts for his isolation, for his efforts to compensate, for his pride in his income, for his willingness to be recognized as a shrewd and cynical rascal. Hence his emphasis on his practicing the very sin that he preaches against and practicing it by preaching against it. Hence his contempt for the peasants he dupes, and hence the stimulus provided by a new audience and the release from his usual role.

The story presents some striking parallels to his own efforts. The impact of gold as unrecognized death sends the revelers back to the egoism and self-indulgence they have usually practiced. It has the same effect in the Pardoner's life. Their idealistic mission to kill Death has its parallel in the Pardoner's performance for the pilgrims. His aim to impress his companions with his cynical skill, and at the same time conceal the physical disability that motivates him, has an evanescence similar to that of the revelers' mission. At the sight of gold, it will quickly dissipate. The Pardoner in his preaching makes others see gold as unrecognized death. That he fails to see the application to his own life, reflects the intensity of his efforts to find some compensating fulfillment for what nature has denied him. This intensity is most clearly expressed in the "I wol's" of his monologue. The image they create of a willful blindness dominates his performance almost to the end. The courtesy he shows the pilgrims in his final blessing marks a moment of escape for the Pardoner. Though he shows no sign of recognizing the death that he has up to that point chosen, he does free himself from his cynical motives and share the blessing and the subsequent mockery with his companions. If distance from his customary haunts and the stimulus of creative effort draw him out of his limited world, the Host's insult sends him back into himself. That Chaucer's comedy can include the struggle of this talented and almost doomed soul speaks for its range.

In the Death that Virginia suffers for her beauty, that the Host vainly seeks distraction from, that the Pardoner is unaware of living, that the revelers would destroy, and that the old man yearns for, the fragment has a unifying theme. The confrontation of old man and revelers carries this theme to its deepest point. What we half recognize in the confrontation is the interdependence of life and death. The old man refutes by his existence the desirability of the mission that the drunken revelers have taken on themselves. It has been, of course, impossible from the start. Once again men's wills—in this case, the Physician's, the Host's, the gentlefolk's, the Pardoner's, and the Knight's—have helped to create an unwilled order which only a "sighte above" can fully appreciate.

3. Fragment E-F—"Mariage"

A return to the question raised by the Wife of Bath, the question of sovereignty in marriage, occurs in three of the four stories in Fragment E-F. The reference in the third story of the series, the *Squire's Tale*, to an early morning hour (F 73) suggests that the Wife's influence, already obliquely present in the quarrel between the Friar and the Summoner and in the Pardoner's confession, was to carry beyond the stories of a single day. No other reference to time or place is made in the fragment, but the worry of the Host over what some of the pilgrims might report to his wife—a worry far from his thoughts when he describes her incitements to violence after the *Melibeus*, would be consistent with the prospect of seeing her that very night.[33] This preparation for a drama of reunion between the Host and his wife constitutes the first evidence that the *Canterbury Tales* would end, not with the tale projected in the Parson's Prologue, but with a scene in the very inn where the pilgrims first gathered. The obsession of Harrie with questions of sex and marriage might have come to a dramatic climax had Chaucer lived to record in his account of the pilgrimage the reunion of the happy couple at the Tabard.

The Host takes pains in calling on the Clerk to instruct him on the proprieties of the situation. He remarks on the Clerk's silence and thoughtfulness and reminds him of his obligations to the group. He insists on a "myrie tale," one free of rhetorical embellishment:

> Speketh so pleyn at this tyme, we yow preye,
> That we may understonde what ye seye.   (E 20)

He shows in his comments a conception of the scholarly life somewhat more sophisticated than the one the Miller assigns to John the Carpenter. But three of the direct comments on learning, the Host's, John the Carpenter's, and "deynous" Symkin's (in the *Reeve's Tale*), share the sense of the scholar's world as an alien country, of his life as self-absorbed, impractical, and incomprehensible. Indirectly, however, the scholar fares better. In the fabliaux of Miller and Reeve, he has sufficient skill in practical matters to outwit those who hold learning in suspicion or contempt. And even the Wife of Bath, who decries the way clerks too old to be any longer interested have written about women, pays her scholar-husband a striking though inadvertent tribute in her enthusiasm for authority. Much as she suffered through the long nights of his reading to her, she listened to him, and recalls almost verbatim what she heard. The Clerk on the pilgrimage has not, as the Host conjectures, been studying "aboute som sophyme." He has heard what the Wife of Bath said about clerks and marriage, and he sets about gently disabusing her on both counts. He has waited patiently to be called on by the Host. He shows good humor and a sophisticated indirection throughout. He indulges in no undignified abuse. His generosity of spirit finds expression in the tribute to "Frauceys Petrak," in his reservations about the story he tells, and in the demonstration he gives of a good-tempered and versatile pedagogy. What Chaucer says of him in the General Prologue is true: "And gladly wolde he lerne and gladly teche" (A 308).

The tale of the patient Griselda not only has an idealistic bent that would appeal to the Clerk but develops in a deliberate and methodical way.[34] The whole first section is devoted to Walter and the petition by his subjects that he marry. It contains a hint of Walter's originality in his questioning the value of heredity in the choice of a wife (E 155 ff.), and of his willfulness in the way he apparently conceives of marriage:

> For sith I shal forgoon my libertee
> At youre requeste, as evere moot I thryve,
> Ther as myn herte is set, ther wol I wyve. (E 173)

This willfulness throws a shadow over the wisdom he shows in his choice, especially when in proposing to Griselda he stipulates:

> I seye this, be ye redy with good herte
> To al my lust, and that I frely may,
> As me best thynketh, do yow laughe or smerte,
> And nevere ye to grucche it, nyght ne day?
> And eek whan I sey "ye," ne sey nat "nay,"
> Neither by word ne frownyng contenance?
> Swere this, and heere I swere oure alliance. (E 357)

On the other hand, the story prepares us for levels of meanings beyond the literal with the reference to the Nativity:

> But hye God somtyme senden kan
> His grace into a litel oxes stalle (E 207)

—with its recall of an Old Testament maiden who drew water from the well on the day she was chosen to be Isaac's wife:

> Grisilde of this, God woot, ful innocent,
> That for hire shapen was all this array,
> To fecchen water at a welle is went (E 276)

—and by the way in which the scene at Janicula's house, and especially Griselda's answer to Walter, brings to mind the Annunciation:

> Wondrynge upon this word, quakynge for drede,
> She seyde, "Lord, undigne and unworthy
> Am I to thilke honour that ye me beede,
> But as ye wole youreself, right so wol I." (E 361)

Not until the story is a third over does the testing of Griselda by Walter begin. Up to that point she passes brilliantly the tests provided by prosperity, handling herself with instinctive grace and modesty and making judgments "of so greet equitee" in disputes she is called on to settle

> That she from hevene sent was, as men wende,
> Peple to save and every wrong t'amende. (E 441)

The testing proceeds over a period of years, each step in the process designed to try more severely Griselda's patience and, more important for the ultimate meaning of the story, her belief in Walter's wisdom and goodness. She suffers the loss of her daughter, of her son, and of her position as his wife. In each instance she remembers her promise in accepting his proposal and does not presume to judge him. He finally devises the cruelest test of all in asking her to prepare the palace for reception of the young noblewoman who is to supplant her. She not only praises the "tendre mayden" in response to Walter's cruel questioning, but tries to provide for her a marriage free of challenge, warning him that

> She koude nat adversitee endure
> As koude a povre fostred creature. (E 1043)

On only one other occasion does Griselda permit herself an implicit criticism of Walter's conduct. Then it comes as a cry from the heart when she thinks back to her wedding day.

Chaucer puts Petrarch's Latin prose into English verse in full awareness of the moral questions it raises.[35] His version does not ignore the cruelty of Walter's conduct, but sets it into fuller relief. One of his rare additions to the story is a comment on Walter's conduct when he first sets out to test his wife's quality (E 459 ff.). Another emphasizes the pathos of her farewell to the daughter she expects never to see again (E 554 ff.). A third gives Griselda a human cry of grief over the change she has experienced in Walter's love for her since the day she was married (E 852 ff.). A fourth condemns the populace for approving the Marquess's treatment of Griselda when they see how lovely his new bride is (E 995 ff.). These additions have a paradoxical effect. They prepare us for the turn that the Clerk gives the tale at the end. They also enhance the figurative meaning of Griselda in the tale.

Most critics have failed to see this last point. They have tended to find Chaucer's emphasis on human feeling in the story an impairment of its value as allegory.[36] This criticism would have validity were the *Clerk's Tale* an example of personification allegory, like the *Romance of the Rose* or the *Faerie Queene*. Then the allegorical meaning would govern the story; the sole function of the literal narrative would be to make the allegory more vividly didactic. In the *Clerk's Tale*, on the other hand, the moral and anagogical meanings rest on the literal and the figural, or allegorical.[37] Behind Griselda stand biblical characters whose experience illuminates hers. Chaucer's recognition of these biblical figures as important to the effect of the story shows itself in the repetition of the "oxes stalle" (E 291), in a context that connects the well with her temperate habits (E 215 ff.). Griselda, coming from the well, puts her waterpot beside the threshold in an ox's stall as she responds to Walter's summons. Rebecca, whose choice as Isaac's wife was associated with her visit to the well, is the least important of the biblical parallels. More important is Jesus and his Old Testament prefigurement in the Nazarite Samson. The parallel here should also not be overemphasized. But the people feel that Griselda has been sent from heaven to save people and to amend every wrong (E 440–41), and her innocent suffering does not make her question her lord's wisdom and goodness or repent having given him her heart "in hool entente" (E 861). The grace of God in an ox's stall also suggests that other principal in the Nativity, whose choice by her Lord resulted in the apparent death of her innocent Son. Chaucer gives the most important of the biblical parallels explicit mention in a stanza that also clarifies the Clerk's purposes in telling the story:

> Men speke of Job, and moost for his humblesse,
> As clerkes, whan hem list, konne wel endite,
> Namely of men, but as in soothfastnesse,
> Though clerkes preise wommen but a lite,
> Ther kan no man in humblesse hym acquite
> As womman kan, ne kan been half so trewe
> As wommen been, but it be falle of newe.   (E 938)

The story of Job, who refused to see worldly prosperity as the reward of virtue, and whose losses and sufferings did not impair his faith, furnishes a consistent parallel, even to the restoration and happiness at the end. The very things that make Griselda's sufferings unjust strengthen the relationship to Job and the anagogical meaning of the story, spelled out at the end by the Clerk as Petrarch's moral:

> For, sith a womman was so pacient
> Unto a mortal man, wel moore us oghte
> Receyven al in gree that God us sent. (E 1151)

If faith in God and good works in the world received their just deserts always, who could distinguish virtue from sharp practice?

As the stanza with the mention of Job suggests, the Clerk has some special purposes in mind in telling the story of Griselda. These purposes become even clearer when he addresses the pilgrims in his own right at the end of the tale and sings the song composed in honor of the Wife of Bath. He has, of course, shown her that a clerk can speak well of women, even of married women. The ideal of conduct represented in Griselda would hardly appeal to the Wife of Bath. Even Petrarch admitted the undesirability of having wives

> Folwen Grisilde as in humylitee,
> For it were inportable, though they wolde. (E 1144)

The Clerk goes even further in his concessions. After saying that it would be difficult to find three, or even two, Griseldas in a whole town, he admits in the first stanza of his song that any man testing his wife and expecting to find a Griselda will certainly fail: "Grisilde is deed, and eek hire pacience" (E 1177).

He then turns to wives and advises them to behave in accord with Alice's advice: "Lat noon humylitee youre tonge naille" (E 1184). Follow Echo, he tells them:

> Beth nat bidaffed for youre innocence,
> But sharply taak on yow the governaille. (E 1192)
>
> . . . .
>
>   Ye archewyves, stondeth at defense,
> Syn ye be strong as is a greet camaille;
> Ne suffreth nat that men yow doon offense.
> And sklendre wyves, fieble as in bataille,
> Beth egre as is a tygre yond in Ynde;
> Ay clappeth as a mille, I yow consaille. (E 1200)

The Clerk enjoys his mockery of the Wife's theories. He continues for two more of his stanzas to adapt elements from her monologue to the rhyme scheme of his song. The result is a pattern of conduct every bit as outrageous as Griselda's, but at the opposite extreme. Like the good teacher he is, the Clerk leaves unexpressed the moral of his song. He has "stynted" of "ernestful matere." The "sooth" of his "game" is something the players can figure out.

The versatility of the Clerk's performance is striking. His answer to the Wife is all indirection. His allegory has roots in at least three archetypal stories: *Cinderella*, *Cupid and Psyche*, and the Book of Job. It also has a literal level that suggests the difficulty of faith. Like Griselda, we are up against a logical dilemma. Either God was wrong when he created us, or he is wrong now in what he asks us as a consequence of our weakness to bear. Logically what we mean by God cannot exist. The illogical universe which faith sees an impossible God creating may well turn out to be the only possible one in which meaning and value exist.[38]

Two immediate responses to the *Clerk's Tale* exist, and the manuscripts suggest that Chaucer retained both of them.[39] The patience of Griselda has so impressed the Host that he hears none of the "game" of the song; he can think only of how nice it would be if his wife "at hoom had herd this legende ones." His appreciation pays the implicit tribute of rime royal to the tale, skipping back over the special stanza form of the song. In the last two lines he seems about to say something, then quickly changes his mind and subsides:

> As to my purpos, wiste ye my wille;
> But thyng that wol nat be, lat it be stille.   (E 1212g)

His later comment on the *Merchant's Tale* may well illuminate his reasons for silencing himself so suddenly.

In contrast to the Host, the Merchant finds inspiration in the final line of the Clerk's song, expressing the wives' insensitivity to their husbands' wretchedness: "And lat hym care and wepe and wrynge and waille!" (E 1212). Ignoring the Host's comment and reverting to couplets, the Merchant breaks out with a startling confession of his misery:

> "Weping and waylyng, care and oother sorwe
> I knowe ynogh, on even and a-morwe,"

Quod the Marchant, "and so doon other mo
That wedded been."   (E 1216)

His anguish knows no order or control. As a result, we do not get a clear
notion of its cause. He refuses to go into detail on his wife's "hye
malice[.] She is a shrewe at al." He would give anything to be free of
her. The most surprising information of all, he saves until almost the
end: he has been married just two months! Yet he feels he has suffered
more from her than any wifeless man in his whole life, "though that
men wolde him ryve / Unto the herte." His two months' experience
has led him to devise a theory of marriage hardly less extreme than
anything the Wife says:

> We wedded men lyven in sorwe and care.
> Assaye whoso wole, and he shal fynde
> That I seye sooth, by Seint Thomas of Ynde,
> As for the moore part, I sey nat alle.
> God shilde that it sholde so bifalle!   (E 1232)

His zeal for accuracy in the exception to his generalization—"I sey nat
alle"—receives a curious footnote from his tale. When the Host,
delighted to find a fellow sufferer, calls on him politely to "telle us
part" of his knowledge, he refuses to speak of his "owene soore," too
painful a subject to talk about further. In telling January's story, he is
speaking, not of himself, nor even of the majority of husbands like him,
but rather of those few happy husbands—the blind.

The Merchant carries the human comedy one step beyond the
Wife of Bath and the Pardoner.[40] They are aware that they are talking
about themselves, even though they do not realize how much they are
revealing. The Merchant, despite his resolve to tell no more about his
own misery, is making an oblique confession in his tale. The bitterness
with which he castigates the folly of January, the form the tale takes
in going from concept to full actualization, and especially the ambiguities of the opening epithalamion, which seems to be in the narrator's
mind as well as January's, throw inadvertent light on the Merchant's
two-month marriage and the thwarted expectations that must have
preceded it. In a sense the tale fully endorses man's freedom. It shows
us a conception of marriage at the beginning which the protagonist then

wills into complete actuality at the end. A remarkable series of images gives authenticity to the Merchant's icy vision. At the end we know nothing about his wife, but we know a great deal about him. We know whom he blames for his present anguish. We know the kind of world he thinks of himself as inhabiting.

The Merchant wastes no time in presenting to us January's folly. The sixty-year-old has a sudden vision of what marriage can mean to him. He has undergone a conversion, not from the lechery that still grips him, but from his conception of how to gratify his vice. Marriage, he has discovered, will win salvation for his soul and the availability of both a nurse and a mistress for his body, with the additional advantage of producing an heir for his property:

> "Noon oother lyf," seyde he, "is worth a bene;
> For wedlok is so esy and so clene,
> That in this world it is a paradys."
> Thus seyde this olde knyght, that was so wys.   (E 1266)

The narrator then seems to join him in his praise of marriage:

> And certeinly, as sooth as God is kyng,
> To take a wyf it is a glorious thyng,
> And namely whan a man is oold and hoor;
> Thanne is a wyf the fruyt of his tresor.   (E 1270)

The endorsement of January's expectations, the association of himself with January's folly, juxtaposed as it is to his earlier confession of misery, exposes a chapter in the narrator's autobiography and accounts for the length of this praise of marriage, for the patent exaggerations, for the occasional caustic criticisms, for the contradictions, and for the strange choice of exempla. Self-mockery provides a bitter pleasure for the Merchant, so quickly disabused of his illusions about marriage. The vision of the old man, looked after by his tireless and loving wife, "Thogh that he lye bedrede, til he sterve" (E 1292); the question as to how a married man can suffer any adversity; the impossibility of describing or even imagining the bliss of married folk, with the wife cheerfully meeting her husband's demands: " 'Do this,' seith he; 'Al redy, sire,' seith she" (E 1346); the fidelity and wisdom of wives that make their counsel always to be followed; their avoidance of waste and unnecessary expense; their willingness to help a poor husband in his work—the virtue and the joy and the cleanliness of it all, constitute so many strokes of the lash on the folly whose consequences he still shares with January.

It is interesting to see the slight additional bias given to the exempla that Chaucer drew from the *Melibeus*. Rebecca, Judith, Abigail, and Esther there exemplify the wise counsel that women can give. They reflect a certain carelessness about implications, even in the *Melibeus* and its source, since Prudence is using them to persuade her husband to take her advice. In the epithalamion they are at best irrelevant. Rebecca deceives her husband into giving the blessing to Jacob rather than Esau; Judith in her widowhood dazzles the besieging army with her beauty and, after winning her way by an elaborate subterfuge into Holofernes' favor, cuts off his head; Abigail saves her husband from David's vengeance, but in such a way that when she tells him of it he becomes as a stone and dies, freeing her to marry David; and Esther has her people's interests rather than her husband's at heart. A strange set of exemplary wives for January to choose in support of his illusions! Even stranger is the use he makes of Adam and Eve to justify his enthusiasm for marriage:

> The hye God, whan he hadde Adam maked,
> And saugh him al allone, bely-naked,
> God of his grete goodnesse seyde than,
> "Lat us now make an helpe unto this man
> Lyk to hymself"; and thanne he made him Eve.
> Heere may ye se, and heerby may ye preve,
> That wyf is mannes helpe and his confort,
> His paradys terrestre, and his disport.   (E 1332)

The image of paradise to describe the joys of marriage has already appeared, but here it is the paradise with Eve as the proof of what marriage can mean to a man. To fail to *see*, as January does, the part that Eve played in the expulsion from the garden—to be unaware of original sin, of the tree of the knowledge of good and evil—is quite simply to be blind. What January sees in marriage is a Garden of Eden with no forbidden tree. These images of the garden, the tree, and the blindness, linked in the misapplication of the Adam-and-Eve story, recur throughout the *Merchant's Tale*, attract other images, like the wax and the knife, and reach a kind of symbolic epiphany in the final scene.

The *Merchant's Tale* contains a series of disparate parts, which the ideas and images of the epithalamion fuse into a unified whole.[41] January's folly, developed fully in his mind, becomes gradually externalized in the two consultations with his friends, in his marriage to May, in the building of his private paradise, in his physical blindness, and in the scene of his betrayal, presided over by Pluto and Proserpine, so that finally all the aspects of his folly, even its imagery, have actualized themselves. Each of the sections has the same inventiveness, the same wealth of detail, that the epithalamion has, governed by a perverse pleasure in the exposure and castigation of folly.

The consultation that January calls to discuss his ideas of marriage emphasizes, first, January's age and his thoughts about salvation, then the importance of finding him a bride of twenty or younger, pliable to the hand like warm wax (E 1430), and then, in a compounding of the folly, a combination of salvation and the tender bride:

> Wherfore I sey yow pleynly, in a clause,
> I wol noon oold wyf han right for this cause.
> For if so were I hadde swich myschaunce,
> That I in hire ne koude han no plesaunce,
> Thanne sholde I lede my lyf in avoutrye,
> And go streight to the devel, whan I dye.   (E 1436)

January would also hate to see his heritage fall into strange hands for want of legitimate children. He proudly displays his knowledge of why men should marry, and in disclaiming any intention of living in "chastitee ful holily," lights on the image of a tree for his virility:

> Though I be hoor, I fare as dooth a tree
> That blosmeth er that fruyt ywoxen bee;
> And blosmy tree nys neither drye ne deed.
> I feele me nowhere hoor but on myn heed.   (E 1464)

Fruit has appeared earlier to suggest the relationship of a wife to an old man's wealth. The fruit portended by this blossoming out of his head will be strange indeed. The tree he cannot see in the Garden of Eden here springs to mind in a context that suggests lechery. The debate between his brothers follows, with Placebo endorsing his folly in a speech that praises the idea of a consultation and makes a travesty of the fact, and with Justinus giving him some home truths which are rejected out of hand. Placebo, given a second turn, reduces the argument to absurdity:

> "I seye it is a cursed man," quod he,
> "That letteth matrimoigne, sikerly." (E 1573)

The scene ends, after almost two hundred lines, with the decision to marry that January has made before the consultation. It does not advance the plot, but does advance the action. The externalization of January's ideas has begun. The exposure of folly, the dwelling with a masochistic fondness on every detailed instance, continues.

January, as it turns out, needs no help from his friends. He finds May on his own,

> And chees hire of his owene auctoritee;
> For love is blynd alday, and may nat see. (E 1598)

But he must go through again the ritual of consulting his friends. This time he wants no discussion of his decision to marry or his choice of a bride. One thing only pricks his conscience:

> "I have," quod he, "herd seyd, ful yoore ago,
> Ther may no man han parfite blisses two,—
> This is to seye, in erthe and eek in hevene.
> For though he kepe hym fro the synnes sevene,
> And eek from every branche of thilke tree,
> Yet is ther so parfit felicitee
> And so greet ese and lust in mariage,
> That evere I am agast now in myn age
> That I shal lede now so myrie a lyf,
> So delicat, withouten wo and stryf,
> That I shal have myn hevene in erthe heere.
> For sith that verray hevene is boght so deere
> With tribulacion and greet penaunce,
> How sholde I thanne, that lyve in swich plesaunce

As alle wedded men doon with hire wyvys,
Come to the blisse ther Crist eterne on lyve ys?" (E 1652)

Justinus, whose jaundiced view of marriage seems moderate and rational in the world the Merchant creates, is able to reassure him, pointing out that marriage may indeed turn out to be his purgatory, and referring to the Wife of Bath as having made clear what he means. That Alice can intrude into the Merchant's fictional world and become a legend, not just in her lifetime but in her very presence, is one of Chaucer's boldest touches.

The marriage ceremony that "made al siker ynogh with hoolynesse" receives a perfunctory treatment. Not so, however, the wedding feast. The comparison of the music to that created by legendary mythic figures gives way to the actual presence of Bacchus and Venus and Hymen. The feast and the mirth are in fact both at January's expense. Venus laughs,

For Januarie was bicome hir knyght,
And wolde bothe assayen his corage
In libertee, and eek in mariage. (E 1726)

The Merchant sums it up with an oblique reference to his own wedding:

Whan tendre youthe hath wedded stoupyng age,
Ther is swich myrthe that it may nat be writen.
Assayeth it youreself, thanne may ye witen
If that I lye or noon in this matiere. (E 1741)

May's beauty inspires in January impatience to be at his work and a confidence that his sexual prowess may be too much for her. Yet he fortifies himself, before retiring, with all the known aphrodisiacs he can lay his hands on. May's beauty also inspires the squire Damyan, "Which carf biforn the knyght ful many a day" (E 1773). Venus, whose dancing "with hire fyrbrond" at the feast seems at first good-natured mockery, turns out to have hurt Damyan so sorely "with hire brond, / As that she bar it daunsynge in hire hond" (E 1778), that he takes to his bed with the grief and the pain. The ensuing rhetorical extravagance—

O perilous fyr, that in the bedstraw bredeth!
O famulier foo, that his servyce bedeth!
O servant traytour . . . (E 1785)

195

—with its outrage at this anticipated "fruit" of January's hoar blossoms, adds another mockery to the occasion and provides another ironical foreshadowing in the prayer for January: "God graunte thee thyn hoomly fo t'espye!" (E 1792).

The physical ugliness of January's lovemaking and the moral ugliness of his sexual aggression come out strongly in what follows, and help to "place" the inflated rhetoric that expresses outrage at Damyan. Most of these elements coalesce in January's fatuous reassurance to May while he is preparing her for the deliberateness of his sexual technique:

> A man may do no synne with his wyf,
> Ne hurte hymselven with his owene knyf.   (E 1840)

In this couplet Damyan as carver for his master joins the first wife, who gave the apple to her husband before both were driven from the garden for the original sin.

The exchange of letters between Damyan and May proceeds to a rhetorical accompaniment that is entirely cynical, now sympathizing with Damyan's plight (E 1866 ff.), now praising the thoughtfulness of January in noticing Damyan's absence and planning to visit his sickbed (E 1897, 1919), now raising the fatuous question whether it is destiny or chance or some constellation that accounts for May's response to Damyan's love letter (E 1967 ff.), and finally praising as excellent May's "franchise," in contrast to the hard hearts some women show their lovers (E 1986 ff.). This rhetoric has the effect of exposing all the characters as petty and undeserving. The Merchant's intention is another matter. He makes a great deal of fuss over the number of days May remains in bed after the wedding night, pointing out that it just doesn't do for the bride to appear in public until four, or in any event three, days have passed. He is inclined to be mealymouthed, using on one occasion a euphemism (E 1951)—though a few lines later he has May put her lover's missive frankly down the privy—drawing the curtain on what happens after January has his wife take off her clothes on her return from reading Damyan's letter (E 1962 ff.), and apologizing for his frankness when May joins Damyan in the tree (E 2350; cf. 2366 ff., 2376 ff.). The rhetoric is for the Merchant one of the conventions of storytelling, to be brought in whenever an opportunity for it arises.

The compulsion to realize his image of marriage in every detail must play some part in January's decision to make a garden, a private paradise, for his own use with May. The beauty of this garden, "walled al with stoon," provides an apt image for January's ugly envelopment of May. The garden, furthermore, has a "smale wyket" with a single silver "clyket," which January bears about with him always. January intends to enjoy the delights of both his wife and his garden exclusively. The two even become associated in his mind—

> And thynges whiche that were nat doon abedde,
> He in the gardyn parfourned hem and spedde.   (E 2052)

May, whose youth he has thought of as pliable like warm wax, has indeed taken an impression (E 1978) from Damyan. She uses some actual warm wax to furnish him with the shape of the key he needs to get into her garden. Meanwhile, to much rhetorical accompaniment, as if compelled to reflect even the inadvertent aspects of his image of marriage, January has gone blind. This blindness occasions a further bearing-out of the imagery. He and May become literally "o flessh" (E 1335). For after a month or two of despair, during which he wishes someone had slain both him and May so that no one should enjoy her even after his death, he recovers somewhat, taking his adversity with patience:

> Save, out of doute, he may nat forgoon
> That he nas jalous everemoore in oon;
> Which jalousye it was so outrageous,
> That neither in halle, n'yn noon oother hous,
> Ne in noon oother place, neverthemo,
> He nolde suffre hire for to ryde or go,
> But if that he had hond on hire alway.   (E 2091)

The seven negatives in a single clause form a suitable adornment for his jealousy.

The Merchant, having prepared everything for his final scene (with the exception of Damyan's key to the garden, which is provided in the

lines immediately following), steps out for a moment from behind his
fiction and gives us a further glimpse of his purpose in telling the tale:

> O Januarie, what myghte it thee availle,
> Thogh thou myghte se as fer as shippes saille?
> For as good is blynd deceyved be
> As to be deceyved whan a man may se.
>   Lo, Argus, which that hadde an hondred yen,
> For al that evere he koude poure or pryen,
> Yet was he blent, and, God woot, so been mo,
> That wenen wisly that it be nat so.
> Passe over is an ese, I sey namoore.   (E 2115)

This passage might be termed the corollary of eyes to the cynical theory
of marriage that the Merchant is insinuating by his tale. Stated another
way, it might read: Eyes make no difference to the blindness of happy
husbands. Which corollary he then sets out to demonstrate with the
aid of another mismatched couple, Pluto and Prosperpine.

Pluto, Proserpine, and all their fairies have been habitués of January's
garden since the day he had it made. They are present at one end of the
garden on that critical eighth of June, when January invites his love in
the language of the Song of Songs to go to the garden with him, his hand
on her always, and she indicates in sign language to Damyan that he
should get there ahead of them. Pluto is rightly shocked at May's
perfidy. At the very moment when she is proclaiming her virtue to
January—"I am a gentil womman and no wenche" (E 2202)—she
is motioning her lover out from under a bush and into a pear tree. Pluto
foresees what is to happen, finds the whole affair typical of women's
treachery to men, quotes Solomon on the impossibility of finding a good
woman, and proposes to restore January's sight, so that he can "espye"
his "hoomly fo." Pluto proves no match for Proserpine, who first vows
to give May "suffisant answere, / And alle women after, for hir sake"
(E 2267), and then demolishes the case he has made. Not only has she
read her Bible and her classical history, but she shows herself a more
critical reader than her husband. She knows the true meaning of the
passage he has quoted. She knows enough about Solomon to question his
credentials as an authority, especially since he had the nerve to call
women "jangleresses."

I am a womman, nedes moot I speke,
Or elles swelle til myn herte breke.   (E 2306)

Pluto has the good sense to give in, and Proserpine the grace to accept
his capitulation. Their brief argument gives a kind of supernatural
sanction and an eternal time span to the Merchant's vision of the relations between men and women.

The tree, the garden, and the blindness come into their own in the
final scene. There the jealous January is overjoyed with his wife's
appetite for fruit, as a symptom of her supposed pregnancy.

"Allas!" quod he, "that I ne had heer a knave
That koude clymbe! Allas, allas," quod he,
"That I am blynd!" "Ye, sire, no fors," quod she;
"But wolde ye vouche sauf, for Goddes sake,
The pyrie inwith youre armes for to take,
For wel I woot that ye mystruste me,
Thanne sholde I clymbe wel ynogh," quod she,
"So I my foot myghte sette upon youre bak."   (E 2345)

January's head now bears the fruit that his hoar blossoms portended and
that his wife has long desired. There is evidence in the Miller's Prologue
that Chaucer knew the joke about cuckolds' horns.[42] If he did not,
he has unwittingly devised the most striking instance of it in literature.
As January's wife steps from his back into the branches of the tree and
cuckolds him, the branches spring from his head as horns—horns that
everyone but him can see. As long as he jealously embraces the tree,
he remains the image of the betrayed husband, cuckolded in his own
horns. Straightening up, his eyesight restored, he sees simply the limbs
of a tree—a tree his wife soon persuades him is not the tree of evil in
his garden. Marriage for January is still the Garden of Eden without
the forbidden tree, the vision he had of it in the beginning fulfilled.

For the Merchant's sanity, January's happiness and the happiness of
other husbands must be blind. He cannot bear to envisage a genuinely
happy relationship between men and women. The bitterness that he
expresses reflects the disappointment of the same expectations that he
assigns to January, and now castigates as folly. His brief marriage has
sent him from a foolish optimism to a cynical pessimism. As he uses May

to expose January, and then later January to expose May, he thinks of himself as enlightened and disabused. His vision of things is as self-centered and limited as it was before. From not seeing evil anywhere, he now sees it everywhere. He sees it growing from minds like his own and January's, the one fully aware of, the other blind to, the consequences he has willed into being. In contrast to the Clerk, who maintains an amused objectivity vis-à-vis the extremes he depicts, the Merchant has a deep emotional involvement in both the folly and the cynicism. His relentless exposure of the folly gives him a perverse pleasure: the pain is self-inflicted. The torment that he suffers from his shrew of a wife, and that he can scarcely bear to mention, is not.

The *Merchant's Tale*, like the one preceding it, incites the Host into comment on his own marriage. He has a fellow-feeling for January and the Merchant, even though he recognizes the distinction between his own wife and May. The former is "trewe as any steel," and yet a "labbyng shrewe" with a heap of other vices. The Host in confidence admits his regret at being tied to her, then recognizes that he would be foolish to go on enumerating her faults:

> And cause why, it sholde reported be
> And toold to hire of somme of this meynee,—
> Of whom, it nedeth nat for to declare,
> Syn wommen konnen outen swich chaffare.   (E 2438)

This oblique reference to the Wife of Bath shows the extent to which Chaucer's imagination is working dramatically at this stage in the development of the *Canterbury Tales*. The passage could not have been written without the parallel and fully developed account of Goodelief's shrewishness in mind. Between the *Melibeus*, which inspired that account, and the *Merchant's Tale* looms the figure of the Wife of Bath and the impact on the pilgrims made by her monologue. The possibility of an alliance between Goodelief and Alice would frighten braver souls than Harrie Baillie into an unwonted caution. The possibility becomes more ominous with every mile of the pilgrims' journey.

The Host requests a tale of love from the next storyteller, the Squire. The story that results provides an interlude in the discussion of marriage.

Unfinished, it has a bewildering number of strands, to match perhaps the youthful enthusiasm of the teller.[43] As in other instances, Chaucer seems to be experimenting with the combination of several genres. It is a question whether he could have brought them to some meaningful fusion as he did with the Nun's Priest's and the Merchant's tales. The tale starts off in the remote but ideal court of Cambiuskan, with a collection of magical objects, modulates from pure romance to comic realism, and breaks off after a complaint voiced by a deserted falcon against her faithless lover, a tercelet. Of the magical objects, which include a horse of brass, a mirror, and a sword, only a ring that permits the wearer to speak and understand bird language (and also to know the healing properties of herbs) has been used. Far from advancing the plot, the device simply adds another unrelated element. The description of the noble King Cambiuskan includes the striking line "Of his corage as any centre stable" (F 22). The common people indulge in amusing speculation on how the magic of the various objects works; those who have stayed up all night, dancing, eating, and drinking, go "galpying" to their rest and dream the morning away. Canace, who has avoided a hangover by going to bed with the sun, gets up for an early morning walk; the falcon she encounters starts her formal complaint by using Chaucer's favorite line (already employed by the Knight and the Merchant):

> That pitee renneth soone in gentil herte,   (F 479)
>
> . . . .
>
> Is preved alday . . . .   (F 481)

The Squire, after disclaiming his ability to describe Canace (F 34 ff.), skipping over a feast because it is already "pryme," (F 63 ff.), making a bad pun on the knight's style, "so heigh" that he "kan nat clymben over" it (F 105–106), and deferring to Lancelot when it comes to the fine points of social intercourse (F 283 ff.), prods himself into untying the knot, not of his tale, but of Canace's walk:

> The knotte why that every tale is toold,
> If it be taried til that lust be coold
> Of hem that han it after herkned yoore,
> The savour passeth ever lenger the moore,

> For fulsomnesse of his prolixitee;
> And by the same resoun, thynketh me,
> I sholde to the knotte condescende,
> And maken of hir walkyng soone an ende. (F 408)

The Squire then ends the second part of his tale, largely devoted to the falcon's lament, with a promise of adventures and battles "That nevere yet was herd so grete mervailles" (F 660), and with a plot summary that provides for the recovery of her love by the falcon through the mediation of Cambalo, the taking of many a city by Cambiuskan, Algarsif's winning Theodora to his wife with the help of a brass horse, and a seemingly incestuous match, after combat by Cambalo with two brothers, between him and his sister Canace.[44] The description of the horse of brass provides a key to the Squire's imagination:

> For it so heigh was, and so brood and long,
> So wel proporcioned for to been strong,
> Right as it were a steede of Lumbardye;
> Therwith so horsly, and so quyk of ye,
> As it a gentil Poilleys courser were. (F 195)

People wonder "How that it koude gon," and so may we with a tale so "plotly."

The Franklin, impressed by the promise of the Squire, makes the first comment on his tale. He praises him the more highly for the contrast between him and his own son, who gambles and consorts with the wrong people:

> I have my sone snybbed, and yet shal,
> For he to vertu listeth nat entende. (F 689)

The fact that the Knight and his son travel together makes the alienation of the Franklin's son the more painful for him. In the atmosphere of close association that the storytelling has fostered, the revelation of such feelings has become common. The Franklin's recognition of the Squire's quality has the same generous spirit that is one of the main points of the portrait in the Prologue. It sets the tone for his performance as a storyteller.

The Host, missing the generosity and taking offense at what he no doubt takes to be snobbery on the Franklin's part, will have none of the latter's interest in gentle upbringing—" 'Straw for youre gentillesse!' quod oure Hoost" (F 695)—and rudely orders him to tell his tale without any further delay. The Franklin's response is almost too mild:

> I wol yow nat contrarien in no wyse
> As fer as that my wittes wol suffyse.
> I preye to God that it may plesen yow;
> Thanne woot I wel that it is good ynow.   (F 708)

Does the Franklin's deference mean a lack of discrimination on his part? Is he mocking the Host with his praise of his literary standards? Or does his mildness reflect the habitual politeness of a man secure in his relationship with others? In his tale he reverts to the discussion of marriage and continues implicitly his remarks to the Squire, despite the Host's prohibition.

The ideal of marriage projected by the union of Dorigen and Arveragus incorporates the delicacy of feelings, the respect and admiration for women, associated with courtly love. The narrative records their wedding and comments on it in a way that contrasts with the epithalamion at the beginning of the *Merchant's Tale*. Instead of the egocentric fantasies, the dreams of self-indulgence, that inspire January, Arveragus and Dorigen think primarily of each other's welfare. In view of some recent critics' efforts to denigrate the Franklin and his concept of marriage, it is important to see the way he makes the relationship evolve. First comes the service of the knight, "many a labour, many a greet emprise," expressing his love. Dorigen's recognition of his worthiness and her sympathy for his long and humble service lead her to accept him for her husband and her lord, "Of swich lordshipe as men han over hir wyves" (F 743). Then, of his free will, he swears never to assume any power over her against her will, never to show her jealousy, but to obey her in everything as if he were still her lover; and she responds by promising to be his humble, true wife, praying that there may never be strife between them "as in my gilt." The tale thus opens, as it closes, with an instance of the influence that generosity of spirit can have in personal relationships.[45]

The Franklin's comments on the marriage emphasize the relevance to what other pilgrims have said—the Wife of Bath's concern for mastery and for freedom from constraint (F 764–70), the Clerk's stress on patience (F 771–90), the Merchant's ironic concentration on happiness in marriage (F 803–805). He recognizes the human frailty that puts every man in need of forgiveness:

> For in this world, certein, ther no wight is
> That he ne dooth or seith somtyme amys.
> Ire, siknesse, or constellacioun,
> Wyn, wo, or chaungynge of complexioun
> Causeth ful ofte to doon amys or speken.
> On every wrong a man may nat be wreken. (F 784)

His understanding tends to express itself succinctly, in the easy generalizations associated with the proverb, as in the final line of the quotation above, or in his vivid image of the impact "maistrie" has:

> Whan maistrie comth, the God of Love anon
> Beteth his wynges, and farewel, he is gon! (F 766)

Other examples are seen in the transition to the subject of liberty, in the very next line, "Love is a thyng as any spirit free"; and in the paradox of the wife who finds her husband "Servant in love, and lord in mariage" (F 793) because of his commitment to the ideals of courtly love. The Franklin sounds almost too well satisfied with himself and with the pleasant life he leads. His generosity, the absence of any hint of aggression in his comments, and his recognition of a common humanity mitigate this tendency to smugness.

The story he tells has a deceptively bland surface, with its delicacy of emotion, its social elegance, and its operatic speeches. Yet within its limits it makes firm discriminations, authenticates its insights by form, and strengthens narrative conviction by the development of its central image. The firm discriminations, the formal support for insight, and the development of the image are all three operant when Dorigen, refusing Aurelius' suit, thinks of the rocks as a way of expressing her feelings. She has already given him his answer. If she goes beyond a definite refusal, it is out of gentilesse, a sympathy with someone whose unhappiness she is causing.

> "Aurelie," quod she, "by heighe God above,
> Yet wolde I graunte yow to been youre love,
> Syn I yow se so pitously complayne.
> Looke what day that endelong Britayne
> Ye remoeve alle the rokkes, stoon by stoon,
> That they ne lette ship ne boot to goon,—
> I seye, whan ye han maad the coost so clene
> Of rokkes that ther nys no stoon ysene,
> Thanne wol I love yow best of any man,
> Have heer my trouthe, in al that evere I kan." (F 998)

She then makes clear that she has picked what she thinks an impossibility as the condition for her yielding to Aurelius.

What she does not explain to Aurelius is the reason why the rocks came into her mind. She has seen them before, looking out from the Breton coast at the ships sailing hither and yon; she saw them then as a menace to her husband's return. What seems on the surface a promise to commit adultery, under certain conditions, expresses in a deeper sense her concern for Arveragus. She has actually transformed the rocks, which she earlier thought of as a useless element in God's creation, into a symbol for the permanence and strength of her marriage. The two prayers—one by Dorigen before this "rash promise," the other by Aurelius after it—emphasize the extent to which she has succeeded in transforming the rocks. Dorigen first questions God's purpose in creating the rocks; then prays:

> But thilke God that made wynd to blowe
> As kepe my lord! this my conclusion.
> To clerkes lete I al disputison.
> But wolde God that alle thise rokkes blake
> Were sonken into helle for his sake! (F 892)

Meanwhile, her friends, recognizing that the sight of the sea gives her no pleasure, seek amusement elsewhere and eventually arrange the day in the garden where Aurelius reveals his passion.

After the "rash promise," it is Aurelius' turn to pray for the removal of the rocks. But his prayer is both longer and more desperate than Dorigen's. He pleads with Apollo for the miracle of a two-year flood tide high enough to cover all of Brittany's rocks, imagining that if Apollo the sun and his sister the Moon keep the same speed the "spryng flood" will last both night and day. Failing that, he would simply have Apollo and his sister

> to synken every rok adoun
> Into hir owene dirke regioun
> Under the ground, ther Pluto dwelleth inne.   (F 1075)

Another element distinguishing the laments is the consistent paganism of Aurelius'. Not only does he pray to Apollo but he envisions himself going barefoot to the temple at Delphi if his prayers are granted. This taint carries over to the magic wrought by clerks of Orleans, called "folye,"

> As in oure dayes is nat worth a flye,—
> For hooly chirches feith in oure bileve
> Ne suffreth noon illusioun us to greve.   (F 1134)

It is called also "supersticious cursednesse" (F 1272) and "swiche illusiouns and swiche meschaunces / As hethen folk useden in thilke dayes" (F 1293). On the other hand, Dorigen refers consistently to a single deity, creator of mankind in his image (F 880), that, as she puts it, "yaf me soule and lyf" (F 983). The distinction between her religion and Aurelius' does not go so far as explicit Christianity. Dorigen is on her way to the "temple" when Aurelius intercepts her with the word that the rocks are "aweye," and she refers in her subsequent lament only to pagan heroines. To compound the confusing anachronisms, the social arrangements belong strictly to the medieval period. People live in castles, amuse themselves dancing and singing in gardens, seek "worshipe and honour" in the knightly practice of arms, and study law at the University of Orleans.

As the story develops, the rocks have an important role to play. Aurelius' brother, distressed by what has happened, suddenly remembers the "magyk natureel" that some of his fellow clerks studied and the "apparences" he has heard of their making. With such an "apparence," a clerk might make

> To mannes sighte, that alle the rokkes blake
> Of Britaigne weren yvoyded everichon.   (F 1159)

A clerk might be able to change the appearance of things "a wowke
or two," not the reality, and so cure his brother of his despair over
Dorigen.[46] Although the agreement they make with the clerk in
Orleans is "To remoeven alle the rokkes of Britayne" (F 1221), he
directs his efforts

> to maken illusioun,
> By swich an apparence or jogelrye—
> I ne kan no termes of astrologye—
> That she and every wight sholde wene and seye
> That of Britaigne the rokkes were aweye.   (F 1268)

He obtains corresponding results: "thurgh his magik, for a wyke or
tweye, / It semed that alle the rokkes were aweye" (F 1296).

Aurelius at first takes the appearance for the reality. He begins to
discover the reality when he meets his lady at the temple and tries to
tell her what he thinks he has achieved. It takes him twenty-eight lines
of tortured syntax—of expressions of his own agony, of excuses and
self-deprecations, of recognition of her power over him, of reminders
of her promise—before he can come to the point. The speech reflects
Aurelius' growing awareness of the obstacle, present from the beginning
and despite appearances. The rocks and what Dorigen has made them
represent—the strength, the steadfastness, the permanence of her love
for Arveragus—remain. A segment of the speech will show Aurelius'
difficulty:

> For, madame, wel ye woot what ye han hight—
> Nat that I chalange any thyng of right
> Of yow, my sovereyn lady, but youre grace—
> But in a gardyn yond, at swich a place,
> Ye woot right wel what ye bihighten me;
> And in myn hand youre trouthe plighten ye
> To love me best—God woot, ye seyde so,
> Al be that I unworthy am therto.
> Madame, I speke it for the honour of yow
> Moore than to save myn hertes lyf right now,—
> I have do so as ye comanded me.   (F 1333)

Five lines later he can finally bring himself to blurt out in one breath what he has come to tell Dorigen: "But wel I woot the rokkes been aweye."

Ironically, the need for removing the rocks has long since disappeared with Arveragus' return from Britain. His temporary absence, when Dorigen hears from Aurelius about the rocks, forces her to face the situation alone. She never doubts Aurelius' word, but she is astounded by what he has said, knowing that "It is agayns the proces of nature" (F 1345). She returns home and for the two days of Arveragus' absence complains against this stroke of Fortune which will bring her dishonor or death; she can see no other alternative. She recalls all the noble maidens and wives who have chosen death in similar situations. Toward the end of her complaint, a few famous women come to mind who did not die—Penelope, Artemisia, Bilyea, Rodogone, and Valeria. Thus, though she is "Purposynge evere that she wolde deye" (F 1458), her resolution finds expression in words only, in words of diminishing strength. The third night Arveragus returns, finds out what has happened, and makes the painful decision:

> "Ye shul youre trouthe holden, by my fay!
> For God so wisly have mercy upon me,
> I hadde wel levere ystiked for to be
> For verray love which that I to yow have,
> But if ye sholde youre trouthe kepe and save.
> Trouthe is the hyeste thyng that man may kepe"—
> But with that word he brast anon to wepe.   (F 1480)

The respect Arveragus shows for a woman's word has shocking impact. We must, of course, accept the story's convention that everyone involved considers the "rash promise" a binding obligation. The Franklin recognizes the difficulty of the suspension of disbelief:

> Paraventure an heep of yow, ywis,
> Wol holden hym a lewed man in this
> That he wol putte his wyf in jupartie.   (F 1495)

The evidence of Arveragus' respect for his wife as an independent human being, whose obligations are as binding as his own, whose obligations, because of their marriage, in fact bind him, completes the obstacle to Aurelius' purpose and convinces him when he learns of it that the rocks are still there. In the face of a mutual love so strong, which Arveragus' decision has now finally transformed the rocks into symbolizing, Aurelius cannot bring himself to hold Dorigen to her promise. He catches the contagion of gentilesse reflected in Dorigen's grief-stricken cry,

> Unto the gardyn, as myn housbonde bad,
> My trouthe for to holde, allas! allas! (F 1513)

and transmits the germ himself to the clerk.

The Franklin has avoided the inclusion of any Christian doctrine in his picture of the ideal marriage. His tale thus resembles Boethius' *De Consolatione Philosophiae* in its eschewing of revelation and authority. At the crisis, Arveragus shows a clear recognition that his relationship with his wife is not self-contained, that it depends on loyalty to values outside the marriage: "Trouthe is the hyeste thyng that man may kepe" (F 1479). In this acknowledgment of loyalties beyond the human level, the tale implicitly supports Christian doctrine. Marriage of course joins fallible human beings. The Franklin's recognition that all men need "suffrance," that even a marriage like the one between Arveragus and Dorigen will encounter difficulties, constitutes the strongest evidence against condemning him for self-satisfaction, and justifies his use of such a firm, cold image as the rocks to reinforce the meaning of his tale.

The contagion of gentilesse which brings the *Franklin's Tale* to a close pays compliment to three of the pilgrims the narrator admires. One of them, the Squire, shows promise of attaining the kind of principled life the Franklin recognizes as good. The other two, the Knight and the Clerk, have confirmed in their tales their claims to be living it. None of these pilgrims obtrudes his morality. The Franklin, the Clerk, and the Knight join the Nun's Priest in an ease of manner at the opposite extreme from another group of pilgrims, whose assertions of morality have a comic effect.[47] The two most prominent of these last give their tales in the vicinity of Canterbury. The Canon's Yeoman's efforts to make sure that we recognize his condemnation of the wicked canon's con game throw an amusing light on his sympathy for his lazy gigolo of a priest. The Manciple's reiteration of the morality learned at his mother's knee has the ludicrous effect of contradicting its own advice.

At the other pole of the pilgrimage, in the vicinity of London, stand the Host and the Parson. Their quarrel in the Man of Law's Epilogue motivates the Host's swearing and the Parson's silence throughout the journey.[48] When the Host finally calls on the Parson as the last of the storytellers, the latter prays Jesus,

> for his grace, wit me sende
> To shewe yow the wey, in this viage,
> Of thilke parfit glorious pilgrymage
> That highte Jerusalem celestial.   (I 51)

Are we to take the direct morality of the treatise on penitence and the seven deadly sins as a fulfillment of this prayer?[49] The Parson, in the Prologue, is twice represented as a doer first, then a preacher. Chaucer's description of him makes him sound vigorous, outspoken, and interesting. If Chaucer intended the treatise for the *Parson's Tale*, he has not carried out the characterization given in the Prologue, and has, in the final story, violated one of the main thrusts of the pilgrimage—the strength of implicit morality. In any event, the final scene would not have belonged to the Parson. That would have transpired back at the Tabard, with the marriage theme and the Wife of Bath, the Host and his wife, the variety and interaction of character, the "goddes foyson" of incident and meaning reasserting the primacy of a literal world. In his final plan for the ending, Chaucer gave even greater stress to the game of storytelling by turning it into a contest. The literary interest, so marked a feature of the B² fragment, would find a comic fulfillment in the Host's choice for the prize and the critical issues that such a choice would raise. The "soper" shared, as well as the prize "soper at oure aller cost," would epitomize the drama and the community of the pilgrimage; the celebration would give final expression to the living voices of a variety of characters, to the sense of a world in which value is experienced, to the "ernest and game" of a mind sharp, gentle and generous, sophisticated and humorous, "Of his corage as any centre stable."

VII

fReeÒom to chanɢe

"Thou shalt namoore"

THE autonomy for the pilgrims to be themselves and the effort on the part of the author to report accurately on what they are—these two conditions determine the fiction that there is no fiction in the *Canterbury Tales*. The pilgrims will end up precisely where they began, at the Tabard eating a meal. Will they be changed by their experience of the road, of the shrine, and of the storytelling? Or will they be, as is usual in comedy, unaltered by the experience of exposure and revelation, by the association with one another for five days, by the patterned meanings their activities generate? Is the world projected in the *Canterbury Tales* essentially static, with the encounters making no difference in the comic rigidities of character? Certainly for some of the pilgrims the answer would be yes. The Miller evinces no desire for change in his quarrel with the Reeve. Satisfied with the world as he conceives it to be, he enjoys the discomfiture of his characters and remains confident he can shrug off any similar mishaps. Toughness, strength, and virility shield him from the self-doubt that impels the Reeve to regard the story of a carpenter as a challenge. The Reeve, though more sophisticated and more vulnerable, finds himself compelled by his choleric nature and by his inability to envision alternatives, to join battle on the Miller's terms. His tale sees life as a series of battles in which alertness to the enemy's vulnerabilities proves decisive, now for one character, now for another. His portrait in the Prologue shows him living off the vulnerabilities of others. From these tales and from the Shipman's, the Friar's and the Summoner's, we might infer that the fabliau world generally was one in which meaningful change did not occur, in which plot mechanisms dominate and render the characters' responses either irrelevant or ludicrously inappropriate.

To the extent that it mocks the very notion of change, the *Merchant's Tale* strengthens this conclusion about the fabliau world. January's great vision of the difference marriage will make in his life has little of the consequence he imagines. He uses his wife as he has earlier used other women. The lust that possesses his mind imposes on his body beyond its capacities and forces him to artificial stimulants, both internal and external. Marriage does not win him the exclusive ownership of a young woman as he has thought it would. Instead, it exposes his folly, making him the archetype of the mismatched and deluded dotard. Yet the *Merchant's Tale* differs fundamentally from the typical fabliau. It confirms negatively man's freedom. In it we see a man bringing into external being all the elements of an internal vision, even the implicit elements he is not aware of. January chooses. Then he bears the consequences of his freedom. That his choice is folly, that it finds a fulfillment only his blindness makes tolerable, does not alter the fact that the chief agency is his own, that January is the architect of his world. Furthermore, on a different level, the mocking of January's happiness as a husband only partly conceals the change that motivates the Merchant's bitter *Weltanschauung*. Two months of marriage have altered completely his view of life. For him no fate can now be so grim as the one he mocks in January's vision and castigates himself for choosing.

More fundamental, because in the direction of life and further freedom, is the change that has occurred for the Wife of Bath, as she reveals it in her Prologue. The Wife is a figure of high comedy because she fails to recognize the change that culminates her experience of marriage. She continues to preach her doctrine of female sovereignty as the secret of wedded bliss, despite its irrelevance to her relationship with her fifth husband, the only one she can remember vividly, whom she pays the repeated tribute of involuntary blessing. The revelation of love climaxes and transforms the sterile record of forty years—the three old men, the reveler whom she remembers mostly as absent or dead, the many casual and undifferentiated couplings—reconciling her to the loss of beauty and pith, and keeping alive her expectations of an inconceivable sixth husband; but the revelation has made no dent on her stubborn, indomitable intellect. The two stories that were the Wife of Bath's reflect the change that took place, both in Chaucer's conception of her and in her life, when the climactic struggle with Jankyn occurred and her quest for love found its miraculous expression. The story that Chaucer transferred to the Shipman shows the intransigence that belonged to her theory and dictated her conduct with the three old men. It cynically displays the convertibility of money and sex, and depicts a woman capable of handling herself in any contingency. The story that Chaucer finally assigned her reflects the richer paradoxes of the more deeply experienced Wife of Bath. The theory, the love, and the miraculous transformation are all there. The Wife sees the transformation as physical, to be realized in the future. We see it as wish fulfillment, and as reflection of a moment of genuine alchemy when dross became gold.

Several of the pilgrims are confirmed in their freedom, as the Miller, the Reeve, and the Shipman are in the reverse; the free need no moment of discovery to confirm their ability to change; they meet their obligations and the challenges of others with responses adapted to the occasion and directed to the issues involved, rather than to the person. The *Knight's Tale*, which was Chaucer's before the *Canterbury Tales* and the Knight came into existence, explores objectively the relationship of two rivals in love, who before they see Emily are cousins, blood brothers, and fellow sufferers under Theseus' despotic power. Their relationship ends in reconciliation generously brought about by the dying Arcite. Theseus' role suggests the ineffectuality of power wielded willfully. It takes Athens' lord an inordinate time, "By processe and by lengthe of certeyn yeres" (A 2967), to call the parlement that confirms with earthly sanction what the "sighte above" has already clearly prepared. The decisions for once bear their anticipated fruit. This story of chivalry and devoted service, with its implications for order and for the meaningful exercise of power, befits the character already developed for the Knight in the Prologue. The authority of this character, whose worthiness everyone acknowledges, exercises a benign influence over the pilgrimage, stopping the Monk and reconciling Pardoner and Host on the only two occasions when a power stronger than Harrie Baillie's is needed.

Two pilgrims whose powers are more subtle, and who are both as a consequence undervalued by the Host, are Chaucer and the Clerk. Chaucer meets the Host's challenge, and the Clerk, the Wife of Bath's, with a finesse and a versatility that do not involve aggression. In a sense, Chaucer's answer to the Host's insensitivity is not just the *Melibeus* but the whole of the *Canterbury Tales*. The Host says, ". . . the substance is in me, / If any thyng shal wel reported be" (B 3994). But his account of the pilgrimage has not survived. The Clerk's impulse is to learn and teach. His teaching turns out to be as oblique as Chaucer's own. Though the Wife makes little of the Aristotelianism of his performance, she may absorb something from the lesson of his manner. Another character, the Franklin, like the Clerk somewhat belittled by the Host, expresses in his tale his appreciation of the Clerk. He has earlier expressed his admiration of the relationship the Knight has achieved with his son the Squire. That these men influence him by their very presence on the pilgrimage is implicit in the contagion of gentilesse depicted in his tale. His own generosity of spirit responds to theirs, as his compliment to them at the end of his tale acknowledges. But his tale, as the rocks suggest, involves more than a fellowship of good feeling. The mutual forbearance of Arveragus and Dorigen in their marriage recognizes human frailty and mitigates its consequences. Arveragus' regard for the importance of Dorigen's word carries over into marriage the revolutionary respect for women of the courtly love tradition. The Franklin finds in the rocks an image adequate to the change in human relations that he advocates.

The influence on the Franklin of men he admires merely strengthens tendencies already present in his nature. Two pilgrims undergo more drastic changes—what, in a sense, amount to reversals—on the road to Canterbury. When the Yeoman rides with his master the Canon fast enough to overtake the company midway between Ospring and Canterbury, he boasts of his master's talents and shows no sign of disaffection. The Host, with a few searching questions, changes his life. What before has seemed exciting adventure, under the tutelage of a gifted sage, he now rejects. The suddenness of his conversion suggests that doubts about alchemy have been building up. The kind of experience that joining the company of pilgrims represents—the taste of a sunlit world away from the dark and dedicated zeal of experiment—breaks the dam of suppression. The Yeoman is suddenly free from the authority of his mentor, awake to the meaning of the seven years, the hole-and-corner existence, the retrieval from repeated failure of a diminishing capital, the vain loss of breath, and color, and time. He reveals in the enthusiasm of his sudden release a shallow nature, eager to display for the uninitiated the ill-digested terminology of his abandoned craft, unable once he has started to stop short of exhausting his lore and exposing his limitations, proud of all that he has retained from the wasted years. His talk makes clear that though his knowledge of alchemy and of its philosophical basis is limited, he can write the handbook of instructions on how to use alchemy to dupe the unwary. The moral fervor with which he condemns such use is not only excessive but selective; he seems unaware of the greed that motivates the victim. The victim in the episodes that he recounts, a lazy parasite of a priest, kept by the woman he lodges with, escapes criticism in the Yeoman's eagerness to castigate the sharp canon. Despite the reversal in the direction of his life, the Yeoman represents no great gain or loss in the community from which his master flees.

A more subtle and important change occurs when the Pardoner is called on for a tale. His purposes in the beginning are clearly aggressive. He will impress the pilgrims with the success he enjoys. He will shock them into awareness by his flouting of morality. He will astonish them with the tricks and skills he uses against his customary audiences. The change that occurs comes from the unwonted experience of sharing, of belonging for the first time to a community instead of preying on it. It is represented by the difference in tone between the concluding lines of his Prologue, willful and contemptuous—

> What, trowe ye, that whiles I may preche,
> And wynne gold and silver for I teche,
> That I wol lyve in poverte wilfully?
> Nay, nay, I thoghte it nevere, trewely!   (C 442)

—and the blessing at the end of the pitch, as he breaks the spell of his typical performance and returns to the audience actually listening to him:

> And lo, sires, thus I preche.
> And Jhesu Crist, that is oure soules leche,

So graunte yow his pardoun to receyve,
For that is best; I wol yow nat deceyve.   (C 918)

His dropping of the serious manner and his resumption of the pitch, directed now at the pilgrims, represent an effort on his part to carry the association still further. Having impressed the pilgrims with his skill and shared with them a typical performance, he feels secure enough to clown it a little for them, to present the imaginary and ludicrous image of pardon at each milestone, to congratulate them on their luck of having a "suffisant pardoneer" in the company. That the Host fails to respond in kind, that the Pardoner loses his temper, that order has to be restored by the Knight are the consequences of misjudgment on the Pardoner's part. The Host was not the one to ask; the pilgrims' acceptance of the Pardoner does not prevent their laughter at his discomfiture. The Knight goes to considerable effort to effect the reconciliation. Was it his sense of the change in the Pardoner as he spoke that made him solicitous to keep him in the company?

The Pardoner's performance best illustrates the set of complex relationships between ernest and game that the pilgrimage generates. The journey that takes the pilgrims to the shrine at Canterbury takes them from their daily routine, frees them from all but what repeated choice has made them. Even without the fellowship of the Tabard and the Host's plan that seals their association, they would experience the release of holiday and discover in the mirror of unaccustomed activity some self-knowledge denied them in the familiarities of home and habit. The ernest of pilgrimage and the game of journey, reflected in the dual meaning of spring, would work their alchemy without the tales. The Host's plan with its rules exponentially increases the possibilities. It creates, for one thing, a new if temporary community. This community imposes a new purpose on the ernest of pilgrimage. The game of storytelling will enclose and contain the overt religious motives. It will continue after the shrine has been visited and will have its own climax. It will develop its own patterns of value. The autonomy of the agents and the literal accuracy of the narrative add the game of nonfiction to this collection of fiction. In the growth of a character like the Wife of Bath's, in the refusal of pilgrims to tell the tales originally assigned them, in the changes that Chaucer's plans for the pilgrimage underwent, a living reality authenticates itself—an imitation of another living reality in which agents are free.

The pilgrims will end up where they began, eating a meal at the Tabard. But as they approach the end of their journey together, they are different as a group, and many of them different as individuals. Though the guildsmen may keep to themselves as much as possible, they cannot fail to have their horizons somewhat widened by association with the other pilgrims. Everyone knows and is known. All share the common experiences of the road and of the inns. All share the suspense as to the Host's verdict. The Host himself, distracted by the reunion with his wife, faces a moment of truth. The decisions as to the "Tales of best sentence and moost solaas" will extend the negative lessons in critical insight, so marked a feature of the Host's immediate response to the stories. The dramatic, the thematic, and the aesthetic interests of the pilgrimage have possibilities of climactic fulfillment in the final scene at the Tabard. Giving unity to the work is the conflict between "ernest" and "game," between pilgrimage and storytelling, present in Chaucer's original plan and developing over the fourteen years a much more complex and subtle balance. The pilgrimage, incomplete though Chaucer's record of it is, has form for its readers. Lacking any simple interpretation, it has a multitude of meanings and levels of meanings. Freedom and the responsibility of choice figure among the most abstract. They earn their validity in the work from never being explicitly stated, from the integrity of the literal "everich a word," from Chaucer's refusal to explain all mysteries and resolve all contradictions. The emergence of pattern and the evanescence of pattern, the juxtaposition of the significant and the trivial, the range, the variety, the "Goddes foyson" communicate the author's confident enjoyment of his own creation and of the creation he tried to imitate. Essential to value in both, is the freedom so startlingly exemplified by the unlikely image of Chauntecleer, who like the Wife of Bath finds the right words in his moment of crisis and, having escaped from the jaws of the fox, shows that even feathered bipeds learn from experience:

> Thou shalt namoore, thurgh thy flaterye,
> Do me to synge. . . .

ABBREVIATIONS USED IN THE NOTES
AND BIBLIOGRAPHY

CE	*College English*
ChauR	*Chaucer Review*
EIC	*Essays in Criticism*
ELH	*English Literary History*
JEGP	*Journal of English and Germanic Philology*
MLN	*Modern Language Notes*
MLQ	*Modern Language Quarterly*
MLR	*Modern Language Review*
MP	*Modern Philology*
MS	*Mediaeval Studies*
NM	*Neuphilologische Mitteilungen*
PMLA	*Publications of the Modern Language Association*
PQ	*Philological Quarterly*
RES	*Review of English Studies*
SP	*Studies in Philology*
UTQ	*University of Toronto Quarterly*

notes

CHAPTER I

1. Quotations throughout are from *The Works of Geoffrey Chaucer* (2nd ed., 1957), edited by F. N. Robinson. In line references I use the Chaucer Society's designation of the fragments, A, B, C, etc., rather than the Roman numerals, since even the editions that adopt the numerals use the letters as a secondary system.

2. See Robert Hollander, *Allegory in Dante's Commedia*, 61. Hollander is quoting Singleton on Dante, but he has already (p. 51) made clear the relevance to Chaucer's *Canterbury Tales*.

3. The most influential book here is D. W. Robertson's *Preface to Chaucer*; see also Robert M. Jordan, *Chaucer and the Shape of Creation*. The most important books on Chaucer of the decade of the sixties, both provide insight into medieval aesthetics.

4. First pointed out by John M. Manly and Edith Rickert (*The Text of the Canterbury Tales*, II, 493–94) and used by William W. Lawrence (*Chaucer and the Canterbury Tales*, 101) in arguing for some attention to place names but against any effort to define the days of the journey. See edition by Albert C. Baugh, p. 230; and Donald R. Howard, New American Library edition, p. xviii.

5. For a discussion of the element of game, which takes as its point of departure Arnold's criticism of Chaucer for lacking high seriousness, see Richard A. Lanham, "Game, Play, and High Seriousness in Chaucer's Poetry," *English Studies*, Vol. XLVIII (1967), 1–24. Lanham's emphasis on situations of conflict, rather than character analysis, for the understanding of Chaucer's poetry derives to some extent from modern game theory and ascribes to Chaucer a more systematic and consistent attitude than the exploratory and developing one here posited. Johan Huizinga. in his *Homo Ludens*, first published in German (1944), emphasizes the "play-concept" as basic in art, and indeed in all civilization; in his chapter "Play-Concept as Expressed in Language," he considers the earnest-play opposition and characteristically concludes that the play concept is more fundamental and more positive than its opposite.

CHAPTER II

1. This chapter reflects the theories developed in a number of articles: "The Plan of the Canterbury Pilgrimage," *PMLA*, Vol. LXVI (1951), 820–26; "The Development of the *Canterbury Tales*," *JEGP*, Vol. LVII (1958), 449–76; "The Earliest Plan of the *Canterbury Tales*," *MS*, Vol. XXI (1959), 202–10; "The Twenty-Nine Pilgrims and the Three Priests," *MLN*, Vol. LXXVI (1961), 392–97; and "The Design of the *Canterbury Tales*," Chapter 11 in *Companion to Chaucer Studies*, edited by Beryl Rowland.

John H. Fisher, in "Chaucer's Last Revision of the *Canterbury Tales*" (*MLR*, Vol. LXVII [1972], 241–51), suggests a final plan that is not very different from the one presented here. He would include B¹ and D, E-F in the final plan, ignoring the implications of F 698, that there would be fewer than four tales per pilgrim, and of his acceptance of B¹ as originally providing the frame for the first story.

2. Justinus refers to the Wife of Bath as an authority when discussing marriage with January (E 1685 ff.). Chaucer recommends reading the Wife of Bath to Bukton, who is considering marriage ("Lenvoy de Chaucer a Bukton," lines 29–30).

3. Chapter 33, as translated by Charles Swan (1824).

4. Sister Mariella, "The Parson's Tale and the Marriage Group," *MLN*, Vol. LIII (1938), 251–56. For God's commandment on John's and Alisoun's sexual behavior, see E. Talbot Donaldson's amusing discussion in *Speaking of Chaucer*, 165 ff.

5. Robert L. Chapman, "The *Shipman's Tale* Was Meant for the Shipman" (*MLN*, Vol. LXXI [1956], 4–5), was answered by Philip Appleman, "The 'Shipman's Tale' and the Wife of Bath" (*Notes and Queries*, n.s., Vol. III [1956], 372–73), and William W. Lawrence, "The Wife of Bath and the Shipman" (*MLN*, Vol. LXXII [1957], 87–88). Lawrence's definitive essay, "Chaucer's *Shipman's Tale*" (*Speculum*, Vol. XXXIII [1958], 56–68, esp. 60–63), did not prevent Murray Copland (*"The Shipman's Tale*: Chaucer and Boccaccio," *Medium Aevum*, Vol. XXXV [1966], 11–28) from reviving the Chapman thesis. See also Hazel Sullivan's title essay, in *A Chaucerian Puzzle and Other Medieval Essays*, for a more complicated explanation of the Shipman as original narrator.

6. See Robert A. Pratt's analysis of the textual evidence for B 1179 in "The Order of the *Canterbury Tales*," *PMLA*, Vol. LXVI (1951), 1154–57; and Charles A. Owen, Jr., "The Development," *JEGP*, Vol. LVII (1958), 452.

7. The connection between the end of the Man of Law's Epilogue and the Wife's Prologue, pointed out in "The Development of the *Canterbury Tales*" (*JEPG*, Vol. LVII [1958], 452), was also suggested by Robert A. Pratt, in "The Development of the Wife of Bath" (*Studies in Medieval Literature in Honor of Albert Croll Baugh*, 45–79). Professor Pratt and I differ on the way the Wife's Prologue developed. He would connect the account of the three old husbands

(D 193–450), "adapted from Theophrastus and Eustache Deschamps," with lines D 1–6 as the earliest part of the Wife's Prologue. The influence on Chaucer of Deschamps' *Miroir de Mariage*, as John L. Lowes pointed out ("Chaucer and the *Miroir de Mariage*," *MP*, Vol. VIII [1910–1911], 165–86, 305–34), belongs to the period of the revision of the Prologue to the *Legend of Good Women*, that is, 1394 or later. It was in this period that Chaucer was reassigning to the Shipman the tale originally told by the Wife, putting together the B² fragment, and composing the "marriage group." The argumentative material on marriage, which Professor Pratt finds unrelated to the *Shipman's Tale*, has the same misguided concern for orthodoxy that is so marked a feature of the Wife's interruption of the Parson and that appears also in the *Shipman's Tale*. I find it extremely unlikely that Chaucer conceived of the three old husbands as a "Wife's Tale," and then later added their two young successors. As soon as he began to see the husbands in specific terms, he seems to have seen them as contrasts, three good, two bad (D 196). The undifferentiated five of D 1–162 would seem to be the earlier conception.

8. See Germaine Dempster, "A Period in the Development of the *Canterbury Tales* Marriage Group and of Blocks B² and C," *PMLA*, Vol. LXVIII (1953), 1142–59.

9. John S. P. Tatlock, in "The Duration of the Canterbury Pilgrimage" (*PMLA*, Vol. XXI [1906], 478–85), gives a good summary of the distances a group like the one depicted could travel in a day and of the possible overnight lodgings between London and Canterbury. Tatlock points out that the pilgrims do not stop at Rochester, but pass it by, in the B² fragment.

10. See Robert K. Root, "The Manciple's Prologue," *MLN*, Vol. XLIV (1929), 493–96. Pratt ("The Order of the *Canterbury Tales*," *PMLA*, Vol. LXVI [1951], 1144) finds "insufficient justification for separating" fragments H and I. To make this finding, one has to ignore not only the indications as to time and place in the two prologues, but also the dramatic situation. Every man except the Parson could not have told his tale (see I 25) if the two fragments are connected. The Cook would still have his tale to tell. See Wayne Shumaker, "Chaucer's *Manciple's Tale* as Part of a Canterbury Group" (*UTQ*, Vol. XXII [1953], 147–56), for a thorough development of this impossible idea.

11. For discussions of the complicated relationship between the *Legend of Good Women*, the Introduction to the *Man of Law's Tale*, the *Constance*, and the different versions of Gower's *Confessio Amantis*, see Walter W. Skeat (ed.), *The Complete Works of Geoffrey Chaucer*, III, 413–17; John S. P. Tatlock, *The Development and Chronology of Chaucer's Works*, 172 ff.; and Eleanor Prescott Hammond, *Chaucer: A Bibliographical Manual*, 278 ff.

12. Skeat reports (*Complete Works*, V, 141) that Furnivall made the suggestion, which Skeat rejects (*Complete Works*, III, 406). Tatlock (*Development and Chronology*, 188 ff.) discusses the *Melibeus* at some length and argues strongly (195 ff.) for its having been assigned originally to the Man of Law.

Tatlock's position has been accepted by most of those who have considered the question of the development of the tales. See, for instance, Carleton Brown, "The Man of Law's Head-Link and the Prologue of the Canterbury Tales," *SP*, Vol. XXXIV (1937), 8–35; Pratt, "The Order of the *Canterbury Tales*," *PMLA*, Vol. LXVI (1951), 1141–67; and Dempster, "A Period in the Development of the *Canterbury Tales*," *PMLA*, Vol. LXVIII (1953), 1142–59.

13. The first recognition of this dramatic connection between the Man of Law's end-link and the Parson's Prologue appeared in my article on "The Plan of the Canterbury Pilgrimage" (*PMLA*, Vol. LXVI [1951], 824–25. See, for independent accounts, Ralph Baldwin's *The Unity of the "Canterbury Tales"* (pp. 92–95) and Robert M. Lumiansky's *Of Sondry Folk: The Dramatic Principle in the Canterbury Tales* (pp. 239–45). Lumiansky's primary concern is with the suitability of the *Parson's Tale* to the teller. Though I do not agree with his idea that the *Parson's Tale* is the revenge of the Parson "for the treatment he has received from Harry Bailly," I find the rest of his discussion of the Host-Parson relationship illuminating.

14. The usual explanation is that Chaucer did indeed discard not only the contest and the final supper at the Tabard but also the return journey, and made his peace with the Church by retracting in a deathbed repentance most of the works that have won him fame.

Parts of this theory are in dispute, but it has found a wide acceptance in handbooks. See, for instance, Robert D. French, *A Chaucer Handbook* (334 ff.); Robert K. Root, *The Poetry of Chaucer* (152–53, 288); Lawrence, *Chaucer and the Canterbury Tales* (146 ff.); and D. S. Brewer, *Chaucer* (177–78, 188 ff.). Perhaps the most satisfactory presentation of the theory is to be found in Shumaker's "Chaucer's *Manciple's Tale* as Part of a Canterbury Group" (*UTQ*, Vol. XXII [1953], 147 ff.). See also E. Talbot Donaldson, *Chaucer's Poetry* (947–49). The theory has been supported by most of those who find the religious theme dominant in the *Canterbury Tales*. See, for instance, Baldwin, *The Unity of the "Canterbury Tales"* (84); Paul Ruggiers, *The Art of the Canterbury Tales* (40); and Bernard Huppé, *A Reading of the Canterbury Tales* (58, 231–32), who supports the theory with reservations. The same assumptions are behind the conclusion of Alfred David's "Man of Law vs. Chaucer: A Case in Poetics" (*PMLA*, Vol. LXXXII [1967], 223–25). An older version of the theory, which extended the period of repentance to the last seven years of Chaucer's life (see *DNB*), can no longer be maintained.

15. In "Chaucer's Retraction: A Review of Opinion" (*Studies in Medieval Literature in Honor of Professor Albert Croll Baugh*, 81–96), James D. Gordon makes clear the trend toward regarding the Retraction as genuine. He does not consider the theory here outlined, which is substantially the one presented in "The Development of the *Canterbury Tales*" (*JEGP*, Vol. LVII [1958], 449–76).

16. The *De Contemptu Mundi* is referred to in the G Prologue to the *Legend of Good Women* (lines 414–15), but not in the F. The omission of the reference

to the Queen (F 496–97) in the G *Prologue* is usually interpreted as resulting from Richard II's grief over her death in 1394. See Robinson's note on the passage (*Works*, 846). The *Astrolabe* is dated 1391 because of the reference to the year in Part II, 1. For the date of the *Equatorie*, based on references in the text and the accompanying tables, see Derek J. Price (ed.), *The Equatorie of the Planetis* (151 ff.).

17. The close association of Graunson with Richard II, and presumably with Chaucer, would point to the year 1393 for Chaucer's adaptation of the French poet's work in "The Complaint of Venus." The "Envoy to Scogan" is usually dated the same year. See Robinson's notes on the two poems (*Works*, 862–63).

18. "The Man of Law's Head-Link and the Prologue of the Canterbury Tales," *SP*, Vol. XXXIV (1937), 8–35.

19. For a full discussion of when the *Melibeus*, the *Clerk's Tale*, the *Physician's Tale*, and the *Man of Law's Tale* were written, see Tatlock, *Development and Chronology*, 188 ff., 156 ff., 150 ff., 172 ff., respectively.

20. The dates of the composition of the *Squire's Tale*, the *Franklin's Tale*, and the *Prioress's Tale* are discussed in my article "The Development of the Canterbury Tales," *JEGP*, Vol. LVII (1958), 466 ff.

21. Robinson (*Works*, 683) would date the three fabliaux of A in the early 1390's on the basis that they "show little or no acquaintance with the literature" which Chaucer turned to account in the tales connected with the Wife of Bath. Innovations of technique, their relationship to one another and to the *Knight's Tale*, and the fact that the *Cook's Tale* breaks off after such a promising beginning, suggest that they were being composed, as well as incorporated into the first fragment, at the end of Chaucer's work on the *Canterbury Tales*. There is also the growing interest in the churls, whose portraits, along with the Monk's and Friar's, were probably added to the Prologue in the final six years of Chaucer's life (see the next section of this chapter).

22. For the keeping of the sea, and the years (1384–1388) when the staple of wool was in Middelburg, see Robinson's note (*Works*, 657–58) to lines 276–77. The Squire's "chyvachie" is a reference to service in Henry Le Despenser's "crusade" against the French supporters of the antipope Clement, in 1383. If the Squire had been sixteen in 1383, the age probably of Chaucer when he was taken prisoner in France in 1359, then his present age of twenty would date the pilgrimage as taking place in 1387. The most probable date for the Knight to have "begun the board" in Prussia with the Teutonic Knights is 1385 (see Muriel Bowden, *A Commentary on the General Prologue to the Canterbury Tales*, 63 ff.).

23. Other theories about the discrepancy in numbers are discussed in my article, "The Twenty-Nine Pilgrims and the Three Priests" (*MLN*, Vol. LXXVI [1961], 392–97). Skeat comments on the ambiguity of Chaucer's association with the pilgrims (*Complete Works*, III, 388). At first Chaucer seems to be saying that he met twenty-nine pilgrims at the Tabard. But before he describes the process of getting acquainted with them, *they* have become *we* (A 29), and of course he

adds himself in at the end of the list (A 544). Oliver F. Emerson, in a consideration of the grouping, thinks that Chaucer intended the three priests to apply to
the Nun's Priest, the Friar, and the Monk ("Some Notes on Chaucer and Some
Conjectures," *PQ*, Vol. II [1923], 89 ff.).

24. Eleanor Hammond suggested that the five pilgrims in the list at the end
were an afterthought (*Manual*, 254). She also felt that there was considerable
evidence for the theory that the Prologue was not *"aus einem Guss"*; that the tales
of the Miller, the Reeve, the Summoner, and the Friar must have been conceived
at the same time that the characters were created; and that the *Merchant's Tale*
(in her view later than those just mentioned) was forced on the pilgrim. (She
apparently did not notice the difficulty in the rhyme Huberd-berd.) She comments
(pp. 254–56) on social satire as the partial intention of the fabliau tales.

CHAPTER III

1. I should like to acknowledge my indebtedness to Robinson's notes and
Bowden's *Commentary*, and to the many other scholars who have contributed to
our knowledge of the pilgrims and their background.

2. Harold F. Brooks, in *Chaucer's Pilgrims: The Artistic Order of the Portraits in the Prologue* (10–11), comments on the different scales of value.
Baldwin, *The Unity of the Canterbury Tales* (44), has an interesting table,
analyzing the portraits with respect to the number of entries in each devoted to
the categories of "condicioun" (inner character), "whiche" (appearance), "degree," and "array." Jill Mann, in a significant book, *Chaucer and Medieval
Estates Satire: The Literature of Social Classes and the General Prologue to the
Canterbury Tales*, published after this chapter was written, stresses the importance
of what she calls 'medieval estates satire" as providing background material for
almost all the portraits. "The narrator," she concludes, "assumes that each pilgrim
is an expert, and presents him in his own terms, according to his own values, in his
own language" (p. 194). Thus we are led "to discover in ourselves the coexistence
of different methods of judging people, the coexistence of different semantic values,
each perfectly valid in its own context." This discovery suggests "the way in
which the coexistence of the people themselves is achieved" (p. 198).

3. Baldwin, *The Unity of the Canterbury Tales*, 50. See also his discussion
(pp. 54–57) of time-and-space and point of view in the Prologue. For point of
view, see also E. Talbot Donaldson, "Chaucer the Pilgrim," *PMLA*, Vol. LXIX
(1954), 928 ff.; Edgar Hill Duncan, "Narrator's Points of View in the Portrait-
sketches, Prologue to the *Canterbury Tales*," *Essays in Honor of Walter Clyde
Curry*, 77–101; and John M. Major, "The Personality of Chaucer the Pilgrim,"
PMLA, Vol. LXXV (1960), 160–62.

4. Jill Mann (*Chaucer and Medieval Estates Satire*, 101) points out that
Chaucer brings the past into a pilgrim's portrait, "revealing the *habitual* channels
of his thought and conversation." Her statement, "The *Prologue* proves to be a

poem about work," is only in part true. Such portraits as the Prioress's, the Miller's, and the Franklin's would tend to confirm Blake's and Dryden's famous dicta on the pilgrims, rather than Mrs. Mann's mutually exclusive alternatives: "The society it evokes is not a collection of individuals or types with an eternal or universal significance, but particularly a society in which work as a social experience conditions personality and the standpoint from which an individual views the world" (p. 202). Fortunately, Mrs. Mann's alternatives are not alternatives, far less exclusive alternatives, but reinforcing aspects, which her book has paradoxically contributed a great deal toward defining.

5. Modern editors have tended to accept the dichotomy "brave-prudent" for *worthy* and *wys*. See the comments on the passage by Frederick Tupper (*Types of Society in Medieval Literature*, 33 ff.) and Will Héraucourt (*Die Wertwelt Chaucers*, 93–94). Robinson's notes and Bowden's *Commentary* both support this interpretation. But Skeat glosses *worthy* in line 68 as "distinguished" and *wys* as "wise, prudent." Baugh (*Chaucer's Major Poetry*) interprets *worthy* as "full of worth, eminent," and *wys* as "prudent." Jill Mann (*Chaucer and Medieval Estates Satire*, 258, n. 8) finds the usual view "too narrow," and cites six passages where Chaucer uses the adjectives together with "little consciousness of their being opposites." Henry B. Hinckley (*Notes on Chaucer: A Commentary on the Prolog and Six Canterbury Tales*, 6) gives "of social position" as the meaning of *worthy*. The specialized meaning of *worthy* as "brave" seems ruled out by the preceding clause—"And everemoore he hadde a sovereyn prys." If we allow *worthy* its more general meaning, there is then no reason to limit *wys* to "prudent."

6. George Lyman Kittredge, *Chaucer and His Poetry*, 32; Kemp Malone, *Chapters on Chaucer*, 167.

7. For a detailed discussion of the grouping, see Brooks, *Chaucer's Pilgrims*, and Chapter 2, section 5, above. The succession of two groups, two single pilgrims, two groups, three single pilgrims, two groups, makes it easy to remember the twenty-nine. Jill Mann's discussion of the pilgrims (*Chaucer and Medieval Estates Satire*) arranges them in groups related to their background. As a consequence, the juxtaposition of Squire and Yeoman in the Prologue is not seen as significant, and Mrs. Mann agrees with Muriel Bowden in finding the Yeoman attractive and likable (pp. 172–73; 285, n. 15). She also gives the Friar's portrait a far more favorable reading than the one given below, and sees the narrator's moral praise of scoundrels as reflecting the social judgments we all make in order to coexist.

8. E. Talbot Donaldson, "Idiom of Popular Poetry in the *Miller's Tale*," *English Institute Essays* (119 ff.), points out that the vocabulary comes from French rather than English romance. See also John Livingston Lowes, "Simple and Coy: A Note on Fourteenth Century Poetic Diction," *Anglia*, Vol. XXXIII (1910), 440–51.

9. Previous comment on this brooch has assumed an awareness of the motto

on the part of the Prioress. See John Livingston Lowes, *Convention and Revolt in Poetry* (66), for the best-known of these comments. Arthur W. Hoffman, "Chaucer's Prologue to Pilgrimage: The Two Voices" (*ELH*, Vol. XXI [1954], 9–10), goes beyond the Prioress's motivation to give to the secular and religious interpretations of the motto the strongest definition. Whatever the meaning of the motto, the "crowned A" could hardly be religious.

10. See Eileen Power, *Medieval People*, Chapter 3, and her *Medieval English Nunneries c. 1275 to 1535*.

11. See Chapter 2, section 3, and especially note 12, for the *Melibeus* as the prose tale originally told by the Man of Law; Chapter 2, section 2, and especially note 6, for the *Shipman's Tale* as the story originally told by the Wife of Bath.

12. John M. Manly, *Some New Light on Chaucer*, 131 ff., 151–57.

13. Hoffman ("Chaucer's Prologue to Pilgrimage," *ELH*, Vol. XXI [1954], 13–14) suggests this relationship and some of the details here cited.

14. For a thorough consideration of the Pardoner's status, see Alfred L. Kellogg and Louis A. Haselmayer, "Chaucer's Satire of the Pardoner" (*PMLA*, Vol. LXVI [1951], 251–77), especially sections 3 and 4. The question of the Pardoner's dress is taken up in note 151, page 276.

15. I disagree with Kittredge's famous dictum that the Pardoner is the one lost soul of the pilgrimage. Alfred L. Kellogg's "An Augustinian Interpretation of Chaucer's Pardoner" (*Speculum*, Vol. XXVI [1951], 465–81) explores this question thoroughly and concludes that the Pardoner has not gone beyond the point of no return (see esp. p. 475 and n. 65). The Summoner and the Friar have more effectively damned themselves by their corruption of others. For a more favorable impression of the Friar, see Jill Mann, *Chaucer and Medieval Estate Satire* (37 ff.). She finds an impenetrable facade and moral ambiguity in the Friar's portrait, where in my view the implications are clear. The same disagreement applies also to the Physician, the Wife of Bath, the Manciple, and the Reeve—and, in the opposite direction, to the Franklin. There Mrs. Mann finds the generosity and the legal service both suspect.

16. Pointed out for the first time, I think, by Manly and Rickert (*The Text of the Canterbury Tales*, II, 493–94) and since then repeated by a variety of critics for a variety of reasons. See, for instance, Malone, *Chapters on Chaucer* (195), and Francis P. Magoun, Jr., *A Chaucer Gazetteer* (53). Chaucer's awareness of this objection and the measures he took to counter it are discussed in Chapter 1, above.

17. Manly, in *Some New Light on Chaucer*, has shown the correspondence between the data given by Chaucer on some of the pilgrims, and the historical records of contemporaries. Malone (*Chapters on Chaucer*, 186 ff.) argues against assuming a living model, even in the case of the Host, Harrie Baillie. Whatever the relationship with actuality, whether the poet's imitation be of a figure originally in his eye or in his mind's eye, he must still create in his art an illusion of life.

CHAPTER IV

1. Part of this chapter appeared in "Chaucer's *Canterbury Tales*: Aesthetic Design in Stories of the First Day," *English Studies*, Vol. XXXV (1954), 49–56. Cf. William C. Stokoe, "Structure and Intention in the First Fragment of the *Canterbury Tales*," *UTQ*, Vol. XXI (1952), 120–27.

2. Brown, "The Man of Law's Head-Link and the Prologue of the *Canterbury Tales*," *SP*, Vol. XXXIV (1937), 8–35; Charles A. Owen, Jr., "The Earliest Plan of the *Canterbury Tales*," *MS*, Vol. XXI (1959), 202–10; and Chapter 2, sections 3 and 4, above.

3. Criticism of the *Knight's Tale* received a new impetus with William Frost's "An Interpretation of Chaucer's Knight's Tale,, (*RES*, Vol. XXV [1949], 289–304) and Charles Muscatine's "Form, Texture, and Meaning in Chaucer's *Knight's Tale*" (*PMLA*, Vol. LXV [1950], 911–29), with their emphasis on the complexity of the thematic element.

See also Paul G. Ruggiers, "Some Philosophical Aspects of *The Knight's Tale*," *CE*, Vol. XIX (1958), 296–302 (revised as a chapter in Part 3 of his book, *The Art of the Canterbury Tales*); Dale Underwood, "The First of *The Canterbury Tales*," *ELH*, Vol. XXVI (1959), 455–69; John Halverson, "Aspects of Order in the Knight's Tale," *SP*, Vol. LVII (1960), 606–21; Elizabeth Salter, *Chaucer: The Knight's Tale and the Clerk's Tale*; and Kiichiro Nakatani, "A Perpetual Prison: The Design of Chaucer's *The Knight's Tale*," *Hiroshima Studies in English Language and Literature*, Vol. IX (1963), 75–89.

For some disagreements with the above articles, see Edward B. Ham, "Knight's Tale 38," *ELH*, Vol. XVII (1950), 252–61; Paull F. Baum, *Chaucer: A Critical Appreciation*, Chapter 3, Part 3; Michael Lloyd, "A Defence of Arcite," *English Miscellany*, Vol. X (1959), 11–25; W. A. Madden, "Some Philosophical Aspects of *The Knight's Tale*: A Reply," *EIC*, Vol. XX (1959), 193–94; Richard Neuse, "The Knight: The First Mover in Chaucer's Human Comedy," *UTQ*, Vol. XXXI (1962), 299–315.

Recent work has emphasized a variety of themes: (1) Determinism: Dorothy B. Loomis, "Saturn in Chaucer's *Knight's Tale*," *Chaucer und seine Zeit: Symposion für Walter F. Schirmer*. (2) A strongly moralistic "self-determinism": Chauncey Wood, *Chaucer and the Country of the Stars: Poetic Uses of Astrological Imagery*, 69–74; cf. Charles A. Owen, Jr., "The Problem of Free Will in Chaucer's Narratives," *PQ*, Vol. XLVI (1967), 435–39. (3) The humor as undramatic Chaucerian commentary on the action: Edward E. Foster, "Humor in the *Knight's Tale*," *ChauR*, Vol. III (1968), 88–94; Paul T. Thurston, "Artistic Ambivalence in Chaucer's *Knight's Tale*" (Ph.D. dissertation, University of Florida, 1968). (4) The significance of Fortune and man's proper attitude toward her: Merle Fifield, "The *Knight's Tale*: Incident, Idea, Incorporation," *ChauR*, Vol. III (1968), 95–106.

4. Frost, "An Interpretation of Chaucer's Knight's Tale," *RES*, Vol. XXV

(1949), 289–304; Muscatine, "Form, Texture, and Meaning in Chaucer's *Knight's Tale*," *PMLA*, Vol. LXV (1950), 911–29; P. M. Kean, *Chaucer and the Making of English Poetry*, II, 5 ff.; Alan T. Gaylord, "The Role of Saturn in the *Knight's Tale*," *ChauR*, Vol. VIII (1974), 171–90. A. C. Spearing, in his edition of the *Knight's Tale*, goes to the opposite extreme and finds Theseus ineffectual in an absurd world ruled by Saturn.. Underwood sees Theseus as learning from experience but never reaching the full Boethian vision implicit in the tale ("The First of *The Canterbury Tales*," *ELH*, Vol. XXVI [1959], 455–69).

5. Albert H. Marckwardt brought a refreshing originality to the study of the two Theban knights in *Characterization in Chaucer's Knight's Tale*. Two recent articles continue the dispute (without reference to Marckwardt), Rodney Delasanta, "Uncommon Commonplaces in *The Knight's Tale*" (*NM*, Vol. LXX [1969], 683–90), favoring Palamon, and A. V. C. Schmidt, "The Tragedy of Arcite: A Reconsideration of the *Knight's Tale* (*EIC*, XIX [1969], 107–17), favoring Arcite. Muscatine insists on the balance of the two ("Form, Texture, and Meaning in Chaucer's *Knight's Tale*," *PMLA*, Vol. LXV [1950], 911–29).

6. For a full discussion of the relationships of the Knight and tale, with similar conclusion, see Lumiansky, *Of Sondry Folk*, 29–49.

7. The assignment of the tale to the Knight is discussed at greater length in Chapter 2, section 4, above, and in my article "The Development of the *Canterbury Tales*," *JEGP*, Vol. LVII (1958), 453–57.

8. The first serious criticism of *The Miller's Tale*, in E. M. W. Tillyard's *Poetry Direct and Oblique* (pp. 85–92, reprinted in *Discussions of the Canterbury Tales*, edited by Charles A. Owen, Jr.), has been overlooked in the Griffith bibliography and in such discussions of scholarship as D. S. Brewer's otherwise admirable one (Chapter 14 in *Companion to Chaucer Studies*, edited by Beryl Rowland). Pioneering work on the language was presented to the English Institute by E. Talbot Donaldson and incorporated in *English Institute Essays* (1950) as "Idiom of Popular Poetry in the *Miller's Tale*."

9. An unusual series of alliterations in the description, some of them extending over a series of lines, as in A 3245–48, reaches a climax in the five concluding alliterative lines, A 3266–70.

10. Paul E. Beichner, "Absolon's Hair," *MS*, Vol. XII (1950), 222–33.

11. A recent article, Cornelius Novelli's "Absolon's 'Freend so deere': A Pivotal Point in *The Miller's Tale*" *Neophilologus*, Vol. LII [1968], 65–69), concentrates on the scene at the blacksmith's and the change that comes over Absolon, without taking account of the full meaning of A 3754–57 or of the coulter as Absolon's weapon.

12. T. W. Craik (*The Comic Tales of Chaucer*, 1), feels that the Miller is unaware of the parody of the *Knight's Tale*, but he agrees that the Miller intends no insult to the Reeve.

13. Craik (*ibid.*, 5–6, 31 ff.) attributes this quality of the tale to Chaucer rather than the Miller, but differentiates the two tales in similar terms.

14. M. Copland, in a remarkably perceptive article, "*The Reeve's Tale*: Harlotrie or Sermonyng?" (*Medium Aevum*, Vol. XXXI [1962], 14–32), goes more deeply into the distinctions between the two tales.

15. Both Paul A. Olson ("Poetic Justice in the *Miller's Tale*," *MLQ*, Vol. XXIV [1963], 227–36) and W. F. Bolton ("The 'Miller's Tale': An Interpretation," *MS*, Vol. XXIV [1962], 83–94) see the sins of avarice, pride, and lechery as represented by John, Absolon, and Nicholas. They find justice done in the tale.

16. Paul A. Olson, in "*The Reeve's Tale*: Chaucer's *Measure for Measure*" (*SP*, Vol. LIX [1962], 1–17), makes this point clearer through an examination of the images in the portrait and in the tale itself.

17. For a study of the clerks' northernisms, see J. R. R. Tolkien, "Chaucer as a Philologist: *The Reeve's Tale*," *Transactions of the Philological Society* (London), 1934, pp. 1–70.

CHAPTER V

1. Tatlock considers the question of overnight stops and of the distance traveled in a day by groups like the pilgrims, in "The Duration of the Canterbury Pilgrimage," *PMLA*, Vol. XXI (1906), 478–85. See also Chapter 2, section 2, above.

2. The *Shipman's Tale* as original Wife of Bath's and the *Melibeus* as Man of Law's are taken up in Chapter 2, above. On the date of composition of the *Monk's Tale*, including the late addition of the stanza on Bernabò Visconti, Kittredge is entirely convincing (*The Date of Chaucer's Troilus*, 41–52).

3. Baum suggests for the B² fragment the title "The Surprise Group" (*Chaucer: A Critical Appreciation*, 74–84). In "The Plan of the Canterbury Pilgrimage" (*PMLA*, Vol. LXVI [1951], 825), I suggest the literary interest in the stories as a unifying element. Alan T. Gaylord, in a brilliant article, "*Sentence* and *Solaas* in Fragment VII of the *Canterbury Tales*: Harry Bailly as Horseback Editor" (*PMLA*, Vol. LXXXII [1967], 226–35), calls the fragment the "Literature Group," with its main subject the art of storytelling.

4. See Albert H. Silverman, "Sex and Money in Chaucer's *Shipman's Tale*," *PQ*, Vol. XXXII (1953), 329–36.

5. The *OED* and the *MED* agree in citing 1453 as the earliest date for the use of *cosin* to mean "fraud, trickery."

6. Robert A. Pratt, in "The Development of the Wife of Bath" (*Studies in Medieval Literature*, 45–79), suggests that these lines were the last of the Prologue to be written. The elaborate scheme Professor Pratt proposes for the development of the Wife is based in part on his feeling that "the argumentative 'sermon,' with its emphasis on learning and preaching," does not fit "between the Epilogue of the Man of Law's Tale and the tale of the Lover's Gift Re-

gained," whereas "Alice's account of browbeating her old husbands" does (p. 62). See Chapter 2, note 7, above, for argument against Pratt's scheme.

7. G. H. Russell, in a fine appreciation of the art of the tale ("Chaucer: *The Prioress's Tale*," *Medieval Literature and Civilization*, edited by D. A. Pearsall and R. A. Waldron), calls into question the satirical reading of the portrait, finding evidence in the tale that the Prioress's spirituality "is neither feeble nor histrionic" (p. 225). Edward H. Kelly, in another recent appreciation of the art of the tale ("By Mouth of Innocentz: The Prioress Vindicated," *Papers on Language and Literature*, Vol. V [1969], 362–74), tries (unsuccessfully, I think) to exonerate the tale of anti-Semitism by attributing the severe punishment to the provost of the land, where both Jew and Christian are alien. For a balanced view of the portrait and the tale, see Ruggiers, *The Art of the Canterbury Tales*, 175–83.

8. Richard J. Schoeck ("Chaucer's Prioress: Mercy and Tender Heart," *Chaucer Criticism: The Canterbury Tales*, edited by Richard J. Schoeck and Jerome Taylor) sees in the tale a reflection of the Prioress's spiritual poverty, citing evidence that the Church did not condone anti-Semitism.

9. See my article "Thy Drasty Rymyng . . . ," *SP*, Vol. LXIII (1966), 539.

10. Samuel McCracken, "Chaucer's Sir Thopas, B² 1914–1915," *Explicator*, Vol. XVII (1959), item 57.

11. Laura Hibbard Loomis, "Chaucer and the Auchinleck MS: 'Thopas' and 'Guy of Warwick'," *Essays and Studies in Honor of Carleton Brown*, 111–28; and the same author's chapter on *Sir Thopas* in *Sources and Analogues of Chaucer's Canterbury Tales*, edited by William F. Bryan and Germaine Dempster.

12. See Robertson, *Preface to Chaucer*, 369; and Huppé, *A Reading of the Canterbury Tales*, 235 ff.

13. The first critic is William W. Lawrence ("The Tale of Melibeus," *Essays and Studies in Honor of Carleton Brown*, 105). The second is Paul Strohm ("The Allegory of the *Tale of Melibee*," *ChauR*, Vol. II [1967], 40).

14. For a definitive study of the development of medieval allegory in the interpretation of the Bible, see Henri de Lubac, *Exégèse Médiévale: Les Quatre Sens de L'Écriture* (Paris, 1959–61). De Lubac makes clear the importance of the literal, the reality of all four levels, and the reasons for the uniqueness of the allegorical levels in the Bible. A short secular work like the *Melibeus* will not contain within itself the figural allegory through which the life of Christ, as recorded in the new Testament, transforms history and the moral meaning of experience. But the literal level can have actual events as a referent and can suggest the positive morality, that is, *caritas*, as opposed to the cautions and prohibitions of ordinary morality, as well as such eternal truths as man's dependence on God's grace in an ordered universe.

15. See J. Leslie Hotson, "The *Tale of Melibeus* and John of Gaunt," *SP*, Vol. XVIII (1921), 429–52. Cf. Gardiner Stillwell, "The Political Meaning of Chaucer's *Tale of Melibee*," *Speculum*, Vol. XIX (1944), 433–44.

16. For a complete analysis of the manuscript evidence on the the the two versions of the Prologue, see Manly and Rickert, *The Text of the Canterbury Tales*, II, 410–13.

17. Pratt calls him an "antifeminist Monk" ("The Order of the *Canterbury Tales*," *PMLA*, Vol. LXVI [1951], 1158; and "The Development of the Wife of Bath," *Studies in Medieval Literature*, 63, n. 6).

18. This reading of the *Nun's Priest's Tale* owes a special debt to Charles Muscatine (*Chaucer and the French Tradition: A Study in Style and Meaning*, 237–43). It reflects my earlier reading of the tale in "The Crucial Passages in Five of the Canterbury Tales: A Study in Irony and Symbol" (*JEGP*, Vol. LII [1953], 305–309), and my indebtedness to J. Burke Severs ("Chaucer's Originality in the *Nun's Priest's Tale*," *SP*, Vol. XLIII [1946], 22–41). See also Milton Miller, "Definition by Comparison: Chaucer, Lawrence and Joyce," *EIC*, Vol. III (1953), 369–77.

19. The contrast between the widow and Chauntecleer as "a veiled comment on his [the Nun's Priest's] position vis-à-vis the Prioress," pointed out in my article "The Crucial Passages" (*JEGP*, Vol. LII [1953], 309), was misunderstood by Arthur T. Broes ("Chaucer's Disgruntled Cleric: *The Nun's Priest's Tale*," *PMLA*, Vol. LXXVIII [1963], 156–62). He discusses (pp. 159–60) the contrast between the widow and the Prioress, but fails to see Chauntecleer's pride as reflecting the Prioress's, and the widow's frugal dignity as reflecting the Nun's Priest's. In fact, he makes of Chauntecleer "the thinly disguised counterpart of the Priest, a *persona* or *alter ego* through which he can criticize women and enjoy a dominance over them that he has been unable to achieve in his own life."

20. Recent efforts to find in the figure of Chauntecleer solemn allegorical meaning are corrected by Judson B. Allen, in "The Ironic Fruyt: Chauntecleer as Figura," *SP*, Vol. LXVI (1969), 25–35.

21. Corinne E. Kauffman, "Dame Pertelote's Parlous Parle," *ChauR*, Vol. IV (1970), 41–48.

22. The possibility that "my lord" is an archbishop or a bishop and the prayer is a special benediction associated with him is discussed in Robinson's note for line 3445 (*Works*, 755).R. T. Lenaghan, in a sensitive article on the "voices" in the tale—the aspiring *rethor*, the sophisticated fabulist, and the straightforward narrator—sees these last three lines as the only ones belonging to the third voice. Lenaghan does not comment on the narrator's temporary loss of his fiction in overt antifeminism ("The Nun's Priest's Fable," *PMLA*, Vol. LXXVIII [1963], 300–307).

23. Paul's reference in II Timothy 3:16 is clearly to the Old Testament and the Gospels, but Chaucer uses the wider reference common in the Middle Ages— here comically, in the Retraction seriously. Professor Robert A. Pratt, in his definitive article "Three Old French Sources of the Nonnes Preestes Tale" (*Speculum*, Vol. XLVII [1972], 667), points out that in this passage Chaucer is parodying the "tradition," and specifically Marie de France.

24. Lumiansky (*Of Sondry Folk*, 105–12) sees the Host's references to the Nun's Priest's physique as ironical and makes him out to be pale and slender, with "skinny neck, narrow breast, and dull eyes."

CHAPTER VI

1. For different accounts of this development, see my "Development of the *Canterbury Tales*," *JEGP*, Vol. LVII (1958), 452, 463, 469, 473 ff.; and Pratt's "Development of the Wife of Bath," *Studies in Medieval Literature*, 45–79.

2. Germaine Dempster, "A Period in the Development of the *Canterbury Tales* Marriage Group and of Blocks B² and C," *PMLA*, Vol. LXVIII (1953), 1149. The article seeks to establish that the marriage group and fragments B² and C were given their present form in the years around 1396, a position that is generally accepted.

3. The references are B 3116, Prologue of the *Monk's Tale*, a reference to Rochester, which the pilgrims must be approaching and which during the next two stories they must leave behind; G 554–56, 584–90, 624, Canon's Yeoman's Prologue, which show that they spent the night at Ospring, sixteen miles from Rochester, and are now halfway to Canterbury from Ospring, at Boughton under Blee Forest; D 847 and 2294, in which the Summoner first threatens the Friar with two or three tales before they reach Sittingbourne, between Rochester and Ospring, and then indicates that he has carried out his threat, "we been almost at towne;" and F 73, in the *Squire's Tale*, which indicates that it is "pryme," or 9:00 A.M. It is physically impossible to arrange these stories—all linked together in their fragments, as we now have them, at approximately the same time—without doing violence to some of the time-and-place indications, unless we are willing to assign some of them to the homeward journey.

4. See my "Development of the *Canterbury Tales*," *JEGP*, Vol. LVII (1958), 473 ff.

5. Robertson (*Preface to Chaucer*, 330–31) comes out strongly against finding "human" qualities in the Wife of Bath: "Alisoun of Bath is not a 'character' in the modern sense at all, but an elaborate iconographic figure designed to show the manifold implications of an attitude." Jordan (*Chaucer and the Shape of Creation*) pits his theory of inorganic form against what he acknowledges to be "unusual among the pilgrim characters" (p. 213), "a woman infinitely various yet all the more consistently 'human' for the frailties and inconsistencies she displays" (p. 208). The result is a draw, as witness the following: ". . . the composition of the Wife suggests that Chaucer's motivation was primarily thematic, that he was concerned with making an entertaining and artful presentation of the traditional, authoritative, pronouncements on antifeminism, to which end the cumulative individualization of the Wife becomes a means" (p. 211). David S. Reid ("Crocodilian Humor: A Discussion of Chaucer's Wife of Bath,"

ChauR, Vol. IV [1970], 73–89) finds the Wife in the Prologue "manipulated with an entire disregard for naturalistic conventions or psychological possibility, She makes sense only in terms of burlesque and knock-about comedy" (p. 79). He objects also to finding serious moral import in the Wife (as in Robertson's interpretation). The present account is a development of the interpretation first given in "Crucial Passages," *JEGP*, Vol. LII (1953), 301–304.

6. D. S. Silvia's interesting notion ("The Wife of Bath's Marital State," *Notes and Queries*, n.s., Vol. XIV [1967], 8–10), that the Wife is still married to Jankyn but no longer in love with him because he is no longer "daungerous" of his love to her, would be more persuasive if there were any evidence to show that her attitude to her fifth husband has changed. For additional argument against Silvia's theory, see A. V. C. Schmidt, *Notes and Queries*, n.s., Vol. XIV (1967), 230–31.

7. An exception is David Parker ("Can We Trust the Wife of Bath?" *ChauR*, Vol. IV [1970], 90–98), who, taking a suggestion from "The Crucial Passages" (*JEGP*, Vol. LII [1953], 301–304), goes even further than I would in calling into question the Wife's account of her fifth marriage. Parker gives a good defense of the traditional view of the pilgrims as "characters."

8. The chronology within the poem and the chronology of composition are again in conflict, as they were in Fragment A. Work on the Wife of Bath's Prologue and *Tale* was completed before the *St. Cecilia* (as *Second Nun's Tale*) was joined to the Canon's Yeoman's Prologue and *Tale* to form Fragment G.

9. Pratt, in "Development of the Wife of Bath" (*Studies in Medieval Literature* 64), speaks of Jankyn as "beaten to a pulp"—unaccountably, I think. Lumiansky (*Of Sondry Folk*, 124) has the Wife "hit him hard" after a feigned swoon.

10. Tony Slade, in "Irony in the *Wife of Bath's Tale*" (*MLR*, Vol. LXIV [1969], 241–47), points out that this list consists of places frequented by women.

11. See William Frost's introduction (p. 18) to *Age of Chaucer*, Vol. I of *English Masterpieces*, edited by Maynard Mack et al. Lumiansky (*Of Sondry Folk*, 128) makes the same point.

12. Most critics have failed to see that the real problem is the old hag's, not the knight's, in the second half of the tale, and that it will take more than a lecture on gentilesse or cleverly balanced alternatives to win the husband's love. An extreme instance is Rose A. Zimbardo ("Unity and Duality in *The Wife of Bath's Prologue* and *Tale*," *Tennessee Studies in Literature*, Vol. XI [1966], 11–18), who sees the Wife as a Shavian agent of the Life Force. Bernard S. Levy ("The Wife of Bath's *Queynte Fantasye*," *ChauR*, Vol. IV [1970], 106–22) also sees her as converting her husband by means of her lecture but as an agent of the devil. See also Joseph P. Roppolo, "The Converted Knight in Chaucer's *Wife of Bath's Tale*," *CE*, Vol. XII (1951), 263–69.

13. Earle Birney, in " 'After His Ymage': The Central Ironies of the 'Friar's Tale' " (*MS*, Vol. XXI [1959], 17–35), forces the issue somewhat in seeing a

connection between the archdeacon's implacability with "lecchours" and "smale tytheres" and the widow Mabely (whom he calls the "smallest tither in all Chaucer"). She becomes the instrument of the summoner's downfall when falsely accused of lechery by "this specialist in its detection" (p. 19). Birney remarks in the beginning of his article on the failure of critics to appreciate the inherent qualities of the *Friar's Tale*, a failure which his article goes a long way towards correcting. See also A. C. Cawley, "Chaucer's Summoner, the Friar's Summoner and the *Friar's Tale*," *Proceedings of the Leeds Philosophical and Literary Society*, Vol. VIII (1957), 173–80; Janette Richardson, "Hunter and Prey, Functional Imagery in Chaucer's *Friar's Tale*," *English Miscellany*, Vol. XII (1961), 9–20; Paul E. Beichner, "Baiting the Summoner," *MLQ*, Vol. XXII (1961), 367–76; Adrien Bonjour, "Aspects of Chaucer's Irony in 'The Friar's Tale'," *EIC*, Vol. XI (1961), 121–27.

14. Richard H. Passon ("'Entente' in Chaucer's *Friar's Tale*," *ChauR*, Vol. II [1968], 166–71) stresses the religious orthodoxy of the tale as compared to analogues where damnation is effected through the sincerity of somebody else's "curse." He ends by pointing out that the uncharitable "entente" of the Friar in telling the story is given emphasis by the hypocrisy of his concluding prayer.

15. John V. Fleming, in "The Summoner's Prologue: An Iconographic Adjustment" (*ChauR*, Vol. II [1967], 95–107), points out that the story parodies the vision of Caesarius of Heisterbach in *Dialogus Miraculorum*, a vision appropriated almost at once from the Cistercian Monks by the Dominican Friars and attributed to their founder. In the revised version, Saint Dominic has a vision of heaven, finds none of his order there, and weeps. Christ shows him his order under the mantle of the Virgin. Fleming continues in this article the exploration of the connections between the *Summoner's Tale* and antifraternalism begun by Arnold Williams in "Chaucer and the Friars" (*Speculum*, Vol. XXVIII [1953], 499–513 and carried on by Fleming in "The Antifraternalism of the *Summoner's Tale*" (*JEGP*, Vol. LXV [1966], 688–700). He shows in the latter article that the spiritual Franciscans were themselves an important source for criticism of the "ordres foure," and suggests that their view of money as excrement may be behind Thomas's "gift."

16. Earle Birney's "Structural Irony within the *Summoner's Tale*" (*Anglia*, Vol. LXXVIII [1960], 204–18) stresses the internal ironies, especially those resulting from the relationship of the friar and the disaffected Thomas. Other recent articles on the *Summoner's Tale* include Thomas F. Merrill, "Wrath and Rhetoric in *The Summoner's Tale*," *Texas Studies in Literature and Language*, Vol. IV (1962), 341–50; John F. Adams, "The Structure of Irony in *The Summoners' Tale*," *EIC*, Vol. XII (1962), 126–32; Paul N. Zietlow, "In Defense of the Summoner," *ChauR*, Vol. I (1966), 4–19; and Bernard S. Levy, "Biblical Parody in the *Summoner's Tale*," *Tennessee Studies in Literature*, Vol. XI (1966), 45–60.

17. Pointed out in my article "Thy Drasty Rymyng . . .," *SP*, Vol. LXIII

(1966), 561–62. The lines are D 1883–84, 1905–1906, 1911–12, 1939–40. We have already noted the use of the rhyme by Chaucer in the portrait of the Friar in a passage that mimics the Friar's voice, and by the Wife of Bath in the beginning of her tale. The only other use of the word *freres* as a rhyme in Chaucer comes in Thomas's angry response to the friar's remarks, D 1950.

18. The pun on *ferthyng* is pointed out in most of the recent essays on the *Summoner's Tale*, including those of Birney, Adams, and Fleming. Fleming also notes the pun on *fundament*, D 2103, as confirming the reference to the spiritual Franciscans' evaluation of gold ("The Antifraternalism," *JEGP*, Vol. LXV [1966], 698f.). For the first note on *ferthyng*, see J. Edwin Whitesell, "Chaucer's Lisping Friar," *MLN*, Vol. LXXI (1956), 160–61.

19. For different interpretations of the sermon on anger, see the articles already cited (note 16, above) by Merrill and Zietlow. I first suggested this interpretation of the exempla, and the function of anger in distorting the tale, in "Morality as a Comic Motif in the *Canterbury Tales*," *CE*, Vol. XVI (1955), 230–31.

20. Birney, Adams, Levy, and Zietlow all treat the problem of division as if it could be of real concern to the friar, forgetting that the fart given the friar has long since dispersed. In redressing the balance and rebutting those who had tended to award victory in the quarrel to the Friar (see especially Father Beichner's "Baiting the Summoner," *MLQ*, Vol. XXII [1961], 367–76), Zietlow goes to the extreme of praising the Summoner's "intelligent control." Levy points out the relevance of the wheel to the symbolism of Pentecost, which is also present in "wind," in fire, and in eloquence. He rightly emphasizes the Summoner's exposure of the friars' (both John's and Huberd's) claims to special grace.

21. Furnivall, for the Chaucer Society, placed it third of the fragments, hence its designation C. Pratt shifted the B² fragment from its place in the Ellesmere order, after the *Pardoner's Tale*, to a point near the beginning (attached to the Man of Law's Epilogue), thus leaving the *Pardoner's Tale* to be followed only by the *Second Nun's Tale*, the Canon's Yeoman's Prologue and *Tale*, the Manciple's Prologue and *Tale*, and the Parson's Prologue and *Tale*. The Ellesmere editor, in the first effort to put the tales in "Chaucerian" order, had the C fragment almost exactly in the middle, with eleven tales preceding and ten following.

22. See Lumiansky, *Of Sondry Folk*, 205 ff.; John Halverson, "Chaucer's Pardoner and the Progress of Criticism, *ChauR*, Vol. IV (1970), 188; and my "Development of the *Canterbury Tales*," *JEGP*, Vol. LVII (1958), 469.

23. The reference, in the digression on governesses (C 72–104), to the court scandal of 1386–1388 involving John Holland and John of Gaunt's daughter Elizabeth, who had been under the care of Katherine Swynford (Chaucer's sister-in-law and John of Gaunt's mistress), places the *Physician's Tale* in the early period of work on the *Canterbury Tales*, 1387–1391. For a relationship in language with the *Parson's Tale*, see my note "Relationship between the *Physician's Tale* and the *Parson's Tale*, *MLN*, Vol. LXXI (1956), 84–87.

24. Professor Frederick Tupper's theory that the pilgrims followed the Pardoner into the tavern had a much greater influence than his "sins" theory. The former, set forth in "The Pardoner's Tavern" (*JEGP*, Vol. XIII [1914], 553–65), was accepted by F. N. Robinson in the first edition of the Cambridge Chaucer (p. 834) and retained in the 1957 edition (p. 729). G. G. Sedgewick did not accept it ("The Progress of Chaucer's Pardoner, 1880–1940," *MLQ*, Vol. I [1940], 440 ff.), and Gordon Hall Gerould explained the ale-stake as a reflection of the final lines of the Summoner's portrait (*Chaucerian Essays*, 57). Robert E. Nichols, Jr., ("The Pardoner's Ale and Cake," *PMLA*, Vol. LXXXII [1967], 498–504) interprets the ale and cake as a theme reverberating through the sermon and the tale and, in their suggestion of the Eucharist, giving an ironic counterpoint to the revelers' ironically successful quest (see especially the "turnen substaunce into accident" of C 539). The interpretation would be more impressive if the Pardoner did not insist on the corniness of his ale.

25. The present account is an expansion of "The Crucial Passages" (*JEGP*, Vol. LII [1953], 304–305). The section on the *Pardoner's Tale* acknowledged indebtedness to Sedgewick ("The Progress of Chaucer's Pardoner, 1880–1940," *MLQ*, Vol. I [1940], 431–58). As Sedgewick pointed out, we are all indebted to Kittredge, whose ground-breaking article on the Pardoner appeared in the *Atlantic Monthly* in 1893 (No. 72, pp. 829–33). There is also Walter C. Curry's interesting diagnosis of the Pardoner's eunuchhood, "The Pardoner's Secret" in *Chaucer and the Mediaeval Sciences*, first published in 1926 (2nd ed., 1960, pp. 54–70). Halverson, in "Chaucer's Pardoner and the Progress of Criticism" (*ChauR*, Vol. IV [1970], 184–202), endeavors to continue Sedgewick's survey for the intervening thirty years, and to put forward suggestions of his own. Halverson stresses the importance of the gentils' protest as motivating the "put-on" of the Pardoner's performance. The Pardoner exaggerates in order to protest the "real self" and to pay back the gentils. In an issue of the *Chaucer Review* devoted to the Pardoner, David V. Harrington ("Narrative Speed in the *Pardoner's Tale*," *ChauR*, Vol. III [1968], 50–59) seems to be applying Jordan's principle of inorganic structure to the Pardoner's performance. He sees narrative speed and rhetoric supplanting character, and interprets "each shift in the Pardoner's behavior as part of a pattern dramatizing the conjunction of superb moralizing with depraved personality." Ian Bishop, in "The Narrative Art of *The Pardoner's Tale*" (*Medium Aevum*, Vol. XXXVI [1967,] 15–24), an article not mentioned by Halverson, stresses the economy of the tale, the anonymity of all the characters except Deeth; he gives a restrained account of the religious implications of "Deeth shal be deed" (C 710). Cf. A. C. Spearing's introduction to his edition (Cambridge, 1965).

26. Ruggiers (*The Art of the Canterbury Tales*, 122–23) uses a theme from the *Parson's Tale*—the good or evil resulting from the possession of gifts—to draw a nice parallel between the *Physician's* and the *Pardoner's Tale*. The gifts

of nature and of fortune in the *Physician's Tale* and the abuse of the gift of grace in the *Pardoner's Tale* both lead to death.

27. Malone, *Chapters on Chaucer*, 177–80; Speirs, *Chaucer the Maker*, 169. Kean (*Chaucer and the Making of English Poetry*, II, 96–109) gives thorough consideration to the adaptation by Chaucer of "the methods of allegorical satire" and concludes that the "whole complex—prologue, introduction, tale, and end-link—is designed as a whole, round and complete," and that the result "is certainly towards a naturalistic conception of character" (p. 108).

28. Halverson ("Chaucer's Pardoner," *ChauR*, Vol. IV [1970], 196–97) regards this section as part of the "put-on," the intentional exaggeration that the Pardoner hopes will shock and convince the pilgrims. For an interpretation closer to the one given here, see Huppé, *A Reading of the Canterbury Tales*, 209–19, esp. 214–15.

29. Christopher Dean ("Salvation, Damnation and the Role of the Old Man in the Pardoner's Tale," *ChauR*, Vol. III [1968], 44–49) thinks the old man, third and most impressive of the warning figures in the tale, "embodies or manifests . . . in some manner Christian goodness." He reflects two aspects of God, his mercy and his justice. Most recent interpretations do not accept the old man as Death, nor as a completely allegorical figure. Nor do they accept W. J. B. Owen's naturalistic reading ("The Old Man in *The Pardoner's Tale*," *RES*, n.s., Vol. II [1951], 49–55). See Halverson, "Chaucer's Pardoner" (*ChauR*, Vol. IV [1970], 192–93), for references.

30. William B. Toole ("Chaucer's Christian Irony: The Relationship of Character and Action in the *Pardoner's Tale*," *ChauR*, Vol. III [1968], 37–43) points out that the old man's longing for death stands in ironic contrast to the revelers' quest for eternal life.

31. The indefinite nature of the old man is stressed by Michael D. West, in "Dramatic Time, Setting, and Motivation in Chaucer," *ChauR*, Vol. II (1968), 172–87.

32. Lumiansky, for instance (*Of Sondry Folk*, 201–23), and Charles Mitchell ("The Moral Superiority of Chaucer's Pardoner," *CE*, Vol. XXVII [1966], 437–44. J. Swart (Chaucer's Pardoner," *Neophilologus*, Vol. XXXVI [1952], 45–50) attributes the plan to the Pardoner's drunken "superbia." Kean (*Chaucer and the Making of English Poetry*, II, 104) suggests that the Pardoner is launching a direct and "personal attack on the Host" with the aim of conquering "this difficult part of his audience," that is, those whose masculinity makes them instinctively unfriendly. Kean attributes to the Host an intention in what he calls his "ruthless and accurate counterattack" seemingly belied in his surprised response to the Pardoner's anger (C 958–59). Kellogg ("An Augustinian Interpretation of Chaucer's Pardoner," *Speculum*, Vol. XXVI [1951], 474), after seeming to accept the seriousness of the Pardoner's effort, approaches the interpretation here presented: "If this be carried off even in jest. . . ."

33. Even if Chaucer canceled the "Host stanza" at the end of the *Clerk's Tale*, this worry is more explicit in the Epilogue to the *Merchant's Tale* (E 2426–40).

34. The best criticism of the *Clerk's Tale* appeared in Raymond Preston's book *Chaucer*, 202–203, 250–57; in James Sledd's article "The *Clerk's Tale*: The Monsters and the Critics," *MP*, Vol. LI (1953), 73–82; in Elizabeth Salter's *Chaucer: The Knight's Tale and The Clerk's Tale* (Studies in English Literature, No. 5, general editor, David Daiches); and in Alfred L. Kellogg's "Evaluation of the *Clerk's Tale*: A Study in Connotation," Chapter 16 of *Chaucer, Langland, Arthur: Essays in Middle English Literature*. J. Mitchell Morse's effort to relate the tale to the philosophical developments in fourteenth-century Oxford ("The Philosophy of the Clerk of Oxenford," *MLQ*, Vol. XIX [1958], 3–20) should also be cited.

35. Chaucer, of course, used the anonymous French translation of Petrarch as well as Petrarch's Latin. See J. Burke Severs, *The Literary Relationships of Chaucer's Clerkes Tale* (Yale Studies in English, No. 96).

36. See Salter, *Chaucer: The Knight's Tale and The Clerk's Tale*, 55–62; Bertrand H. Bronson, *In Search of Chaucer*, 103–14; Jordan, *Chaucer and the Shape of Creation*, 198–207. Sledd ("The *Clerk's Tale*," *MP*, Vol. LI [1953], 73–82) and Ruggiers (*The Art of the Canterbury Tales*, 216–25) stand out against this tendency. The point made here about the allegory is to some extent anticipated by Ruggiers (p. 219).

37. See Hollander, *Allegory in Dante's Commedia*, especially the first chapter, for a clear exposition of the primacy of the literal level and the importance of the allegorical or figural as limiting and helping to define the other two levels. See also Chapter 5, note 14, above. Kean (*Chaucer and the Making of English Poetry*, II, 125 ff.) points out many of the figural parallels, but concludes that Griselda's "lapses into naturalism tend to give the lie to behavior which seems, in other places, to show her to us as a figure of symbolical depth and resonance." Kean feels that this type of story "needs a firmer choice between naturalism and the special formalism of allegory . . . a stronger didacticism than Chaucer's urbanity" permits him (p. 129). Kellogg ("Evaluation of the *Clerk's Tale*," *Chaucer, Langland, Arthur*) also anticipates many of the figural parallels pointed out for Griselda. He gives the best explanation to date of the composite of Walter's meanings (see esp. p. 308). He has a fine appreciation of the love Griselda shows for Walter despite her lord's apparent cruelty (pp. 312–13): "If Griselda's perfection be viewed as a figure of the human spirit struggling through prosperity and adversity to attain union with the heavenly bridegroom, it is her love which drives her on."

38. This implication of the Griselda story, as Chaucer's Clerk presents it, is at the opposite pole from the tendency to sentimentalize man's plight.

39. The "Host stanza" was retained in the Hengwrt, Ellesmere, and *a* MSS. As Manly remarks, "Strangely enough it is preserved almost solely in MSS containing the latest work." Mrs. Dempster, though acknowledging it as genuine,

238

thinks it was canceled ("A Period in the Development of the *Canterbury Tales*," *PMLA*, Vol. LXVIII [1953], 1142–46).

40. What follows is a development of my interpretation in "The Crucial Passages" (*JEGP*, Vol. LII [1953], 297–301). Bertrand H. Bronson changed the direction of criticism of the *Merchant's Tale* with his article "Afterthoughts on the Merchant's Tale" (*SP*, Vol. LVIII [1961], 583–96), questioning its connection with its prologue and its teller, and stressing the comic elements. Jordan (*Chaucer and the Shape of Creation*, 132–51) finds the tale "less a unified presentation than a composite of several narrating attitudes and positions, often mutually contradictory," each assumed by the poet to maximize the effect of the particular situation (p. 150). David L. Shores ("*The Merchant's Tale*: Some Lay Observations," *NM*, Vol. LXXI [1970], 119–33) takes issue with Bronson and Jordan on the question of unity, but agrees that the effect of the tale is comic rather than "bitter." Norman T. Harrington ("Chaucer's Merchant's Tale: Another Swing of the Pendulum," *PMLA*, Vol. LXXXVI [1971], 25–31) finds the work unified, bitter, and "remarkably daring." Harrington recapitulates recent criticism. See also Kean, *Chaucer and the Making of English Poetry*, II, 156 ff. Kean calls January, the Pardoner, and the Wife of Bath the "three most complex figures of the *Canterbury Tales*." But, except in footnote 16, page 250, he does not consider the Merchant.

41. Jordan (*Chaucer and the Shape of Creation*, 138) attributes the epithalamion to "the familiar Chaucerian innocent, here undertaking the glorification of marriage." The position is hard to refute, since January's view of matrimony at this point is ignorant and foolish. That another mind than January's is also present emerges in the bitter comment of E 1318 and 1356–57, in the piling up of extravagance and fatuity, and in the relationship of the imagery to the rest of the tale. Jordan concedes to some extent this last point when he says that "one passage is no more crucial than any other. One can drop his finger at random anywhere in the text and find something about marriage, and any of the foolishness in the tale (of which there is much) can be interpreted as 'blindness' " (pp. 146–47). The climax of the story involves literal blindness, a garden designed for delight, a tree in which an evil deed occurs, and a miracle of restored sight which does not undeceive—details that do not require much interpretation.

42. See A 3151–62 and Robinson's note on 3161, which was no doubt influenced by Skeat (*Complete Works*, V, 96).

43. The youthful enthusiasm is caught in different degrees by two articles in a 1966 issue of *Chaucer Review*: Harry Berger, Jr., "The F-Fragment of the *Canterbury Tales*," Part I, *ChauR*, Vol. I (1966), 88–102; and John P. McCall, "The Squire in Wonderland," *ibid.*, 103–109. See also D. A. Pearsall, "The Squire as Story-teller, *UTQ*, Vol. XXXIV (1964), 82–92; and Robert S. Haller, "Chaucer's *Squire's Tale* and the Uses of Rhetoric," *MP*, Vol. LXII (1965), 285–95. The disparate qualities of the tale were pointed out in a seminal article by Gardiner Stillwell, "Chaucer in Tartary," *RES*, Vol. XXIV (1948), 177–88.

44. Haldeen Braddy has found the incest motif in oriental analogues. See his article "The Genre of Chaucer's *Squire's Tale*," *JEGP*, Vol. XLI (1942), 279–90; and the second of "Two Chaucer Notes," *MLN*, Vol. LXII (1947), 173–79.

45. The interpretation of the *Franklin's Tale* here presented is a development of my "Crucial Passages" (*JEGP*, Vol. LII [1953], 295–97). Since 1953 a tide of criticism directed at the Franklin has set in. The most severe of these critics have taken exception to the Franklin's ideals of marriage and of gentilesse—Robertson, for instance (*Preface to Chaucer*, 470–72), and Donald R. Howard ("The Conclusion of the Marriage Group: Chaucer and the Human Condition," *MP*, Vol. LVII [1960], 223–32) from a religious point of view; Lumiansky (*Of Sondry Folk*, 180–93) and Alfred David ("Sentimental Comedy in *The Franklin's Tale*," *Annuale Mediaevale*, Vol. VI [1965], 19–27) from a social point of view. Three recent articles have combated this trend: Lindsay A. Mann, " 'Gentilesse' and the Franklin's Tale," *SP*, Vol. LXIII (1966), 10–29; Berger, "The F-Fragment of the *Canterbury Tales*," Part II, *ChauR*, Vol. I (1967), 135–56; and A. M. Kearney, "Truth and Illusion in *The Franklin's Tale*," *EIC*, Vol. XIX (1969), 245–53. See also Kean, *Chaucer and the Making of English Poetry*, II, 142 ff.

46. Chauncey Wood (*Chaucer and the Country of the Stars*, Princeton, 1970, Chapter 6, "Time and Tide in the *Franklin's Tale*,") sees the clerk as taking advantage of a natural phenomenon rather than making the rocks appear to vanish by magic. The clerk's deceit is then seen as typical of the false values in the tale, which reflects the Franklin's epicureanism.

47. See my article "Morality as a Comic Motif in the *Canterbury Tales*," *CE*, Vol. XVI (1955), 226–32.

48. A detailed account of the quarrel appears in my article "The Earliest Plan of the *Canterbury Tales*," *MS*, Vol. XXI (1959), 205 ff.; and in Chapter 2, section 3, above.

49. For a discussion of the "Parson's Tale," see my article "The Development of the *Canterbury Tales*," *JEGP*, Vol. LVII (1958), 458–64; and Chapter 2, section 3, above. For a review of scholarly opinion on the Retraction (not, however, complete), see Gordon, "Chaucer's Retraction: A Review of Opinion," *Studies in Medieval Literature*, 81–96.

BIBLIOGRAPHY OF WORKS CITED

Adams, John F. "The Structure of Irony in *The Summoner's Tale*." *EIC*, Vol. XII (1962), 126–32.

Allen, Judson B. "The Ironic Fruyt: Chauntecleer as Figura." *SP*, Vol. LXVI (1969), 25–35.

Appleman, Philip. "The 'Shipman's Tale' and the Wife of Bath." *Notes and Queries*, n.s., Vol. III (1956), 372–73.

Baldwin, Ralph. *The Unity of the "Canterbury Tales."* Anglistica, Vol. V. Copenhagen, 1955.

Baugh, Albert C., ed. *Chaucer's Major Poetry*. New York, 1963.

Baum, Paull F. *Chaucer: A Critical Appreciation*. Durham, N.C., 1958.

Beichner, Paul E. "Absolon's Hair." *MS*, Vol. XII (1950), 222–33.

———. "Baiting the Summoner." *MLQ*, Vol. XXII (1961), 367–76.

Berger, Harry, Jr. "The F-Fragment of the *Canterbury Tales*." *ChauR*, Vol. I (1966–67), 88–102, 135–56.

Birney, Earle. " 'After His Ymage': The Central Ironies of the 'Friar's Tale'." *MS*, Vol. XXI (1959), 17–35.

———. "Structural Irony within the *Summoner's Tale*." *Anglia*, Vol. LXXVIII (1960), 204–18.

Bishop, Ian. "The Narrative Art of *The Pardoner's Tale*." *Medium Aevum*, Vol. XXXVI (1967), 15–24.

Bolton, W. F. "The 'Miller's Tale': An Interpretation." *MS*, Vol. XXIV (1962), 83–94.

Bonjour, Adrien. "Aspects of Chaucer's Irony in 'The Friar's Tale'." *EIC*, Vol. XI (1961), 121–27.

Bowden, Muriel. *A Commentary on the General Prologue to the Canterbury Tales*. New York, 1948.

Braddy, Haldeen. "The Genre of Chaucer's *Squire's Tale*." *JEGP*, Vol. XLI (1942), 279–90.

241

————. "Two Chaucer Notes." *MLN*, Vol. LXII (1947), 173–79.

Brewer, D. S. *Chaucer*. 2nd rev. ed. London, Toronto, New York, 1960.

————. "The Fabliaux." *Companion to Chaucer Studies*. Edited by Beryl Rowland. Toronto, 1968. Pp. 247–67.

Broes, Arthur T. "Chaucer's Disgruntled Cleric: *The Nun's Priest's Tale*." *PMLA*, Vol. LXXVIII (1963), 156–62.

Bronson, Bertrand H. "Afterthoughts on the Merchant's Tale." *SP*, Vol. LVIII (1961), 583–96.

————. *In Search of Chaucer*. Toronto, 1960.

Brooks, Harold F. *Chaucer's Pilgrims: The Artistic Order of the Portraits in the Prologue*. London, 1962.

Brown, Carleton. "The Man of Law's Head-Link and the Prologue of the Canterbury Tales." *SP*, Vol. XXXIV (1937), 8–35.

Cawley, A. C. "Chaucer's Summoner, the Friar's Summoner and the *Friar's Tale*." *Proceedings of the Leeds Philosophical and Literary Society*, Vol. VIII (1957), 173–80.

Chapman, Robert L. "The *Shipman's Tale* Was Meant for the Shipman." *MLN*, Vol. LXXI (1956), 4–5.

Copland, M. "*The Reeve's Tale*: Harlotrie or Sermonyng?" *Medium Aevum*, Vol. XXXI (1962), 14–32.

————. "*The Shipman's Tale*: Chaucer and Boccaccio." *Medium Aevum*, Vol. XXXV (1966), 11–28.

Craik, T. W. *The Comic Tales of Chaucer*. London and New York, 1964.

Curry, Walter C. *Chaucer and the Mediaeval Sciences*. 2nd ed. New York, 1960.

David, Alfred. "The Man of Law vs. Chaucer: A Case in Poetics." *PMLA*, Vol. LXXXII (1967), 217–25.

————. "Sentimental Comedy in *The Franklin's Tale*." *Annuale Mediaevale*, Vol. VI (1965), 19–27.

Dean, Christopher. "Salvation, Damnation and the Role of the Old Man in the *Pardoner's Tale*." *ChauR*, Vol. III (1968), 44–49.

Delasanta, Rodney. "Uncommon Commonplaces in *The Knight's Tale*." *NM*, Vol. LXX (1969), 683–90.

Dempster, Germaine. "A Period in the Development of the *Canterbury Tales* Marriage Group and of Blocks B² and C." *PMLA*, Vol. LXVIII (1953), 1142–59.

Donaldson, E. Talbot. "Chaucer the Pilgrim." *PMLA*, Vol. LXIX (1954), 928–36.

————, ed. *Chaucer's Poetry: An Anthology for the Modern Reader*. New York, 1958.

————. "Idiom of Popular Poetry in the *Miller's Tale*." *English Institute Essays*. New York, 1950. Pp. 116–40.

————. *Speaking of Chaucer*. London and New York, 1970.

Duncan, Edgar Hill. "Narrator's Points of View in the Portrait-sketches, Prologue to the *Canterbury Tales.*" *Essays in Honor of Walter Clyde Curry.* Nashville, 1954 [1955]. Pp. 77–101.

Emerson, Oliver F. "Some Notes on Chaucer and Some Conjectures." *PQ*, Vol. II (1923), 81–96.

Fifield, Merle. "The *Knight's Tale*: Incident, Idea, Incorporation." *ChauR*, Vol. III (1968), 95–106.

Fisher, John H. "Chaucer's Last Revision of the *Canterbury Tales.*" *MLR*, Vol. LXVII (1972), 241–51.

Fleming, John V. "The Antifraternalism of the *Summoner's Tale.*" *JEGP*, Vol. LXV (1966), 688–700.

————. "The Summoner's Prologue: An Iconographic Adjustment." *ChauR*, Vol II. (1967), 95–107.

French, Robert D. *A Chaucer Handbook.* 2nd ed. New York, 1927.

Frost, William, ed. *Age of Chaucer.* Vol. I of *English Masterpieces.* Edited by Maynard Mack et al. New York, 1950.

————. "An Interpretation of Chaucer's Knight's Tale." *RES*, Vol. XXV (1949), 289–304.

Gaylord, Alan T. "The Role of Saturn in the *Knight's Tale.*" *ChauR*, Vol. VIII (1974), 171–90.

————. "*Sentence* and *Solaas* in Fragment VII of the *Canterbury Tales*: Harry Bailly as Horseback Editor." *PMLA*, Vol. LXXXII (1967), 226–35.

Gerould, Gordon Hall. *Chaucerian Essays.* Princeton, 1952.

Gordon, James D. "Chaucer's Retraction: A Review of Opinion." *Studies in Medieval Literature in Honor of Professor Albert Croll Baugh.* Philadelphia, 1961.

Haller, Robert S. "Chaucer's *Squire's Tale* and the Uses of Rhetoric." *MP*, Vol. LXII (1965), 285–95.

Halverson, John. "Aspects of Order in the Knight's Tale." *SP*, Vol. LVII (1960), 606–21.

————. "Chaucer's Pardoner and the Progress of Criticism." *ChauR*, Vol. IV (1970), 184–202.

Ham, Edward B. "Knight's Tale 38." *ELH*, Vol. XVII (1950), 252–61.

Hammond, Eleanor Prescott. *Chaucer: A Bibliographical Manual.* New York, 1908.

Harrington, David V. "Narrative Speed in the *Pardoner's Tale.*" *ChauR*, Vol. III (1968), 50–59.

Harrington, Norman T. "Chaucer's Merchant's Tale: Another Swing of the Pendulum." *PMLA*, Vol. LXXXVI (1971), 25–31.

Héraucourt, Will. *Die Wertwelt Chaucers, die Wertwelt einer Zeitwende.* Heidelberg, 1939.

Hinckley, Henry B. *Notes on Chaucer: A Commentary on the Prolog and Six Canterbury Tales.* Northampton, Mass., 1907.

Hoffman, Arthur W. "Chaucer's Prologue to Pilgrimage: The Two Voices." *ELH*, Vol. XXI (1954), 1–16.

Hollander, Robert. *Allegory in Dante's Commedia.* Princeton, 1969.

Hotson, J. Leslie. "The *Tale of Melibeus* and John of Gaunt." *SP*, Vol. XVIII (1921), 429–52.

Howard, Donald R. "The Conclusion of the Marriage Group: Chaucer and the Human Condition." *MP*, Vol. LVII (1960), 223–32.

———, ed. *Geoffrey Chaucer's The Canterbury Tales: A Selection.* New York, 1969.

Huizinga, Johan. *Homo Ludens: A Study of the Play Element in Culture.* New York, 1970. (First published in German, 1944.)

Huppé, Bernard F. *A Reading of the Canterbury Tales.* New York, 1964.

Jordan, Robert M. *Chaucer and the Shape of Creation: The Aesthetic Possibilities of Inorganic Structure.* Cambridge, Mass., 1967.

Kauffman, Corinne E. "Dame Pertelote's Parlous Parle." *ChauR*, Vol. IV (1970), 41–48.

Kean, P. M. *Chaucer and the Making of English Poetry.* London and Boston, 1972.

Kearney, A. M. "Truth and Illusion in *The Franklin's Tale*." *EIC*, Vol. XIX (1969), 245–53.

Kellogg, Alfred L. "An Augustinian Interpretation of Chaucer's Pardoner." *Speculum*, Vol. XXVI (1951), 465–81.

———, and Louis A. Haselmayer. "Chaucer's Satire of the Pardoner." *PMLA*, Vol. LXVI (1951), 251–77.

———, et al. *Chaucer, Langland, Arthur: Essays in Middle English Literature.* New Brunswick, N.J., 1972.

Kelly, Edward H. "By Mouth of Innocentz: The Prioress Vindicated." *Papers on Language and Literature*, Vol. V (1969), 362–74.

Kittredge, George Lyman. *Chaucer and His Poetry.* Cambridge, Mass., 1915.

———. "Chaucer's Pardoner." *Atlantic Monthly*, No. 72 (1893), 829–33.

———. *The Date of Chaucer's Troilus and Other Matters.* Chaucer Society, 2nd Ser., No. 42. London, 1909.

Lanham, Richard A. "Game, Play, and High Seriousness in Chaucer's Poetry." *English Studies*, Vol. XLVIII (1967), 1–24.

Lawrence, William W. *Chaucer and the Canterbury Tales.* New York, 1950.

———. "Chaucer's *Shipman Tale*." *Speculum*, Vol. XXXIII (1958), 56–68.

———. "The Tale of Melibeus." *Essays and Studies in Honor of Carleton Brown.* New York, 1940. Pp. 100–110.

———. "The Wife of Bath and the Shipman." *MLN*, Vol. LXXII (1957), 87–88.

Lenaghan, R. T. "The Nun's Priest's Fable." *PMLA*, Vol. LXXVIII (1963), 300–307.

Levy, Bernard S. "Biblical Parody in the *Summoner's Tale*." *Tennessee Studies in Literature*, Vol. XI (1966), 45–60.

———. "The Wife of Bath's *Queynte Fantasye*." *ChauR*, Vol. IV (1970), 106–22.

Lloyd, Michael. "A Defence of Arcite." *English Miscellany*, Vol. X (1959), 11–25.

Loomis, Dorothy B. "Saturn in Chaucer's *Knight's Tale*." *Chaucer und seine Zeit: Symposion für Walter F. Schirmer*. Edited by Arno Esch. Tübingen, 1968. Pp. 149–61.

Loomis, Laura Hibbard. "Chaucer and the Auchinleck MS: 'Thopas' and 'Guy of Warwick'." *Essays and Studies in Honor of Carleton Brown*. New York, 1940. Pp. 111–28.

———. "Sir Thopas." *Sources and Analogues of Chaucer's Canterbury Tales*. Edited by William F. Bryan and Germaine Dempster. Chicago, 1941. Pp. 486–559.

Lowes, John Livingston. "Chaucer and the *Miroir de Mariage*." *MP*, Vol. VIII (1910–1911), 165–86, 305–34.

———. *Convention and Revolt in Poetry*. Boston, 1919.

———. "Simple and Coy: A note on Fourteenth Century Poetic Diction." *Anglia*, Vol. XXXIII (1910), 440–51.

Lumiansky, Robert M. *Of Sondry Folk: The Dramatic Principle in the Canterbury Tales*. Austin, 1955.

McCall, John P. "The Squire in Wonderland." *ChauR*, Vol. I (1966), 103–109.

McCracken, Samuel. "Chaucer's Sir Thopas, B² 1914–1915." *Explicator*, Vol. XVII (1959), item 57.

Madden, W. A. "Some Philosophical Aspects of *The Knight's Tale*: A Reply." *EIC*, Vol. XX (1959), 193–94.

Magoun, Francis P., Jr. *A Chaucer Gazetteer*. Chicago, 1961.

Major, John M. "The Personality of Chaucer the Pilgrim." *PMLA*, Vol. LXXV (1960), 160–62.

Malone, Kemp. *Chapters on Chaucer*. Baltimore, 1951.

Manly, John M. *Some New Light on Chaucer*. New York, 1926.

Manly, John M., and Edith Rickert. *The Text of the Canterbury Tales*. 8 vols. Chicago, 1940.

Mann, Jill. *Chaucer and Medieval Estates Satire: The Literature of Social Classes and the General Prologue to the Canterbury Tales*. Cambridge, England, 1973.

Mann, Lindsay A. " "Gentilesse' and the Franklin's Tale." *SP*, LXIII (1966), 10–29.

Marckwardt, Albert H. *Characterization in Chaucer's Knight's Tale*. University of Michigan Contributions in Modern Philology, No. 5. Ann Arbor, 1947.

Mariella, Sister. "The Parson's Tale and the Marriage Group." *MLN*, Vol. LIII (1938), 251–56.

Merrill, Thomas F. "Wrath and Rhetoric in *The Summoner's Tale.*" *Texas Studies in Literature and Language*, Vol. IV (1962), 341–50.

Miller, Milton. "Definition by Comparison: Chaucer, Lawrence and Joyce." *EIC*, Vol. III (1953), 369–81.

Mitchell, Charles. "The Moral Superiority of Chaucer's Pardoner." *CE*, Vol. XXVII (1966), 437–44.

Morse, J. Mitchell. "The Philosophy of the Clerk of Oxenford." *MLQ*, Vol. XIX (1958), 3–20.

Muscatine, Charles. *Chaucer and the French Tradition: A Study in Style and Meaning.* Berkeley and Los Angeles, 1957.

———. "Form, Texture, and Meaning in Chaucer's *Knight's Tale. PMLA*, Vol. LXV (1950), 911–29.

Nakatani, Kiichiro. "A Perpetual Prison: The Design of Chaucer's *The Knight's Tale.*" *Hiroshima Studies in English Language and Literature*, Vol. IX (1963), 75–89.

Neuse, Richard. "The Knight: The First Mover in Chaucer's Human Comedy." *UTQ*, Vol. XXXI (1962), 299–315.

Nichols, Robert E., Jr. "The Pardoner's Ale and Cake." *PMLA*, Vol. LXXXII (1967), 498–504.

Novelli, Cornelius. "Absolon's 'Freend so deere': A Pivotal Point in *The Miller's Tale.*" *Neophilologus*, Vol. LII (1968), 65–69.

Olson, Paul A. "Poetic Justice in the *Miller's Tale.*" *MLQ*, Vol. XXIV (1963), 227–36.

———. "*The Reeve's Tale*: Chaucer's *Measure for Measure.*" *SP*, Vol. LIX (1962), 1–17.

Owen, Charles A., Jr. "Chaucer's *Canterbury Tales*: Aesthetic Design in Stories of the First Day." *English Studies*, Vol. XXXV (1954), 49–56.

———. "The Crucial Passages in Five of the Canterbury Tales: A Study in Irony and Symbol." *JEGP*, Vol. LII (1953), 294–311.

———. "The Design of the *Canterbury Tales.*" *Companion to Chaucer Studies.* Edited by Beryl Rowland. Toronto, 1968. Pp. 192–207.

———. "The Development of the *Canterbury Tales.*" *JEGP*, Vol. LVII (1958), 449–76.

———, ed. *Discussions of the Canterbury Tales.* Boston, 1961.

———, "The Earliest Plan of the *Canterbury Tales.*" MS, Vol. XXI (1959), 202–10.

———. "The Plan of the Canterbury Pilgrimage." *PMLA*, Vol. LXVI (1951), 820–26.

———. "The Problem of Free Will in Chaucer's Narratives." *PQ*, Vol. XLVI (1967), 433–56.

———. "Relationship between the *Physician's Tale* and the *Parson's Tale.*" *MLN*, Vol. LXXI (1956), 84–87.

———. "Thy Drasty Rymyng . . . ." *SP*, Vol. LXIII (1966), 533–64.

Bibliography

———. "The Twenty-Nine Pilgrims and the Three Priests." *MLN*, Vol. LXXVI (1961), 392–97

Owen, W. J. B. "The Old Man in *The Pardoner's Tale*." *RES*, n.s., Vol. II (1951), 49–55.

Parker, David. "Can We Trust the Wife of Bath?" *ChauR*, Vol. IV (1970), 90–98.

Passon, Richard H. "'Entente' in Chaucer's *Friar's Tale*." *ChauR*, Vol. II (1968), 166–71.

Pearsall, D. A. "The Squire as Story-teller." *UTQ*, Vol. XXXIV (1964), 82–92.

Power, Eileen. *Medieval English Nunneries c. 1275 to 1535*. Cambridge, England, 1922.

———. *Medieval People*. Anchor ed. New York, 1956. (First published 1924.)

Pratt, Robert A. "The Development of the Wife of Bath." *Studies in Medieval Literature in Honor of Professor Albert Croll Baugh*. Edited by MacEdward Leach. Philadelphia, 1961. Pp. 45–79.

———. "The Order of the *Canterbury Tales*." *PMLA*, Vol. LXVI (1951), 1141–67.

———. "Three Old French Sources of the Nonnes Preestes Tale." *Speculum*, Vol. XLVII (1972), 422–44, 646–68.

Preston, Raymond. *Chaucer*. London, 1952.

Price, Derek J., ed. *The Equatorie of the Planetis*. Cambridge, England, 1955.

Reid, David S. "Crocodilian Humor: A Discussion of Chaucer's Wife of Bath." *ChauR*, Vol. IV (1970), 73–89.

Richardson, Janette. "Hunter and Prey, Functional Imagery in Chaucer's *Friar's Tale*." *English Miscellany*, Vol. XII (1961), 9–20.

Robertson, D. W., Jr. *A Preface to Chaucer: Studies in Medieval Perspectives*. Princeton, 1962.

Robinson, F. N., ed. *The Works of Geoffrey Chaucer*. 2nd ed. Boston, 1957.

Root, Robert K. "The Manciple's Prologue." *MLN*, Vol. XLIV (1929), 493–96.

———. *The Poetry of Chaucer*. 2nd ed. Boston, 1922. (First published 1906.)

Roppolo. Joseph P. "The Converted Knight in Chaucer's *Wife of Bath's Tale*." *CE*, Vol. XII (1951), 263–69.

Ruggiers, Paul G. *The Art of the Canterbury Tales*. Madison and Milwaukee, 1965.

———. "Some Philosophical Aspects of *The Knight's Tale*." *CE*, Vol. XIX (1958), 296–302.

Russell, G. H. "Chaucer: *The Prioresse's Tale*." *Medieval Literature and Cililization: Studies in Memory of G. N. Garmonsway*. Edited by D. A. Pearsall and R. A. Waldron. London, 1969. Pp. 211–27.

Salter, Elizabeth. *Chaucer: The Knight's Tale and the Clerk's Tale*. Studies in English Literature, No. 5. David Daiches, general ed. London, 1962.

Schmidt, A. V. C. "The Tragedy of Arcite: A Reconsideration of the *Knight's Tale*." *EIC*, Vol. XIX (1969), 107–17.

Schoeck, Richard J. "Chaucer's Prioress: Mercy and Tender Heart." *Chaucer Criticism: The Canterbury Tales.* Edited by Richard J. Schoeck and Jerome Taylor. Notre Dame, 1960. Pp. 245–58.

Sedgewick, G. G. "The Progress of Chaucer's Pardoner, 1880–1940." *MLQ*, Vol. I (1940), 431–58.

Severs, J. Burke. "Chaucer's Originality in the *Nun's Priest's Tale.*" *SP*, Vol. LXIII (1946), 22–41.

———. *The Literary Relationships of Chaucer's Clerkes Tale.* Yale Studies in English, No. 96. New Haven, 1942.

Shores, David L. "*The Merchant's Tale*: Some Lay Observations." *NM*, Vol. LXXI (1970), 119–33.

Shumaker, Wayne. "Chaucer's *Manciple's Tale* as Part of a Canterbury Group." *UTQ*, Vol. XXII (1953), 147–56.

Silverman, Albert H. "Sex and Money in Chaucer's *Shipman's Tale.*" *PQ*, Vol. XXXII (1953), 329–36.

Silvia, D. S. "The Wife of Bath's Marital State." *Notes and Queries*, n.s., Vol. XIV (1967), 8–10.

Skeat, Walter W., ed. *The Complete Works of Geoffrey Chaucer.* 7 vols. Oxford, 1894–1897.

Slade, Tony. "Irony in the *Wife of Bath's Tale.*" *MLR*, Vol. LXIV (1969), 241–47.

Sledd, James. "The *Clerk's Tale:* The Monsters and the Critics." *MP*, Vol. LI (1953), 73–82.

Spearing, A. C., ed. *The Knight's Tale.* London and New York, 1966.

Speirs, John. *Chaucer the Maker.* London, 1951.

Stillwell, Gardiner. "Chaucer in Tartary." *RES*, Vol. XXIV (1948), 177–88.

———. "The Political Meaning of Chaucer's *Tale of Melibee.*" *Speculum*, Vol. XIX (1944), 433–44.

Stokoe, William C. "Structure and Intention in the First Fragment of the *Canterbury Tales.*" *UTQ*, Vol. XXI (1952), 120–27.

Strohm, Paul. "The Allegory of the *Tale of Melibee.*" *ChauR*, Vol. II (1967), 32–42.

Sullivan, Hazel. "A Chaucerian Puzzle." *A Chaucerian Puzzle and Other Medieval Essays.* Edited by Natalie Grimes Lawrence and Jack A. Reynolds. Miami, 1961. Pp. 1–46.

Swart, J. "Chaucer's Pardoner." *Neophilologus*, Vol. XXXVI (1952), 45–50.

Tatlock, John S. P. *The Development and Chronology of Chaucer's Works.* Chaucer Society, 2nd Ser., No. 37. London, 1907.

——— "The Duration of the Canterbury Pilgrimage" *PMLA*, Vol. XXI (1906), 478–85.

Thurston, Paul T. "Artistic Ambivalence in Chaucer's *Knight's Tale.*" Unpublished Ph.D. dissertation, University of Florida, 1968.

Tillyard, E. M. W. *Poetry Direct and Oblique.* London, 1934.

Tolkien, J. R. R. "Chaucer as a Philologist: *The Reeve's Tale.*" *Transactions of the Philological Society* (London), 1934, pp. 1–70.

Toole, William B. "Chaucer's Christian Irony: The Relationship of Character and Action in the *Pardoner's Tale.*" *ChauR*, Vol. III (1968), 37–43.

Tupper, Frederick. "The Pardoner's Tavern." *JEGP*, Vol. XIII (1914), 553–65.

———. *Types of Society in Medieval Literature.* New York, 1926.

Underwood, Dale. "The First of *The Canterbury Tales.*" *ELH*, Vol. XXVI (1959), 455–69.

West, Michael D. "Dramatic Time, Setting, and Motivation in Chaucer." *ChauR*, Vol. II (1968), 172–87.

Whitesell, J. Edwin. "Chaucer's Lisping Friar." *MLN*, Vol. LXXI (1956), 160–61.

Williams, Arnold. "Chaucer and the Friars." *Speculum*, Vol. XXVIII (1953), 499–513.

Wood, Chauncey. *Chaucer and the Country of the Stars: Poetic Uses of Astrological Imagery.* Princeton, 1970.

Zietlow, Paul N. "In Defense of the Summoner." *ChauR*, Vol. I (1966), 4–19.

Zimbardo, Rose A. "Unity and Duality in the *The Wife of Bath's Prologue* and *Tale.*" *Tennessee Studies in Literature*, Vol. XI (1966), 11–33.

index

Index